EIGHTY IS NOT ENOUGH

ONE ACTOR'S JOURNEY THROUGH AMERICAN ENTERTAINMENT

*For my Pal
Frank
Good Luck
Dick Van Patten*

Dick Van Patten
AND ROBERT BAER

**PHOENIX
BOOKS**

Library of Congress Cataloging-in-Publication Data

Van Patten, Dick.
    Eighty is not enough! : one actor's journey through American
entertainment / Dick Van Patten and Robert Baer.
        p. cm.
    ISBN 978-1-60747-700-6 (hardcover)
1. Van Patten, Dick. 2. Actors–United States–Biography. I. Baer, Robert. II. Title.
    PN2287.V337A3 2009
    792.02'8092–dc22
    [B]

                                                    2009034311

Book Design by: Marti Lou Critchfield

Printed in the United States of America

Phoenix Books, Inc.
9465 Wilshire Boulevard, Suite 840
Beverly Hills, CA 90212

10 9 8 7 6 5 4 3 2 1

FOR MOM
WHO WAS THERE FOR ME AT THE BEGINNING

AND

FOR PAT
WHO'S BEEN THERE FOR ME EVER SINCE

TABLE OF CONTENTS

1

KNOCKOUT

John Henry was down. It was only the first round, but I knew it was over. Above the roar of the crowd, I could hear the excitement in the announcer's voice as I moved closer to the old Emerson radio against the back wall in the dressing room. I waited as the referee down the street at the Garden began the count.

It was 1939. I was ten years old, and Joe Louis was my hero. As I stood there pressed up to the radio, Joe's opponent, a tough but aging former light-heavyweight champion named John Henry Lewis, was on the canvas. It was his second trip down in the first two minutes of the fight. The first time, Joe had knocked him clear through the ropes. Ten seconds later, the referee called the fight, and I raced out of the dressing room, bursting to tell the very next person I saw that the great Brown Bomber was still Champion of the World.

Fredric March stood in the wings of Broadway's Center Theater. He was growing anxious, his entrance cue fast approaching. March was starring in *The American Way*—a popular Broadway spectacle, directed by the great George S. Kaufman, telling the story of a German-American named Martin Gunther, a man torn by mixed loyalties to his old and new countries in the late 1920s. Gunther's divided loyalties would be further tested by the prejudice rising against his family as tensions in America later mounted along with the emergence of Hitler and the Nazis in Europe.

I reached the wings. I was playing Gunther's grandson, Karl. Taking Fredric March's hand, we waited together for our cue. At the moment, I was only vaguely aware that Fredric March was special. Standing there with him, I wouldn't have known why. I wouldn't have known that he won the Academy Award for *Dr. Jekyll and Mr. Hyde* in 1932, nor that just a year before he was again nominated for his acclaimed performance in the smash hit, *A Star is Born*. None of that mattered to me. I had far more important news to relate.

"Louis won!" I blurted out. I was beside myself with excitement as I looked up, expecting March to be just as thrilled as I was. Instead, he glared back. Instantly, I saw something was wrong. This was Rockefeller Center. The play was a tremendous

7

production with a cast and crew of over two hundred and fifty people. The seats were packed with New Yorkers who came to the theater in the hope of finding some small relief from the stress of ten years of the Great Depression and new anxieties over an impending World War. I wasn't aware of all that, but I could tell that Fredric March was mad—and worse still, he was mad at me.

"Get your mind on your acting," he snapped. "This is more important than the fight." His tone startled me. For a moment I was devastated. We stood there waiting in silence. But seconds later the cue came, and we stepped out together under the bright stage lights of Broadway.

As we did, I found myself transforming. Quickly I became Karl Gunther, another young boy living in an entirely different world than mine. And just as fast, I forgot all about the fight. The old guy was right. The show really was more important. For the next seventy years in this line of work, I've come to realize that the show is *always* more important. That's a lesson I first learned from Fredric March—and one I'd never forget.

That night—and every night—my Mom was backstage. Josephine Acerno Van Patten—everyone called her "Jo"—was quite simply the most extraordinary person I've ever known. Consider what she accomplished: in the midst of the Great Depression, Jo had this crazy idea that her two kids could be stars on Broadway. Without money, connections, access or advantages of any kind, she somehow, through sheer force of will, turned that crazy dream into reality. When she passed away in 1975, my father wrote poignantly to my sister Joyce and me, reminding us of just how important she was to our success: it was Mom's "persistence and doggedness that put you where you are today."

Dad was right. But it's also true that her pursuit of that dream cost her dearly; probably even her marriage. She made that sacrifice, not because she wanted to, but, I believe, because she had no choice. Unrelenting ambition was something written in her nature. She felt it every minute of every day. Most important, she could never settle for not trying. It was one thing to fail, but, for Mom, it was unforgivable not to try. And so, my mother was utterly relentless, a force of nature, the likes of which I've never seen.

When I think about my mother in those early days in the 1930s and 1940s, I'm reminded of the ongoing debate about whether parents should bring their children into the world of entertainment. It's something people will forever debate. The clash of opinion in my own family is striking. My sister Joyce and I have such different memories of life as child actors that I sometimes think we must have come from different homes.

I tend see the positive; some might—and do—say that I stress the positive to the point of being blind to reality. But for me, my mother made this wonderful life I've enjoyed possible, and I find it hard to imagine what I would have done without her ambition and drive. Joyce, however, has always been more sensitive to the downside. Joyce, so highly intelligent, has deeply felt the very real underside of a life where getting that bigger and better role became the only measure of things. She rebelled against a world that placed such a high premium on show business success. Joyce left home early and carved out her own wonderful and successful life. As her older brother, I could not be more proud of what she has accomplished, both as a person and a performer.

So the question remains, do child actors lose their youth? Are they exposed too soon to the often cutthroat and unforgiving world of entertainment? Is there a price to be paid later when an overly-protected and idealized childhood is insufficient training for the real challenges of life that inevitably lurk around the corner? After years thinking about this question, I've come to believe there's no one simple answer. What works for some, doesn't work for others. That's not a cop-out; it simply reflects the fact that people are different.

I played a television dad in *Eight Is Enough*. But playing a character in a television show doesn't magically turn you into that character. Actors pretend to be policemen, doctors, and scientists, but that hardly gives them the courage of a cop, the judgment of a doctor, or the brilliance of a scientist. Oddly, I've known actors who confuse their real and fictional persona. Nothing is more absurd. Like everyone else, what I've learned about being a father has come from my own life, my own family and from the challenge of raising my own children.

Still, like any father, there were things I could bring to the role of a TV dad that may have contributed some authenticity to the show. Also, it's inevitable that during a long-running show, relationships develop among the various characters, both on and off camera. Those relationships are as varied as they are in real life. There are the good things: admiration, pride, caring, and compassion; there are also the bad things, the worst of which is jealousy. Through the years I've tried to keep in touch with the casts of both *Eight Is Enough* and *I Remember Mama*. I've always considered them like second families. And like any family there have been successes and disappointments, even tragedies. There is a great deal of pressure on performers—especially young performers—when they come off a successful show. I've felt it myself, and I've seen many others confronted by it.

Over the past eighty years, I've been fortunate to see firsthand the many great changes in American entertainment. Most remarkable was the advent of television, and I've never lost my astonishment at its awesome power. I participated in the transition from radio to television in the late 1940s, and the power of the new medium was immediately recognizable. Recently, I was struck again by the magnitude of television's place in American culture in a very personal way.

In the recent presidential election, Americans were fortunate to have two exceptional candidates in terms of their personal integrity and character. The nomination and election of the first African-American as President of the United States certainly reflects a tremendous advance from the days of my own youth when segregation and racial bias were still ugly stains on America. Regardless of one's political views, all Americans should be proud of this extraordinary moment in our history.

Most astonishing to me, however, was that at a key moment in the campaign *Eight Is Enough* actually enjoyed a brief resurgence on the world stage. On the night of President Obama's historic acceptance speech at Denver's Invesco Field, I was watching at home with my family. About midway through, I nearly fell off my chair as the Democratic nominee made a clear reference to *Eight Is Enough*. "We love this country too much to let the next four years look just like the last eight," Obama told the massive throng of supporters. "On November 4, we must stand up and say: 'Eight is enough.'"

The next day in an article titled, "Somewhere, Dick Van Patten is Smiling," television writer Michael Malone noted: "Even Dick Van Patten's wise Bradford patriarch character couldn't have predicted what would happen next." He was right. No sooner than Obama said it, some eighty-thousand people began chanting in unison "Eight is enough, Eight is enough," as literally tens, if not hundreds of millions of viewers watched worldwide. I sat there, not only "smiling," but absolutely astonished.

Numerous writers commented on President Obama's reference to the show. David Remnick gently lampooned the phrase in *The New Yorker*, noting that John F. Kennedy in his acceptance speech had cited the prophet Isaiah, Oliver Cromwell,

Henry II, and Lloyd George, while Barack Obama chose to cite an old television show. Remnick wrote: "For the culturally disadvantaged, 'Eight Is Enough' is a reference to a Dick Van Patten sitcom of the late seventies." Roger Catlin of the *Hartford Courant* wondered if "future historians [will] get all of its references centuries from now?" Will they know, Catlin wrote, that Obama was "gently referring to the 1970s sitcom starring Dick Van Patten?" And comedian Jon Stewart of *The Daily Show* also "picked up on the pop cultural reference." The next day, Stewart poked fun at the line by constructing a mock speech made up only of television shows. Pretending to be a presidential candidate, Stewart announced: "We must take it *One Day at a Time*! To restore *Good Times* and *Happy Days*. Whether you're *Married with Children* or just *Friends*, *Cheers* to you. *Monday Night Football*."

I was delighted by the President's reference to our show. But it also underscored the enormous power of television. Remnick, among the most prominent writers in America, argued that Obama's "homey sloganeering"—which, according to Remnick, included the reference to *Eight Is Enough*—"worked." In other words, Obama's policy platform was best served when joined with a vision of what is good about America. Without overstating its significance, I think it's fair to say that the ideal of an American family and a positive way of life was, for many people of President Obama's generation, at least partially represented by the Bradford family. But never in my wildest dreams did I expect to hear it alluded to at this historic moment. I hope all the hundreds of people associated with the show were as thrilled as I was.

* * *

For nearly eight decades I've had the great fortune of playing thousands of roles before millions of people. I've enjoyed every step of the journey. Now, I look back with a mix of emotions; sadness for the people who are gone, nostalgia for times that have passed, but immense gratitude for the wonderful opportunities that came my way. I've titled this book *Eighty Is Not Enough* not just for the obvious play on words, but as a way of expressing the single idea that has governed my entire life; that every moment of life is precious; that every step we take is an adventure; that every day on earth is a gift from God.

I imagine that anyone turning eighty would say, "Eighty is not enough." I hope that thought is moved less by a fear of what comes after this journey than a love of life itself. The truth is, I still wake up early to meet the new day. While I don't jump out of bed with the nimbleness of my youth, I've retained a desire to see what's new for today and what's on the horizon for tomorrow. I don't believe that will ever change. My son, Jimmy, has recently described me as someone who enjoys the simple things in life: "My dad can find something awesome in a can of coke," he says. I think he's right. There is so much in this wonderful life we take for granted—things, as Jimmy says, we should really experience with a sense of awe.

I've also made more than my share of mistakes. I'll talk about some of that; and I hope to do so in a way that's honest, but without being hurtful to others. Revealing things backstage is always a bit dicey. But it's the challenges we confront as much as our triumphs, the failings as much as the victories that reveal the full measure of our lives. When I decided to set down my memoirs, it was with the idea of showing that an imperfect life, as mine has been, can still be a wonderful life.

2

EARLY DAYS

My career began in a baby carriage. That's how Mom always told it. Pushing me up and down the streets of Kew Gardens in the late 1920s, people would stop and comment to her: "You should bring that baby to a modeling agency!"

Most mothers hearing such flattery would be both delighted—and satisfied. But not Jo. Immediately she began imagining the possibilities. Mom had already been dreaming about Broadway and the world of entertainment she had come to love, but I was still too young for that. So why not get started with some modeling.

Attitude, I'm convinced, is the first step toward success of any kind. Nothing is more important than the ability to see or imagine something that appears unlikely, or even ridiculous, and still hold firmly to a belief that you can make it happen—even in the face of skepticism and ridicule. And that was Mom's strength. Once the idea of turning me into a child model entered her head, she never let it go, and she had the kind of self-confidence to think that nothing was outside her grasp.

And so after a few baby-carriage compliments, Jo was on the hunt. She poured through newspapers and magazines looking for pictures of child models. As she did, she became even more convinced she could make it happen. First, she asked around and learned the names of all the modeling agencies in Manhattan; then she began taking me on the E-Train from Kew Gardens across the East River for interviews at the studios in Manhattan.

Jo began at the top. In 1932, when I was three years old, she brought me for a test at John Robert Powers, the biggest modeling agency in New York City. The Powers agency, on 277 Park Avenue in Manhattan, took a look at me and signed us up.

The photo shoots were done at studios spread across Manhattan from 42nd Street to downtown—which even today is the center of New York's modeling locales. Looking back, the technology of the 1930s seems archaic. This was long before digital photos or even Polaroid. Today, we have cellular phones that take pictures that are often as good as those produced by the best equipment in 1933. And color photography was only just beginning to be marketed with the introduction of Kodachrome film two years later.

I hated the shoots. Dressed in the clothes they were advertising, I had to sit there still as a corpse for fear of blurring the shot if I dared to move. The photographer held up a stick with a little fake bird on the end, while in his other hand he kept a rubber ball attached to the camera, which he squeezed as he took the picture. And right before shooting, he would bark out the same monotonous instructions over and over again: "Watch the birdie! Watch the birdie! Stand still! Don't move! Now watch the Birdie!" There were, of course, times when I did move, ruining the picture. Then he'd become exasperated and yell at me: "Do it over! Now don't move! Don't move!" This would go on for hours, and the truth is I couldn't wait until it was over. I was just a kid who wanted to be running around and playing games rather than stuck in those studios standing perfectly still for hours and wondering why they needed so many darn photographs. What's the big deal, I thought. Just take the picture and let me out of here.

Even worse, as I got older I took some ribbing from the kids in the neighborhood. They knew I was going to Manhattan for these modeling jobs and would call me a sissy. That was horrible. I remember them yelling at me on the avenue: "Hey, Dickie, tomorrow we're going to play punch ball," knowing full well that I had a modeling job. Kids can certainly be cruel.

While I hated modeling, modeling didn't hate me. I've made a point of never taking myself too seriously as an entertainer, but it's true that I was a photogenic kid. Once I started with the Powers agency, the jobs just kept coming. I modeled for everything: Wonder Bread, toothpaste, endless clothing lines, and everything else imaginable. I was in all the Montgomery Ward catalogues wearing children's clothing, especially the stylish pea caps that were so popular in the 1920s and 1930s.

My modeling was a financial bonanza for the family. In the middle of the Depression, I was getting five dollars an hour—more money at four years of age than most working men in the country. I now wonder how many hundreds or thousands of desperate people I passed by on the E-Train headed to these jobs. How many people would have given anything for the few bucks I made just by standing still for a photographer?

My modeling career peaked when, at age seven, I appeared on the cover of *The Pictorial Review*, one of the top magazines in the country. In 1935 making the cover of *The Pictorial Review* would be like being on the cover of *Life* magazine in the 1960s or maybe, *Vanity Fair*, today. Also, it was a color picture—which was rare in those days.

My mother considered that cover shot for *The Pictorial Review* one of our greatest achievements. She kept a copy hanging on the wall at the foot of the staircase, conspicuously placed so nobody who entered would miss it. The picture remained there for many years after I left home, and even my nephew Casey, who lived with Mom before his marriage in 1974, remembers the photo still on the same wall, some forty years after it first appeared on the newsstands of New York City. Mom took those baby-carriage compliments seriously and that cover shot was as meaningful to her as anything we would ever accomplish.

But modeling was just the beginning. Although it proved to be a needed financial boon, and certainly elevated Mom's status among her friends who perused the magazines and were bombarded with pictures of her little Dickie modeling all the children's clothing, still it was not really entertainment. Being a mainstay at John Robert Powers was great, but Mom had her sights on bigger things—especially the Broadway stage. She was working on that all through the modeling years, although the road we took was anything but a straight path.

3

MR. PERSONALITY

The 1930s was a decade of pageants and contests. I like
to believe it's not so long ago when it seemed like every mother in
America was marching their children down the boardwalk at the
world-famous Atlantic City Baby Contest, or when throngs of
beautiful young ladies vied for recognition in the endless stream of
beauty contests held by every town, county and state—not to
mention Miss America.

In the fall of 1934, when I was five years old, Mom
learned of a talent contest for children held at the Willard Theater
in Woodhaven, Queens, just a short distance from our home. I was
already a precocious kid and beginning to enjoy some success on
the modeling circuit, so the opportunity to step up to a stage
performance seemed only natural. It was also what mom really
wanted. The Willard Theater was a long way from Broadway, but
I still remember her excitement the night I stood at a microphone
on the Willard stage reciting a poem with the title, "Why I Love
My Mother." Frankly, I wasn't too impressed with my performance,
but I did come home the winner.

The Willard prize sent me across town for the final round
at the Loews State, the beautiful old theater on 44th and Broadway
in Manhattan, which is still among the most prominent theaters in
New York City. The same contest I won in Queens had been held
in all the five boroughs of New York, and the winners got to
perform in the finals at the Manhattan Loews.

I still remember the night. Just five years old in October
of 1934, I arrived at the theater smartly dressed in short pants,
blazer, and a little blue pea cap that I wore proudly as I stepped
onstage for the big show. When my turn came, I walked out to the
microphone and recited the same poem. As a tactical matter, I was
a little uncertain about reciting poetry. Other kids were singing and
dancing while all I did was recite my poem. But Mom knew better
than me. And, once again, I came out on top. Now I was the proud
winner of New York's Loews/MGM Screen and Voice Contest
for 1934.

The most extraordinary part—and something of which I
was pretty much oblivious—was that two of the contest judges

were Eleanor Roosevelt, the First Lady of the United States, and Fiorello La Guardia, the Mayor of New York City. I don't recall actually meeting them at the time. The finals were recorded, and it may have been that the First Lady and the Mayor viewed the film privately before making their choice. Anyway, my mother was ecstatic. We now had our first brush with the world beyond Kew Gardens. Eleanor Roosevelt and Mayor LaGuardia were already legendary figures, and I'm still grateful to them both for selecting the kid with nothing more than a navy pea cap and a poem about his mom.

In retrospect, I also find it remarkable that the contest was filmed. Today everything is filmed; at a moment's notice we turn our telephones into video recorders and store them as electronic files. But this was 1934. The "talkies," beginning with Al Jolson's *The Jazz Singer* in 1927, were only seven years old. It would take another five years before the world would know *The Wizard of Oz* or *Gone with the Wind.* To make an actual sound film of the contest meant it was something they took seriously, no doubt as a promotional piece for MGM and Loews. Winning the top prize was also a nice résumé item—one Mother was planning to use in the years ahead as she continued her relentless drive to make me an entertainer.

The personality contest was also important in showing that I had no fear of the stage. Perhaps this experience at such an extremely young age helped remove the specter of stage fright— a condition that haunts many established actors, as well as those who might otherwise have tried their hand at acting. At an early age, speaking in front of a large crowd seemed as natural to me as talking at the dinner table.

I also learned to memorize. I was too young to read, and so the poem was recited by heart. Since then I've never had a problem memorizing lines. I recall years later riding on the subway to performances of *I Remember Mama*, reading and memorizing the entire scripts before the train pulled into Penn Station.

Of course, acting on soap operas also requires a good memory. For two years in the 1960s I played a character on *Young Doctor Malone,* and each day we were handed a script which had to be ready the next day. And my role was relatively small. Memory block is fatal to an actor. I've seen it end a number of careers, and it's usually sad—especially if the lapses are associated with aging.

In over seventy-five years onstage, I've been lucky to be free of both stage fright and memory lapse, and I suspect that at least a part of that good fortune is the result of standing in front of several thousand people at the Loews Theater and spouting off that poem about Mom. For me, it was the right way to launch my stage career. After all, it was Mom who made it all possible. I hope that as she sat there among all those thousands of people watching her little boy talk about how much he loved her, she knew it was much more than just a recitation for the contest.

* * *

Like most kids my age, I loved *Our Gang*. Spanky, Farina, Buckwheat, Pete, the black-eyed bulldog, and the whole gang were taking the entertainment world by storm in the 1930s. This wasn't the more familiar television show, *The Little Rascals*, which began in 1955, but the film shorts, which years before the advent of television, were among the most popular shows in the country.

Mom decided I should get in on it. As always, she shot right for the top. At the time, Laurel and Hardy were the biggest comedy team in the country, and Mom discovered that Stan Laurel was connected to the producer of *Our Gang*, Hal Roach. So in 1934, when I was six years old, she wrote a letter directly to Stan Laurel, asking if he could help me get an audition for a part. She included some of my modeling pictures.

To our great surprise, Stan responded. Among my most prized mementos is the letter he wrote to my mother in 1934. In it he described me as "a cute little tyke" and at the end, predicted: "There are great things waiting for you." Seventy-five years later, I still have that letter in a frame in my home. And as it turned out, Stan Laurel was exactly right. Great things were waiting—although there would be many twists and turns along the way.

4

LAND OF BROKEN DREAMS

In the spring of 1935, we lived on the first floor of a two-family house in Woodhaven, Queens. We were crowded there—my grandmother, Florence, my Aunt Margie, as well as the four of us. Joyce was just a few months old, and she and I shared a bedroom in the back of the house, my grandmother and aunt had their own rooms, and my parents had to sleep in the living room.

In 1935, my Aunt Anna died, and the funeral was held for three days at our house. My parents put flowers on the front door and brought the casket right into the living room, and Anna was laid out right next to my parents' bed. I remember the creepy feeling that kept me up at night while Mom and Dad slept soundly right next to the dead body.

In her will, Anna left my grandmother a few thousand dollars, and so Florence decided to use the inheritance to take a trip to California and visit some of her relatives. Since we had just received the letter from Stan Laurel, Mom began thinking about ways to parlay the inheritance into opportunities.

She asked Florence to take me with her. In addition to Stan Laurel's letter, she had made a more dubious Hollywood connection, one supposedly arranged by a beautician on Jamaica Avenue named Anthony who claimed his brother worked as a makeup artist at MGM and could get me an audition for the *Our Gang* comedy show. Florence, like my father, possessed an inquisitive mind and an adventurous nature, and she immediately agreed, probably without really thinking through what she was getting herself into.

Once the money came, she and I took off on a long trip to see America, visit her relatives in San Francisco, and to try to turn my small accomplishments into a career opportunity. Although only six years old, I had already been modeling for several years, and I was the winner of the Loews/MGM Sound and Screen contest. With these various résumé pieces, my mother was sure that someone would be interested in giving me a job.

I'll never forget the train ride. We took off from Penn Station and switched to the Pacific Limited in Chicago. With Florence's inheritance, we went in style. Pork-chop dinners were served every night in a beautiful dining car, resplendent with white linen tablecloths and fancy silverware. I came to see for the first time the vast and beautiful American countryside, standing for hours on the viewing platform of the train's observation deck as we roared across the Great Plains and over the Rocky Mountains.

We stopped in Arizona, and I recall seeing Native Americans for the first time in my life. They were selling jewelry and other trinkets at the train station. We stopped in the middle of the desert in Needles, California, which they told us was the hottest place in the country. I was really in the spirit of the western motif, and I wore my star-spangled cowboy outfit and ten-gallon hat every single day. We also saw the Grand Canyon, and I can still remember my amazement at this remarkable natural wonder.

And I could not have had a better travel companion. I loved my grandmother, and she was not only full of enthusiasm for the trip, but an encyclopedia of interesting anecdotes about every place we passed. It was a glorious five days on the train to the West Coast.

But the rest of the trip wasn't so much fun. Florence was a very different woman than Mom. In fact, my grandmother didn't really approve of pushing children into the entertainment world. She was, moreover, more reserved and uncomfortable with the idea of trying to maneuver her way into some executive's office. If someone said "no" to my mother, that was just the start of the conversation. She knew how to push, plead, threaten, and manipulate to turn that "no" into a "yes." But Florence accepted "no" as "no"—and that was a frame of mind ill-suited for the competitive business of motion pictures.

Arriving in Hollywood, Florence took me to Stan Laurel's office. I still have the note she wrote on a photo taken that day: "We called on Mr. Laurel of Laurel and Hardy." But, when we got there we were politely brushed away. And Florence didn't put up much of a fight.

Discouraged, we went to the MGM studios where we thought my winning the MGM sponsored Personality Contest at the Loews would get us in the door. It didn't. Instead Florence and I ran headfirst into a bunch of disinterested functionaries guarding against the star-seekers who even in 1935 were arriving in Hollywood from all over the country.

My mother didn't take the news well. She was as unyielding as the studio guards. On the phone at the hotel, I could hear Florence patiently listening as Mom railed on about how she should have just barged in on Hal Roach and Stan Laurel. But

Florence couldn't do that. It was sad. I'll never forget standing at the gate of MGM Studios with my Grandmother as the guards told us to go away. Even at age six, I could sense a profound conflict in Florence. She didn't want to be pushy; she didn't want to cause a scene, but at the same time, she knew she would end up fighting with Mother for failing to get us in.

I have no doubt that had Mom been there, dealing with all those guardians of the inner sanctums, she would have viewed their denials as little more than a minor inconvenience. One way or another Mom would have gotten us inside. In short order, we would have been talking with people who could make things happen. But she was three-thousand miles away, and, instead, Florence and I just stood on the street with the gate closed. For me, it was a poignant moment—and not because we didn't get in or because I lost out on opportunities—in truth I was too young to fully appreciate all that. It was sad because I hated to see my Grandmother sad and helpless.

But things got even worse. My mother was infuriated with what she regarded as Florence's timidity, indifference, and even incompetence. Mom was unable to see that others might have difficulty doing things that came so natural to her. The result was a profound rift arising between Mom and Florence. It lasted the rest of their lives, and they never spoke again.

And so, the joy of seeing America from the deck of the Pacific Limited was a little tainted. No doubt, my mother was more to blame for the ensuing conflict. She had no right to expect from others what they couldn't give. Florence's inaction was not, as my mother thought, a betrayal and Mom should have known better and let it go.

Florence died of pneumonia in 1940, when I was twelve. It was a terrible blow for me, but even more so for Joyce who was really the apple of her eye. When Joyce and I first heard that Florence had been taken seriously ill, we went running down Queen's Boulevard to the Kew Gardens Hospital, praying that we would find her okay. But it was too late. They told us Florence had died. Joyce and I sat there in the hospital room unable to stop crying.

In the end, I've tried not to be judgmental, either about Grandmother or Mom. Just as Florence couldn't find a way past those guards, Mom couldn't find her way to reconciliation. It was Mom's nature that accounted for her seeming intolerance, but it was that same nature that made her the person who turned two obscure kids from Woodhaven into child stars. And so I've made my peace with that aspect of Mom's character. I also believe that

Joyce, who suffered more from Mom's relentless ambition, has come to terms as well. In the end, I'm forever grateful to my mother for dragging me to all those auditions. By doing so, she gave me this wonderful life. At the same time, I loved Florence dearly and I hope, and believe, that by now they've made their own peace together in a far better place.

5

STAGESTRUCK

My mother was born in 1907 in Queens, New York. The daughter of Vincent and Rose Acerno, both Italian immigrants who arrived separately in America in the 1890s, Mom moved with her parents and five younger siblings to Catherine Street in the crowded, vibrant neighborhood of Manhattan's Lower East Side. There they were part of that melting pot of migrants who poured into New York City from every part of the world in the early years of the twentieth century.

There was considerable poverty in the immigrant community. Conditions were certainly an improvement from the circumstances back in Italy that prompted my grandparents and so many millions of their neighbors to brave a voyage to America in search of opportunity. Still, it was a tough life on Catherine Street.

My grandfather, Vincent Acerno, always made a decent living so my mother never experienced hunger or lack of shelter. But she witnessed poverty all around her. I believe that youthful experience in the immigrant communities of the Lower East Side played a large part in shaping her character and sharpening her determination to move out and get ahead. She spoke Italian at home and was very conscious of the prejudice against Italians and Jews that was fairly widespread at the time.

In 1917, at age ten, Mom and her family moved to Lincoln Place in Brooklyn, where they stayed for five years. Eventually, they bought a bungalow in Ravenhall, a small town near Coney Island. At age fifteen, they moved again to Woodhaven, Queens, where they lived until she married my father.

In Woodhaven, Mom attended Richmond Hill High School, where she excelled at athletics. She was particularly good at both swimming and field hockey, unusual choices for women at the time. Eventually she became an instructor in Physical Training at the Kew Forest Public School in Queens.

Unlike Mom, my father came from an old Dutch family. His mother, Grandmother Florence who took me to California, was a Tyler and proud of her family's distant relationship to President John Tyler. Her husband, my paternal grandfather, John Van Patten, came from Saranac in upstate New York, eventually moving to

Brooklyn where he met and married my grandmother. A milkman in Brooklyn, John died at age thirty-six of pneumonia in 1912, and my father, who was just five years old at the time, barely remembered him.

With my grandfather's death, the family needed money to survive. Florence took in roomers, and for a long time they lived off the rent. Because of their circumstances, my father went to work at a relatively early age. His first job was turning off the street lamps in Green Point. This was around 1915, and the streets were lit with old kerosene lamps. Early each morning Dad would make his rounds on roller skates to turn off the flames.

At eighteen, Dad met my mother at a local dance contest in Richmond Hill. Dad was a judge and Mom a contestant. With Dad's support, Mom won and soon afterwards they began dating. In the spring of 1925, she brought Dad to her senior prom at the Hotel Nassau in Long Beach. Dad later recalled the evening as "a beautiful spring night on the ocean front. The Nassau was still an elegant hotel. The chandeliers in the ballroom sparkled." They danced The Charleston and The Black Bottom together, and Mom gave Dad her sorority pin, which as Dad later told us was tantamount to a betrothal.

Mom continued school at Savage, a Physical Training Academy on 59th Street in New York City. Dad proudly attended her graduation ceremony held at the Mecca Temple—later City Center at West 54th Street. After the ceremonies, Mom was the star of the dance production. "She had all the grace and style of a professional," Dad told me and Joyce. "You would have been proud of her!"

They married in 1927. The wedding took place at the Republican Club on Woodhaven Boulevard. It was a typical Italian wedding—"robust, noisy and unorganized." Dad recalled how he and Mom sat at the front of the room while the relatives put envelopes with money into a white satin bag. Later that night, in their room at the Hotel Astor, they sat on the bed and counted their take.

My parents were inseparable. They played bridge together five nights a week and developed a mutual love for the theater. Through the years, they went to a play in New York City every Friday night. On one of these excursions in 1928, they saw Edna Ferber's *Showboat*. Mom was dazzled by the show and always described that night as a turning point for her. She was pregnant with me at the time, and I can't help but think that the enthusiasm of both my parents was somehow sensed by their unborn child.

Mom later told me that she was stage-struck at *Showboat*. Edna Ferber's courageous story, centering on an interracial marriage, became an instant classic. Mom and Dad heard the Ziegfeld Theater ring out with *Old Man River*, the timeless, plaintive ballad of life's relentless movement, like the currents of the Mississippi River that "just keeps rollin' along." Over sixty-five years later in 1995, my parents' two children worked together in a revival of that great production that had so moved and inspired them to believe that their children could one day be a part of this marvelous world of entertainment.

6

BROADWAY

On December 27, 1935, I took my first step onto a Broadway stage. I'd just turned seven, and already we'd made it onto the Great White Way.

I had good company that night at the Shubert. Melvyn Douglas, one of the biggest stars in America, played my father in a short-lived show called *Tapestry in Gray*. A drama set in World War I, *Tapestry* told the story of a doctor who operated on the bullet-riddled face of a wounded soldier. A careless nurse prematurely removed the soldier's bandages, and her mistake scarred him for life. Melvyn Douglas played the doctor, and Elissa Landi was the nurse.

Melvyn was among those great actors who would win all the awards—an Oscar, a Tony, and an Emmy. A few years before I met him, he starred alongside a famous Broadway actress, Helen Gahagan, and they married shortly afterwards. Later Helen Gahagan would launch a second career in politics, becoming well known as the Congresswoman who ran against Richard Nixon for the California Senate in 1950 and was dubbed by Nixon, "The pink lady." She got him back, though, derisively referring to Nixon for the first time as "Tricky Dick"—an unwelcome moniker he never shed.

I landed the part because of my great shock of blond hair. It actually made me look like Melvyn's son. I still remember opening night, walking onstage and looking out into that great darkness that every stage actor knows. I wasn't nervous. I guess I was too young to be nervous. I also remember that the director, Marion Gering, had to tell me my lines because I couldn't read yet. I listened to him and memorized them. It was a good start.

I didn't talk much with Melvyn Douglas. He seemed like a very private person. But I loved Elissa Landi. She was warm and accessible. I thought she was wonderful—and beautiful too. Elissa was about thirty years old at the time of *Tapestry* and already an accomplished actress. The previous year, 1934, she had won acclaim for her role in the film, *The Count of Monte Cristo*.

Elissa always found time to talk with me. And I quickly became very attached to her. One day she said: "Dickie, I have a present for you." She handed me a box. I ripped off the paper, and it was a game with racing bears. I loved it—just as I've always loved all things about animals.

I was twenty years old when I heard that Elissa had died of cancer at age forty-three. I was deeply saddened. She was so full of life and to have it cut down so early just seemed wrong. Elissa Landi was my very first friend on Broadway, and now seventy-three years after she gave me that game of racing bears, I can still see her gorgeous smile, and it brings me back to those days that are so long gone.

Tapestry, unfortunately, bombed. Five weeks was all the critics and audience could take. When it closed, no one was more disappointed than my mother. She had worked so hard to get me on that Broadway stage. Finally, she saw it happening with two giant stars like Melvyn Douglas and Elissa Landi. And just as quickly it was over.

Still, Stan Laurel's prediction held true. Within several months of his letter, I was on Broadway alongside two of the biggest stars in America. Stan had said, "There are great things waiting for you"—and he was right. For a seven-year-old, it was quite a beginning.

Most important, I was a happy kid. I genuinely enjoyed my life onstage. Unlike many other children, I never really internalized any of the pressures associated with performances. That's not to say I was immune to the curves that come our way in childhood. In fact, at age seven, I was about to find out about another side of life, one I was not at all prepared for.

7

THE LAST CASUALTY

Every child—whether an actor or not—is going to learn that life is tough. Some of my very favorite scenes from *Eight Is Enough* involved those moments when one of the children would go crashing headfirst into some harsh reality. They would, of course, come to me, as the father, with their problems, and I would have to explain—or attempt to explain—what no child is anxious to learn; that life is often difficult and sometimes terribly unfair. I came to that knowledge myself on a bright summer afternoon in 1935.

You don't hear much about it nowadays, but Italian families in New York City were closely following Italy's invasion of Ethiopia in October of 1935. It was in the newspapers, on the newsreels, and we would hear about it in school. Every day there were pictures of Mussolini and Haile Selassie, the Ethiopian king who was eventually defeated after putting up a courageous defense.

We kids were unaware of the dark side of this war. We didn't know that innocent people were dying or that a country was being torn apart. And we certainly didn't see that the war was a prelude to a far darker alliance with Nazi Germany that would soon throw the entire world into chaos. For us, the war was nothing more than the inspiration for a kids' game like "cops and robbers," only we played, "Italians and Ethiopians."

We began by choosing sides. Since all of our relatives were supporting Italy, the losers had to be the Ethiopians. There were no rules, we just chased each other around, throwing things, and pretending we were fighting the war.

One afternoon after school, we stopped at my house in Woodhaven, Queens, and everyone left their school books on our porch as we went into the woods to play "Italians and Ethiopians." We chose sides, and I was one of the Italians. So was Renee, my aunt who was actually just my age, and my friend, Robert Johnson. At the edge of the woods, there was a hill that sloped down to the tracks for the Long Island Railroad. We started running down the incline, pretending to be having our little war, with everyone throwing pebbles at each other. At the bottom of the hill Renee and I crossed the tracks.

Just after crossing, I looked back. I saw my friend, Robert Johnson, trip. As he fell, I watched his chin land directly on the electrified third rail. I can still see him as if it were yesterday. Robert's face and his arm were touching the electric rail, and instantly I felt sick as I saw smoke rising out from his head.

It was a horrible sight, and for a moment I was frozen with fear. I was just seven years old and didn't know what to do. Renee and I began screaming and crying out, and then we took off running for home. We reached the house where we found my Uncle Albert. We told him what had happened, and he dashed out of the house. Uncle Albert was actually a great track star. In the 1920s he beat two world champions, Glenn Cunningham and Gene Vesky, in the mile at Madison Square Garden. But I doubt he ever moved a step faster in his life than he did that day. When he got to the tracks, Albert found Robert's body just as we had left him. He was dead. Albert came back to the house and told us it was too late. Our friend was gone.

Our parents had warned us not to go near those tracks. I remember them talking about the dangers of the third rail. They came home shortly afterwards, and soon they were both crying. I never saw that before, and I never remember them so angry with me. While all this was going on, I still remember seeing Robert's books on our porch. It was so sad. He was dead, and all his school books were still there as if waiting for him to come get them.

It made the headlines the next day in *The Long Island Press*. My father wrote a letter to the Railroad expressing his anger that there was not a fence around the tracks. Things were different in the 1930s. People didn't pay as much attention to safety issues as they do today. But, after a while, they did build that fence. It was the middle of the Depression, but they came up with the money.

Robert's parents were foreigners, either German or Swedish. They were superintendents of an apartment building about a block from my house. I don't think they spoke English. One day I remember walking by their building, and they were outside. I could tell they were visibly shaken just by seeing me. I felt terrible and avoided that house in the future. There was no way I could understand the depth of their grief, but from the day Robert Johnson died on that track, I've understood that life can be tough and terribly fragile.

8

THE ETERNAL ROAD

In the decade from 1935 to 1945, there were many plays on Broadway responding to events in Europe, especially the rise of Hitler and the Nazis. As children, Joyce and I were fortunate to have been a part of several of these major productions: I was in *The Eternal Road, The American Way,* and *The Land Is Bright,* while Joyce had a starring role in *Tomorrow the World.* When I look back on those plays, I find it remarkable to see the insight and sensitivity of the various writers, directors, and producers concerning the dark clouds hovering over Europe and the world.

The Eternal Road was among the biggest productions in the history of American theater. We had a cast of over 350 people, and the sets were so huge and extravagant they had to literally tear out the orchestra pit, as well as a large portion of the seating in New York's Manhattan Opera House.

The play began as the brainchild of Meyer Weisgal—who in 1933 conceived an idea he thought of as "our answer to Hitler." Weisgal approached the great German émigré director Max Reinhardt, and in 1934 they met to discuss the project at Reinhardt's home in Salzburg—a locale ironically situated within view of Hitler's summer home in Austria. The group of people involved grew as the composer Kurt Weill, the writer, Franz Werfel, and the designer, Norman Bel Geddes all joined in.

The Eternal Road told the story of a European dictator persecuting the Jewish population of his country. At the outset, many of the Jews fled an angry mob, finding refuge in a synagogue. There the Rabbi, played by Sam Jaffe, comforted a young boy by recounting the history of the Jewish people.

Originally Reinhardt intended to give the part of Isaac to my friend, Sidney Lumet. But, Sidney had a problem with the role, through no fault of his own. There comes a climactic moment in the play when Abraham takes his son, Isaac, to the top of a mountain, places him on an altar, and raises his hand to kill him. At that point, Isaac cries out in the voice of a frightened child: "Father!" According to Weisgal, Max Reinhardt rehearsed Sidney "for days on that single word." But, Sidney, a few years older than me, was maturing, and during the course of the rehearsals his voice started changing, making it impossible for him to sound like a child. In the end it worked out well for both of us. I got to play Isaac, and Sidney, who like many people in the play had been recruited from the prestigious Jewish Theatre on Second Avenue and Second Street, stepped into a bigger role as the young boy to whom the Biblical story is told by the Rabbi.

My audition for Max Reinhardt was really strange. Reinhardt couldn't speak English so he had his assistant, Norman Von Mendelssohn, interpret everything. But Von Mendelssohn also had to tell me what to say because I still couldn't read very well. So there we were with Von Mendelssohn feeding me the lines in English so that I would say them, and then Max Reinhardt would listen to it in a language he didn't understand and then give instructions in German, which Von Mendelssohn would translate for me.

But the worst for me was the makeup. Every night, Mom would cover my whole body with greasy paint so that I looked brown. It would take twenty-five minutes while I stood on a chair in the dressing room. The next day at school back in Queens, the kids would make fun of me because of the tell-tale smudges of makeup left over from the previous night's performance. This happened every day, and I came to dread going to school after the show.

The sets, designed by Norman Bel Geddes, were spectacular. They cost a half million dollars, an astronomical sum in those days. In fact, they were so elaborate that the *New York Times* wrote a lengthy review devoted just to the set production. Bel Geddes literally built a mountain on the stage that went winding up to heaven with a synagogue at the base.

On opening night, construction was still in progress. Max Reinhardt's son, Gottfried, recalled his arrival at the theater that afternoon. "My primary objective," he recalled, "was the first workable toilet." But Bel Geddes had ripped out all the bathrooms. So when nature called, patrons had to run next door to the Hotel New Yorker.

Nothing seemed ready for curtain call. As Gottfried Reinhardt surveyed the disastrous-looking scene of 350 actors scurrying about with no apparent rhyme or reason, and the unfinished construction of these massive and intricate sets, an exasperated Meyer Weisgal was heard to mutter: "Tonight the Jews *need* a miracle!"

According to Gottfried, they got it. He described three acts of "extraordinary power and poetry, moving and uplifting." He believed it to be a great cultural moment for the Jewish people, as well as for all suffering people throughout the world. "The Jewish destiny was captured to its very core," Reinhardt exclaimed, "and, yet, the overall effect was universal." And the critics agreed.

I was, of course, too young to attend the production party honoring Max Reinhardt that night at the Waldorf Astoria. Mayor La Guardia was among the dignitaries, but the highlight was a brief tribute from Albert Einstein, a great supporter of the efforts of Jews fleeing persecution in Europe—just as he had done several years earlier. It is both thrilling and humbling to think that Albert Einstein watched me go up that mountain and cry out, "Father!" in the retelling of the great Biblical story of Abraham and Isaac.

The Eternal Road was an extraordinary show that captured the fear of what was happening in Europe—and what was yet to come. It was specifically about the Jewish people, but its message against tyranny and racism was, as Gottfried wrote, universal. I played a very small role in that wondrous production, but it's one I'll never forget.

9
MENAGERIE

On the third floor of our Victorian house in Kew Gardens, Queens, I built my own menagerie. In retrospect, my life has always been connected in some way to animals. I've been watching, riding, and betting on horses for seventy-five years. Over the past decade, I've represented Natural Balance dog food, both as a spokesman and part owner. But, it was back in the days of my Queens menagerie that this infatuation with animals, and not just the cute ones, really took off.

I'm not sure how it began, but by the time I was seven years old, my aunt Marjorie was taking me all over Brooklyn, the Bronx, and Queens to sample the different pet shops. And every week, I would get a different pet to add to the menagerie. I bought chameleons, snakes, horn toads, even pet rats.

One favorite was my alligator, Oscar. In those days, you could buy alligators at a pet shop. Today it's against the law, but at the time the pet shops had big aquariums filled with baby alligators. They cost a dollar each. One day, Aunt Marjorie brought me to a pet store at 121st Street and Jamaica Avenue in Queens, and I bought Oscar. He was about a foot long, and he ate raw hamburger meat twice a day.

In time, Oscar began growing. Finally, he got so big he couldn't fit in the aquarium anymore, so I put him in the bathtub. For a month nobody could take a bath. That's when my Grandmother started yelling at me: "Get that alligator out of the bathtub." I didn't know what to do, so I brought him to the Central Park Zoo. The people at the zoo were very nice. They said I could come and visit whenever I wanted. For a while I used to go back and look at Oscar in the cage where he sat in a pool with all the other alligators and giant turtles. I guess he could still be there because alligators live a very long time, sometimes up to seventy years. But more likely Oscar has gone to his reward in animal heaven.

There was also a reptile show at Grand Central Station. It was located in a building above the tracks and run by a man named Dr. Ditmars. He was famous for his trips to Africa and other exotic locales where he captured various species of snakes and other reptiles, all of which he related in his best-selling books.

My Aunt Marjorie brought me to the show and introduced me to Dr. Ditmar. He asked if I'd like to have a snake. I said, "Sure." He opened a burlap bag and took this big black snake—called a milk snake even though it's black—and stuffed it in the sack. I still recall him handing it to me and nonchalantly saying: "Here you are, son."

We got on the subway, with me holding the snake in the burlap bag. When we arrived home, my father was fast asleep in his bed. That's when I got a brilliant idea on how to give someone a heart attack. I took the snake out of the bag, held it up in the air and yelled out: "Dad, Dad, look what I got!" The poor guy opened his eyes out of a fast sleep and saw this big black snake right in front of his head. He jumped out of bed and screamed. I'll never forget the look on his face. Imagine opening your eyes and having a black snake staring straight back at you. Needless to say, Dad wasn't too pleased with me for a few days.

Along with the alligator, chameleons, and snakes, I had rabbits, and even a big goat, that I kept in the backyard. But I also loved the more traditional pets. My first dog, Skippy, was a black and white cocker spaniel. My mother bought him for me when I was six years old. Later we added a cat, Beauty, and, while cats and dogs are supposed to be natural adversaries, these two became fast friends. In fact, when Skippy died, it seemed to affect Beauty more than anyone. Beauty must have found Skippy first after he died because I still remember walking into the backyard and seeing Beauty just sitting there motionless in front of Skippy as if protecting the dog's corpse from desecration. There was no doubt in my mind that Beauty was mourning the loss of a good friend.

If the various animals in the menagerie were my best friends in the animal kingdom, my closest friend growing up among the humans was my grandfather—Mom's dad, Vincent Acerno. Later he would be my best man when I married in 1954, and through the years he influenced me, for good or bad, as much or more than anyone in my life.

10

AND THEY'RE OFF

My grandfather was a bookie. I know that sounds terrible, but until 1941, horse betting was legal in the United States, and bookmaking was a legitimate, if not a wholly respectable, profession. Many argue that the most serious criminal involvement in horse-racing, including mob-controlled betting, really exploded only after bookmaking was criminalized in 1941. Whether that justifies the bookmaking profession is a complicated question—one I'll leave for others to decide. What I do know is that for over forty years, my grandfather got up every morning and headed to the racetrack just like any other man going to a job to support his family.

Vincent was born in Potenza, Italy, in 1881. Set at the top of the Italian boot, Potenza is a mountain town high in the Southern Apennine range. I'd never met anyone from Potenza until I happened to mention my lineage to Mel Brooks's wife, the marvelous actress, Anne Bancroft, and it turned out her parents also hailed from Potenza. They would have been there just before the turn of the century, and it's certainly possible that in such a relatively small town our grandparents could have been neighbors.

Vincent was tough as nails. He hung out with a rough crowd from the Lower East Side tenement houses. One of those local toughs was a funny guy with a big nose from Catherine Street named Jimmy Durante. Over the years Vincent and Jimmy became good friends, and Vincent would go to see Jimmy perform at Feldman's Bar on Coney Island where Durante got his start as a singing waiter. Like so many things, it has faded away, but the singing waiter was a common attraction at the time.

Years later in the 1970s, I caught one of Jimmy's shows at the Dunes in Las Vegas. Afterwards, my wife Pat and I went backstage and asked an usher to tell him that Dick Van Patten wanted to see him. A few minutes later the guy returned and said Jimmy doesn't know anyone named Dick Van Patten. So I told him to say it's Vincent Acerno's grandson. Moments later, Durante came running out all excited: "So you're Vincent Acerno's grandson!" Then he gave me his trademark line: "What can I do for ya!" It was thrilling to hear him reminisce about the old days with my grandfather in New York City. He was so nice that it's easy to see why Vincent became such close friends with him and why he reached such great heights as a comedian.

Growing up, I idolized my grandfather. I loved to hear him talk about New York City in the "good old days." The great year, he assured me, was 1920: Man o' War ruled the racetracks, Jack Dempsey was champ, and Babe Ruth first put on a Yankees uniform. The great tragedy of Vincent's life was watching Man o' War lose to a horse appropriately named, "Upset"—a race that prompted the Saratoga racetrack to be dubbed "The Graveyard of the Favorites."

Before the First World War, Vincent and his younger brothers, Johnny and Mickey, worked at a newsstand at the Hoboken Ferry station in New Jersey. They were just kids, teenagers really, and each day they took the ferry across the Hudson River to Hoboken. Along with the newspapers, they also sold daily racing forms. One day a bookmaker asked them to pick up bets for him from the commuters who passed through the newsstand.

It wasn't long before they started generating business. They worked for the guy for a few months, and things were going smoothly. Then one day they took a lot of bets on a particular race, and the bookmaker never showed. Stuck holding the bets, they were a nervous wreck. If there were a lot of winners, they wouldn't have had the money to pay.

But they got lucky. There were only a few winners, and they ended up making more money in a day than they ever earned selling newspapers. That got them wondering why they should turn their bets over to another bookmaker when they could do it for themselves. So they continued taking bets at the newsstand, paying off the winners and keeping the profits. In a very short time, the three Acerno boys were the main bookies at the Hoboken Ferry.

But Vincent and his brothers wanted bigger and better things. The next step was getting in the door at a racetrack. To do that, a prospective bookmaker needed both money and political pull. It cost one hundred dollars a day to set up a bookie's stall inside the grounds, and the competition to get in was so fierce you had to have the backing of someone with clout. Vincent knew a guy at Tammany Hall named Pete Hamill, a politician from the same section of the Lower East Side where the Acerno boys had grown up, and Hamill helped get them in the door at the Saratoga racetrack.

There were forty or fifty bookmakers working in front of the Grandstand inside Saratoga. I remember seeing my grandfather sitting up on a big high stool, like all the bookies, with a large blackboard next to him. He hired a guy to write down the odds for each race. They controlled the odds, which they fluctuated with each race. When someone bet a lot of money on a long shot, to protect themselves from a disastrous upset, they would immediately lower the odds. It was perfectly legitimate. They just had to work it out so regardless of who won, they made money.

For many years, Vincent earned a good living as a racetrack bookie. Then in 1940 the New York State Legislature passed a law disallowing anyone but the State from taking bets. In short, the government took over horse betting.

The day that law passed was one of the few times in my life I ever saw my grandfather upset. It ended the bookmaking profession, and he was out of work. He always believed that the law promoted the development of criminal syndicates. And it was true that as soon as the State took over, the mob moved in. They had always been involved outside the racetrack, but now with the government holding a legal monopoly on horse betting, the opportunities for illegal betting skyrocketed.

After the state takeover, Vincent continued working at Roosevelt Raceway as a ticket seller. But that also ended abruptly in 1942 when all American racetracks were shut down due to the war. In fact, the Santa Anita track, where the legendary Seabiscuit ran, was turned into an internment camp for Japanese Americans.

As a child, my grandfather took me to the Belmont track nearly every day. He taught me all about the racing business, and by the time I was ten years old I could handicap the horses. I also came to know my way around the racetrack. There was something about the grass, the horses, the jockeys, and then the excitement of the races that thrilled me even as a child.

At the time, I was unaware of the downside. I didn't yet fully understand that if you spend enough time around a racetrack, you're going to see some broken lives. Gambling can be an addiction as strong as any drug. There were times in my life when I felt that compulsion, and moments when it might have sent me, as it had so many others, spiraling downward into self-destruction.

When the tracks closed in 1942, Vincent retired. In his later years, he would head to Woodhaven Park every day to play pinochle with a group of old guys from the neighborhood. He looked forward to the games, although he had to walk five blocks up a steep hill from his house on Woodhaven Boulevard to the Park.

One day he didn't make it. On December 13, 1959, Vincent, 78 years old, fell in the snow. It was freezing, and he couldn't get up. I can't imagine what his last thoughts were as he lay there dying on that terrible winter night. I'm told that people who freeze to death experience a warm, calm feeling just before dying. I hope that happened. Perhaps Vincent was thinking about his great Man o' War or Dempsey knocking out Tunney, but I really hope and believe that in his final moments his mind turned to my grandmother, Rose, his wife for over fifty years, a truly wonderful woman who put up with more than her share of troubles from Vincent, but who loved him right to the end.

I was home in Bellerose with Pat and the kids when my Aunt Lucille called with the news. When I heard my grandfather was dead, it was one of the few times in my life that I've actually cried. I had to go over to the police precinct and then to the morgue to identify the body. At the morgue, they opened up a curtain, and there he was. There's no way to prepare for that. This was my grandfather, my best man, my closest friend, and there he was just a body on a slab of steel. It's a terrible shock to anyone when they open that curtain. It certainly was for me. I remember the cop asking me, "Is that your grandfather?" I said, "Yeah." But that body wasn't really Vincent Acerno. It was just a shell once occupied by a man full of life, who left his mark on me and everyone else he met.

The next day, I went to the park to hang a note on the bulletin board. I thought his friends should know he was gone. But a guy who worked at the park stopped me. "Take that down," he barked. I guess it violated some park rule. It's funny how some small things stick with you. I thought it was petty and mean-spirited, but I didn't say anything. Still, it always bothered me that he wouldn't let me notify the guys at the pinochle game that Vincent wouldn't be back.

But back in the late 1930s, Vincent was still very much alive, and one thing he never missed was a chance to see his grandson perform on Broadway. I was already beginning to build a small reputation as a child actor, and when *The Eternal Road* closed in May of 1937, Mom was busy plotting our next move.

11

A Broadway Résumé

In the winter of 1937, Mom heard about an upcoming play requiring an extensive and challenging child role. She thought this was our big chance. We went to the Longacre Theater on West 48th Street, and I auditioned for the role of a ten-year-old boy in a play called *On Borrowed Time*.

It wasn't meant to be. Two other youngsters attracted the director's attention, and it seemed to me that he had settled on these two fellows from the outset. Still, there was a smaller part for me, and a small part was better than none at all. Also, the director, a young man named Joshua Logan, was making his Broadway debut, and he had very much impressed my mother. Her instincts proved correct as Logan went on to become a legend in American theater and film, directing such Broadway classics as *South Pacific, Annie Get Your Gun,* and *Mister Roberts*, the latter a play where Joshua and I would again cross paths many years later.

It was always fun when there were other kids in a play. Once we came offstage, we were all equals. And we always found ways to enjoy ourselves in this adult world into which we'd been placed. The two boys, Peter Minor and Peter Holden, were each about a year younger than me. I like to think they got the part because I was too old. That's what my mother told me. In truth, they were both excellent. Peter Minor had opened the play on the road in New Haven, but when we arrived on Broadway, he became ill, and Peter Holden took it over and never let it go.

I'm not aware of either boy moving on to other roles or having careers in entertainment, but they certainly had the talent, and, at least for a time in 1938, Peter Holden dazzled New York City and the Broadway critics. Brooks Atkinson of the *New York Times* affirmed that Peter had, indeed, "won the hearts of the audience."

On Borrowed Time was a play about death—or more to the point—a play about what would happen in a world without death. Even as a child, I thought it was an interesting idea. Set in the post-World War I years, it opened with the sudden demise of a young boy's parents in a car crash. Their death leaves him in the care of his grandparents, who love him deeply. But the boy's aunt wants to adopt him. Her motives, however, are suspect. She knows his parents left a large sum of money that she could only get her hands on if the boy, named Pud, was in her custody.

Pud's grandfather sees through the designs of the aunt and determines that she should never get custody. But, it's not so easy. Soon, Granny dies, and then death comes for Gramps. Taking a human form, "Death"—who is dressed in a business suit and refers to himself as "Mr. Brinks"—tells Gramps it's time to go.

But Gramps has a card up his sleeve, which involves a special power he learned about at the expense of another young boy who keeps going into Gramps's tree and stealing his apples. That was my role. At first he can't catch me, but then Gramps, who has a birthday wish coming, blurts out in anger at me: "I wish you would stay up in that tree." With that, I became magically stuck. My repeated attempts to jump down were to no avail.

Eventually I did manage to loosen my clothes and drop from the tree. But, Gramps's now turned his new powers on Mr. Brinks, wishing him into the tree. It's never fully explained how I managed to get down, but Mr. Brinks couldn't. Still, it established the plays principal conflict: what would happen to the world if Death were caught in a tree and was unable to get on with his daily work?

Death on holiday sounds great—at least at first. And in my eightieth year it seems even more appealing than before. But as the old adage goes—be careful what you wish for because you just might get it.

With Mr. Brinks in the tree, the play confronts the unforeseen consequences of a world without death. Those who should die naturally, linger on. They endure great and pointless suffering. One of Gramps's friends, a doctor, discovers that death has been suspended. He recognizes the problems of life without death and tries to talk Gramps into letting Mr. Brinks out of the tree.

Things offstage were getting as dicey as they were onstage. Shortly before taking the part, I had switched from public school to Holy Child, a Catholic school run by the Saint Joseph's nuns. One of the very first things the nuns drummed into our impressionable heads was that cursing of any kind was a serious sin.

The lesson must have stuck. Although I've certainly had my share of vices, I never really felt comfortable around a lot of cursing, and I seldom do it myself. It just rarely seems appropriate to me. I've heard about people who learn to curse while serving as soldiers, and I imagine that living under that kind of stress one might be more inclined to let out some colorful language. In any event, my reticence to curse was never more pronounced than during the days when the Sisters of Saint Joseph hammered into me the dire consequences in store for anyone with a foul mouth.

That brings us to the crisis of *On Borrowed Time*. Back in 1938, Gramps was originally played by Richard Bennett, a giant on the American stage for half a century who had made his Broadway debut as far back as the 1890s. Bennett was Joshua Logan's absolute first choice for the part. In his memoirs, Logan confirms that "[O]ne actor and one actor alone seemed perfect: Richard Bennett." When it turned out Bennett was available and interested, Logan was sure he had a winner. But, again, be wary what you ask for!

It wasn't long before we all realized that Bennett, now sixty-eight years old, was having serious difficulty with the role. Throughout rehearsals, he mumbled his lines almost incoherently. Logan later claimed he was not at first concerned because in the theater world there are actors who "save" their best performance for the live audience. But no one on the set was buying that. It was perfectly clear that something more was going on here—this was not just an actor keeping his powder dry for the big night. Even all of us kids could see that Bennett wasn't just mumbling. On the contrary, he just couldn't remember his lines.

When the play opened at the Shubert Theater in New Haven Connecticut, Bennett literally froze onstage. Fortunately Peter Minor, who knew the entire play by heart, managed to walk inconspicuously across the stage and whisper his lines to him. As good as Peter was, it was still obvious to the audience. In fact, Bennett, calling upon his considerable stage instincts, said to Peter: "Thank you, son. That's real thoughtful of you." The audience laughed, no doubt wanting to give some support to this elderly man who was clearly struggling. Had it stopped then, everything would have been fine. But it didn't.

Throughout the entire run, Bennett was irascible. He took criticism hard, which made it doubly difficult for Joshua Logan. Still, Logan was not about to see his upcoming Broadway debut fall apart, and so he kept after Bennett to remember his lines. He also tried to help him by placing extra prompters offstage.

Notwithstanding Logan's best efforts, the situation deteriorated, and the fighting between Bennett and Logan escalated to a point where these two Broadway giants were cursing up a storm at every rehearsal and before and after each performance. It was the first time I had seen real battles backstage between a director and actor, and it wasn't pretty.

And it still would all have been just boring adult stuff to me, except that I had been taught so well by the nuns to bow my head and bless myself each time I heard a curse word. So for several weeks during the road show of *On Borrowed Time*, my most prominent memory is dropping my head like a bobbing-head doll while repeating every two seconds, "Bless me, Bless me" as Logan and Bennett raised the roof with streams of obscenities that rang out in theaters from Hartford to Boston.

In his book, Josh Logan is generous to Bennett. He omits the knock-down, drag-out sessions that gave this poor Catholic kid a sore neck every night. Logan largely blamed the producers who were concerned that the show's investors would pull out if something wasn't done. The truth is that even we kids realized that something had to be done, and as we approached Broadway, it was obvious there needed to be a change. Logan finally fired Bennett and pulled in a wonderful character actor, Dudley Diggs, who memorized his role in a weekend. On opening night on February 3, 1938, at Broadway's Longacre Theater, he and Peter Holden gave stunning performances and won over both the crowd and the critics.

A year later, *On Borrowed Time* was made into a movie, with the great Lionel Barrymore playing Gramps. The film was a hit, and any other year it may have gone home with some Oscars. But that was 1939, the magical year of American film with *Gone with the Wind*, *The Wizard of Oz*, *The Third Man*, *Wuthering Heights*, and *Mutiny on The Bounty*. Still, *On Borrowed Time* has its place as a charming fantasy—one that raised serious questions about the way we confront our own mortality. It did so, moreover, at just the right time, as the country was not yet fully consumed with the horrors of the war that waited just around the corner.

* * *

I was nine years old during the run of *On Borrowed Time* in 1938, and it was time for another life lesson. This time it had to do with the loss of things we hold dear. During the run, we moved a short distance from Kew Gardens to Richmond Hill. It's always sad for a child to leave an old neighborhood and old friends, but in this case it wasn't such a shock because my new home was just a few blocks away. What really did bother me, however, was leaving our old Victorian house, which had been the home of my menagerie. Although I did, like Noah, transport all of my reptiles and other friends to the basement of our new brick Tudor home, it was a traumatic experience.

After we left the house, the owners sold it to developers who were about to turn the lot into an apartment building. One day I rode over on my bicycle. The men were working, and I watched while they literally tore the house down. I saw that big iron ball crashing right into my bedroom. It was terrible. The feeling of loss cut deeply as they thoroughly destroyed the place that held all my most precious memories. I've always valued my home and family as a shelter against the vagaries of life. Our early experiences, of course, help shape our future behavior. I think the image of that wrecking ball laying waste to my very first home in Kew Gardens accounts for my lifelong desire for stability and permanence at home.

12

THE FAMILY HEARTH

Today it's hard to imagine a world without television. Over the past half century, it's become such a central part of every household—and not just in America. *Eight Is Enough*, for example, was an international hit. It played in various European countries under such titles as *La Famiglia Bradford, Otto Bastano, Huit, ça suffit!*, and *Con Ocho Basta*. Today television shows are broadcast around the world almost as soon as their release in the United States. The enormous influence and power of television is, for good or bad, an integral fact of our world. Television has become the centerpiece of every home, and even the advance of computers has done little to diminish its stature.

But there was a time before television. Until a few years after World War II, as my old friend and producer Bob Evans points out in his memoirs, radio was "king." Bob captures the times perfectly: "No matter how poor you were everyone in America had a church-shaped Philco or Edison in their living room. It was the family hearth."

And the shows broadcast over the "family hearth" were as diverse as our television programming. Just as today, families gathered around their radios to listen to their favorite shows, ranging from detective stories, mysteries, soap operas, comedies, and variety shows—even cartoons broadcast by real actors. And following those shows required a fertile imagination. As Larry King has recently noted, radio created a genuine "theater of the mind." Unlike the passivity of watching television or movies, radio made you work—everyone became involved in the creative process of putting flesh and bones to the names and places described by the great radio actors. With radio everyone participated. If a million people heard a program, then the story played out in a million different "theaters of the mind"—a million unique creations prompted by the writers and actors, but brought to life in every single unique imagination.

Among the most popular cartoons of my childhood was *Reg'lar Fellas*. Written and drawn by Jerry Devine, it was known to everyone who picked up a newspaper. In 1941, NBC decided to turn *Reg'lar Fellas* into a radio show. I landed the part of Jimmy

Duggan, the lead character. Others were Raymond Ives Jr. as Puddin' Head Duffy, Eddie Phillips as Wash Jones, and Dickie Monahan as Dinky Duggan, my younger brother. Also, Skippy Homeier had a small part as the sissy in the group. He would later star with my sister, Joyce, in the Broadway hit, *Tomorrow the World*. In May of 1941, *Reg'lar Fellas* replaced *The Jack Benny Show* for the summer at the prime-time spot on Sunday night. The show was first recorded live at 7 p.m. Later we all returned to the studio to broadcast a 10 p.m. performance for the West Coast.

Reg'lar Fellas was one of several hundred shows I worked on during twenty years in radio. Among the most popular were *Young Widder Brown, Henry Aldrich, David Harem,* and *Duffy's Tavern.* Each of them were hits that lasted for years. In fact, my schedule was so hectic that on Thursdays I did *David Harem* at 11:00 a.m. then went to *Young Widder Brown* at 3:45 p.m. and ended with *Henry Aldrich* at 8 p.m.

But there was one show that stands above the rest: *Miss Hattie.* Running for two years in the early 1940s, *Miss Hattie* was unusual for two reasons: first, there were only two regular stars. Most of the shows had large ensemble casts. I played one of the roles, Teddy, the nephew of the widow, Miss Hattie Thompson. Second, my co-star was the great Ethel Barrymore.

It would be impossible to exaggerate the stature of Ethel Barrymore. Known as "the first lady of the American theater," Ethel was the sister of John and Lionel Barrymore and easily the biggest stage actress of the first half of the twentieth century. As a young woman, she was engaged to Winston Churchill, and, although they never married, the two maintained a close friendship throughout their lives. Many giants of Broadway, like Alfred Lunt and Lynn Fontanne, with whom I eventually worked, came of age when the theater world was ruled by the Barrymores. In fact, by the time I worked on *Miss Hattie* with Ethel Barrymore, there was already a theater named after her on Broadway.

Although I was just thirteen years old when we began our radio program together, I recognized that Miss Barrymore was viewed differently by others, almost with a sense of awe. Perhaps my mother was the one most astonished—and delighted—that her child was actually sharing the limelight with this icon of the American stage. It was especially fortuitous because Ethel actually did very little work on the radio. Born in 1879, Ethel was the granddaughter of John Drew, patriarch of one of the oldest American theater families. One other such elite theater family in the mid-19th century was the Booths. On occasion, I marvel at the brevity of time, considering that I worked with a woman whose grandfather may well have known and acted with John Wilkes Booth, the man who assassinated President Lincoln.

Recently I listened to an old recording of *Miss Hattie.* This particular episode is a courtroom drama called, *Teddy Thinks He's Blind in One Eye.* Hearing Ethel Barrymore perform not only kindles old memories, but reminds me of a very different age of acting. Her voice was a model of perfect enunciation. It possessed a dignified quality, almost like an elevated British accent—which makes sense given her relationship with Churchill. Like her brothers, John and Lionel, Ethel represented a classical style of acting that reigned over Broadway for many years.

Listening to *Miss Hattie*, I also noticed my own voice sounded remarkably like Mickey Rooney. Mickey was the biggest child star in America, and like everyone my age, I loved his *Hardy Boy* movies. While I don't recall ever consciously making an effort to imitate Mickey's intonation, it may well have been in the back of my mind. Actors, like singers, often begin by copying those they admire before fully developing their own style. Of course, it may also be that as a youngster I just happened to sound a bit like Mickey.

One aspect of live radio programming that people may not fully realize is that shows were often broadcast in big theaters to large crowds. Throughout the years, I played radio programs in front of thousands of people at the biggest theaters in New York City and many other cities, and the pulse of the audience could be as integral to a good performance as it is in the theater.

I always deeply admired the radio actors. They were what I call "fast actors." They learned their parts quickly, and the best ones could change character at a moment's notice. My favorites were Richard Widmark, Frank Lovejoy, and Agnes Morehead—and I had the good fortune to work with all of them.

The radio actors also had to be adept with a live mike. Unlike today's film or television shows, the radio shows were all broadcast live. As a result there was the occasional screwup, which could be fatal. One such instance involved, *Uncle Don*, one of the most popular kid shows in America. I well recall the scandal that ended Uncle Don's career—one that involved a moment when Uncle Don, like many of our politicians, came to appreciate the dangers of a live mike only after it was too late. One evening, just as the show was ending, Uncle Don gave his trademark, "This is your Uncle Don, saying, 'Goodnight, Kiddies.'" He should have left it at that. Instead, without realizing he was still on the air, he muttered, "That should hold the goddamn brats." Needless to say, there was an abrupt demise to Uncle Don's career.

At the same time my radio career took off, Broadway was again reacting to events abroad, and Mom was anxious for me to land a part in a giant new spectacular, directed by George S. Kaufman. The play, written by Moss Hart, was to be a celebration of the American way of life. But, it was also a warning against dangers threatening that way of life, from within as much as from aggressive foreign powers. It was interesting to hear President Obama, in his recent inaugural address, warn that we must "reject as false the choice between safety and our ideals." We should protect our American way of life without sacrificing the principles that make us who we are. Striking that balance is, perhaps, the greatest challenge confronting any free nation, and it was no different in the late 1930s than it is today.

13

THE AMERICAN WAY

In the winter of 1938, the drums of war were sounding in Europe, and Americans were already embroiled in a debate over what we should do when the fighting started. Broadway, as always, responded to the situation—this time with a patriotic extravaganza titled, *The American Way*—one that raised serious questions about national loyalties.

The play was a massive production, staged at my favorite venue in New York City, the Center Theater on 47th Street in Rockefeller Center. The Center, which was later transformed into New York's first Ice Theater, was modeled on Radio City Music Hall, which is next door. The Center was a gorgeous playhouse, with three balconies as well as dressing rooms with mirrors instead of walls, so the actors could see themselves from every angle before heading onstage.

The Center was enormous, seating around four-thousand people. It was also enormous underground. One day I discovered a secret passageway in the basement that wound around all the way to Radio City Music Hall. In time, the forty other kids in the play and I were exploring those old tunnels. Although I was the only child with lines in the play, there were no hierarchies among us. In fact, I even developed my very first crush on a young girl named Connie Large. Regrettably, she didn't reciprocate. I don't know what ever happened to Connie, and although she broke my heart back in 1939, I hope she's had a happy life.

The American Way told the story of Martin Gunther, a German immigrant, played by Fredric March. Gunther brought his family to the United States late in the 19th century, and when World War I broke out, he found himself in the midst of a terrible internal conflict. His wife, played by Florence Eldridge—who was married to Fredric March in real life—was opposed to their son fighting in the war, fearing he might be forced to kill the children of their friends and family back in Germany. There's a scene I still remember vividly when the townspeople, in a fit of xenophobia, gather outside the Gunther home, throwing bricks through the windows. The mob yelled, "Slacker, Slacker," a word that at the time had a different connotation than today. Rather than "lazy," it meant "coward," and the mob was angry that Gunther's son, played by David Wayne, had not yet enlisted. They got their way, and despite his mother's reservations, the young man signed up and died in the war, leaving the Gunther family angry and bitter.

Things then moved ahead to 1927, at which time I entered as Karl, Martin Gunther's grandson. My initial entrance was the moment when Fredric March scolded me for talking to him about the Joe Louis fight. I remember my first lines: "What about Lindy? Did he get there yet?" Staged in 1939, this act of the play was set twelve years earlier on the night of Charles Lindbergh's historic flight across the Atlantic. Everyone listened for news of his progress on the radio as he headed toward Paris.

Lindbergh's flight took place in May of 1927, over a year before I was born. But Lucky Lindy was still a hero to me. My parents talked a great deal about the kidnapping of his child, which took place in 1934, when I was five years old. We listened to reports from the trial on the radio, and I remember when Bruno Hauptmann was executed in 1936. Recently, I saw the courtroom where the historic trial was held in Flemington, New Jersey, and was told that each year a local theater group performs a reenactment of the trial in the same courtroom.

The American Way ends with Karl, now grown up in 1939, joining a German Bund, whose members are sympathetic to the Nazis. Again his Grandfather tries to convince his wife and grandson that they are Americans now and should reject these flirtations with the racist propaganda emanating from the Third Reich—propaganda that too often found a home among impressionable young men in the German-American Bunds.

The play raised this dilemma of divided loyalties. Such divisions are an inevitable problem in a country of immigrants. Even as a ten-year-old in 1939, I understood that if we went to war our soldiers might be fighting against relatives or friends back in Europe. In fact, I understood the issues in this play in a very personal way because of the alliance between Mussolini and Hitler. On the Italian side of my family, there was strong sentiment against our involvement in the war. My mother's sisters, aunt Lucille and aunt Beatrice, were especially vocal in their support of isolationism.

There were many prominent people in the country who shared their view. The most famous was Lindbergh himself. At the time, Lindy was a leading spokesman for the America First movement, which opposed our intervention in the War. His passion for isolationism brought accusations of anti-Semitism and of being a Nazi sympathizer against him. Those charges were largely laid to rest after Pearl Harbor when Lindy reenlisted in the Air Force and flew fighter planes in the Pacific Theater. There were many other distinguished people in the America First movement, both liberals and conservatives, including a young Gerald Ford, who would, of course, become President of the United States and Potter Stewart, later a Supreme Court Justice.

I was twelve years old when my aunts took me to an America First rally at Madison Square Garden in 1941. I still recall the impassioned speech of an actor named Eddie Bracken, who clearly believed his outspoken support of the movement would destroy his career. That night he told the Garden crowd: "I'll never work again." But the cause, he insisted, was important enough that he was willing to make the sacrifice. As it turns out, Bracken did work again and actually had his biggest hit film, *The Miracle of Morgan's Creek*, only a few years later in 1944. He continued to have a successful career, ultimately receiving two stars on the Hollywood Walk of Fame. But that night, he definitely felt he was putting his career in jeopardy, and regardless of whether his position was ultimately correct—and I believe it was not—he, nevertheless, followed his conscience.

Coincidentally, years later, I worked with Eddie on an episode of the *The New Dick Van Dyke Show*. He was a very nice man, and I was tempted to mention having seen him at the Garden, but I decided against it.

Several months after *The American Way* opened, Hitler invaded Poland. I recall the massive headlines announcing the invasion. With the start of the war, the questions raised by Moss Hart when he first drafted the play had now become even more relevant to the audiences at the Center Theater, who, like everyone, struggled with the question of whether or not to take up arms in Europe.

Even at age ten, I understood that this play, like *The Eternal Road*, was something more than just entertainment. It was clear that theater could actually affect people's lives. I imagine Fredric March understood exactly that when he told me to get my mind off the boxing match and on the play. There were important things happening in the world, and a play like *The American Way* became a part of the public conversation about those events. In its own way, it helped to shape the manner in which people understood the world that seemed to be crashing in on them. Looking back, I realize that this was theater at its best.

14

THE GREAT FAIR OF '39

But, of course, I was still a kid. And foremost on my mind in early 1939 was not impending war, but the arrival of the New York World's Fair. In fact, everyone awaited with great anticipation the Grand Opening on April 30, 1939. President Franklin Roosevelt inaugurated the fair by delivering one of the first televised speeches ever, viewed by some two-hundred people with televisions sets in the New York area. The fair was also a source of work in the Depression, and a lot of the kids on *The American Way* left for better pay in a play called *The American Jubilee*, at the World's Fair.

The fair was held at Corona Park in Flushing Meadow, Queens—the same location as the 1965 fair. That was just a short distance from our home in Kew Gardens, and after school let out, I went to the fair nearly every day. My favorite place was the Amusement Area where each day they put on different shows.

For some reason I've always had an odd attraction to the bizarre. And there was plenty of that at the fair. As often as possible, I would go see Olga, the Headless Girl. They said Olga had been in a train crash, lost her head, and miraculously was still living without it. They even had a giant picture of the train wreck. There wasn't much to the show—just Olga sitting there with a tube coming out of her neck.

It may be that Olga really did have a head, but they sure fooled me. I honestly believed it was true; that this girl was living without a head. It sounds crazy, but it looked absolutely real. Years later a magician told me it was all done with mirrors. If so, that was some trick. It was so convincing that I never missed a chance to see headless Olga at the fair.

My other favorite exhibit would be considered tasteless today—and properly so. It was the Midget Village—an entire miniature town, with houses and everything, where little people lived. At the time, it simply didn't occur to me that this was cruel or insensitive. Again, it appealed to my penchant for oddities, something that has stayed with me my whole life.

On a typical day I hustled from Olga to the Midget Village and then to the Parachute Jump, where they raised you 250 feet in the air with your feet dangling, and then dropped you like a rock. The plummet was an incredible rush. Today with bungee jumping, skydiving, soldiers parachuting from airplanes, and swat teams rappelling down the sides of buildings, the Parachute Jump may not seem so extraordinary. But in 1939 nobody had ever heard of anything like a free-fall from the sky in a parachute. In fact, on opening day of the fair, the Parachute Jump generated its own controversy when the pulleys malfunctioned, and a young couple was stuck at the top for seven hours. The next day there was a picture on the front page of the *Daily News* of the terrified lovers. After the World's Fair ended, they moved the Parachute Jump to Coney Island, and I used to take the plunge over there as often as possible.

I also loved Billy Rose's Aquacade, which starred Rose's wife, Eleanor Holm. The show was performed in a tremendous pool. At the outset, the pool was empty. Then, suddenly, it filled with water. At the same time some fifteen girls suddenly appeared in the pool. Everyone was amazed, wondering how they all got in there. Later I learned the girls entered from trap doors placed underneath the pool. The women performed synchronized swimming, which would become popular in a series of MGM films in the 1940s starring Esther Williams.

For me, the world's greatest comedians were Abbott and Costello. They also performed at the 1939 World's Fair, in a show called *Streets of Paris*. I was just eleven, and Bud and Lou were not yet famous. In fact, their very first movie, *A Night in the Tropics*, came a year later in 1940, and top billing actually went to the leading man, Allan Jones, who had worked with The Marx Brothers in *Night at the Opera*. In *Streets of Paris*, Abbott and Costello were billed only as "radio sensations." But their ascent to the top had just begun, and a year later in *Buck Private*, a war movie, they exploded into national stardom.

Their rise began with a Broadway version of *Streets of Paris*—as things turned out that production at the Broadhurst Theater would be their only Broadway show. It was only modestly successful on Broadway, but then they were hired to do four shows a day at the World's Fair. The fair had become such a tremendous event that all the entertainers were trying to get in it.

Streets of Paris was essentially a burlesque, and it co-starred the famous stripper Gypsy Rose Lee. It also had Bill "Bojangles" Robinson, the wonderful dance partner of Shirley Temple. I used to hear the barker yell out: "Come and see the world's funniest comedy team and ten beautiful girls with nothing on but a great big smile." I was dying to get in, but I was underage. I thought about trying to sneak in, but never got past the barker. Anyway, it whetted my appetite to see these two new comics.

Ten years later, I would come to know Lou Costello personally, mostly because of our mutual penchant for a good card game. After *Streets of Paris*, Lou moved to Hollywood to pursue his movie career. But he often returned to New York, and in the 1950s, he would call me up and ask if I could put together a game of cards. I would immediately round up a bunch of guys, and we headed to Lou's suite at the Essex House where we played all night. Lou was a serious player, and he was in every pot. For me, win or lose, I was just happy to be around the man who was, in my view, the funniest comedian in America.

You get to know people pretty well at the poker table. But, in all the time I spent with Lou Costello, I never once saw any evidence of the deep tragedy he carried with him through most of his adult life. It was a well-known story. The whole country seemed to be in shock when Lou's first child, Lou Jr., drowned in their swimming pool a few days short of his first birthday. What compounded the shock, and mystified many, was that Lou insisted on going on air that night for the regular broadcast of *The Abbott and Costello* radio show. I remember listening to the program, and like everyone else, I noticed nothing out of the ordinary. Lou seemed to be his regular hilarious self.

When it was over, Lou left the studio, and Bud Abbott took the mike and told the audience he had some personal comments. Bud then informed millions of radio listeners that Lou's child had died earlier in the day. It was one of those moments you never forget—like a presidential assassination or the moon landing. In her book, *Lou's on First*, Lou's daughter, Chris Costello, provides a moving account of the whole day, including Abbott's speech. Bud explained: "Ladies and Gentlemen, now that the program is over, and we have done our best to entertain you I would like to take a moment to pay tribute to my best friend, and to a man who has more courage than I have ever seen displayed in the theater. Tonight the old expression, 'The show must go on' was brought home to us on this program more clearly than ever before. Just a short time before this broadcast started, Lou Costello was told that his baby son—who would have been one year old in a couple of days—had died."

Through the years I've heard people wonder how in the world Lou could have performed that night. His son had just died.

It seemed inconceivable that anyone could perform, much less perform comedy, under such circumstances. But Bud Abbott explained after the broadcast that Lou performed so that "you, the audience, would not be disappointed." I'm sure there is much truth in that. Lou was the consummate professional. As Fredric March taught me, the show is the important thing.

At the same time, I wonder if there might have been some small relief for Lou in stepping away, if only momentarily, from the crushing reality that must have overwhelmed him on that terrible day. Afterwards, Lou's celebrity status continued rising, as he made over twenty-five films in the fifteen years after his son's death. And in the contact we had in those all-night card games at the Essex House, I never saw any sign of depression or lingering sadness. But it was always present. His daughter, Chris, tells us that, for Lou, the child's death "clouded everything else he did for the rest of his life." As the father of three boys, I have no doubt that's true.

Lou Costello came from Paterson, New Jersey, and today there is a statue downtown in Costello Park. Lou richly deserves it.

15

THE LAND IS BRIGHT!

I loved the Polo Grounds. Home of the New York Giants baseball team, it had one of America's greatest sporting traditions dating back to the days of John McGraw, Leo Durocher, later Willie Mays and finally the New York Mets who, in the early 1960s, played their first three seasons there while awaiting the construction of Shea Stadium.

On a chilly December day, I went to see the Dodgers and Giants with my Grandfather's brother, Uncle Mickey, and my cousins, Donald, Richard and Renee. Younger sports fans might be wondering why those two great New York baseball rivals would be playing in December. But old-time New Yorkers will recall that there were actually two professional football teams in New York City, and they were also named the Dodgers and the Giants. The Giants, of course, still play in Giant Stadium across the river in New Jersey's Meadowlands, but the Brooklyn Dodgers football franchise closed in 1944.

We were sitting in the upper deck of the Polo Grounds that afternoon, and I honestly don't remember who won the game. But when it ended, it took a few minutes for us to make our way out of the stadium and into the streets of Harlem. When we emerged, we were immediately struck by a tremendous excitement out on the streets. Above the din, newspaper vendors were shouting in that distinctive voice unique to their trade: "Extree! Extree! Read all about it! America bombed by the Japanese!"

Like everyone there, we wanted a newspaper. But it wasn't so easy. For the first and only time in my life, I saw a massive line of people trying to buy one as they exited the Polo Grounds and heard the news. I doubt many people there had even heard of Pearl Harbor—I know I hadn't. But as we waited in line it became more and more clear that the Japanese had attacked us. I was two days short of my thirteenth birthday, and while I didn't comprehend the full import of the news—nor did anyone else at the time—I did realize that the debate over the conflict had now been decided by the enemy: the United States would be entering the war. The next day we huddled around the radio at home and once again listened anxiously as the familiar voice of Franklin Roosevelt explained that the day before "was a day that will live in infamy."

I've mentioned how my maternal aunts Lucille and Beatrice had taken me to an *America First* rally at Madison Square Garden where a number of celebrities, including actor Eddie Bracken, had opposed our involvement in the Second World War. Coming from an Italian family, many of whom had been brought up in immigrant communities along the Lower East Side, there were strong feelings among some family members against involvement in a war that might pit us against Italy and potentially in a fight against family members still back in Potenza. As *The American Way* had shown, these divided feelings run deep in a country of immigrants.

But the attack on Pearl Harbor put an end to that. Much like what occurred in the aftermath of September 11, 2001, most of the country put its differences aside and united in a joint cause against the Japanese military dictators as well as the European Fascists. Regrettably, not everyone acted perfectly as actions were taken by the government against Japanese Americans, who were interned in California. Notwithstanding this, the country was united as never before.

Ironically, at the time of the Pearl Harbor attack, I had just begun working in a Broadway play that had been designed precisely to encourage our entrance into the War. *The Land Is Bright*, written by the Pulitzer Prize–winning author Edna Ferber—whose *Showboat* had so influenced my parents—and directed by George S. Kaufman, opened at the Music Box just two months before the attack.

Ferber's play related the saga of the fictional Kincaids, a rich American dynastic family. Their enormous wealth had been accumulated in the 1800s, when family patriarch, Lacey Kincaid, through unethical financial practices, had made a fortune. Like *The American Way*, *The Land Is Bright* told the story through several generations, beginning with the original period of Lacey Kincaid's wealth accumulation, and then moving to the profligate behavior of his children during the Roaring Twenties. One critic noted the exceptional performance of Diana Barrymore, the daughter of John and grandmother of Drew Barrymore—who was sensational as the wild and dissolute flapper who recklessly squandered her enormous wealth on booze and parties.

The final scene took place in contemporary 1941 at the family's plush Park Avenue apartment. By this time, the new generation of Kincaids began to recognize the gravity of their past sins. I played Timothy Kincaid, the ten-year-old great grandson of

Lacey Kincaid. Ferber and Kaufman used my character to help move the family toward a final commitment to the country that had given them so much.

The Land Is Bright was certainly a nationalist play. Still, it was one recognizing that our democracy—indeed our destiny as a nation—was bound to events outside our borders. Burns Mantle of *The Daily News* wrote about the transformation among the Kincaids: "The second world war took the great grandchildren in hand and did something to them." The contrast between the terrible realities of war and the Kincaid's privileged lives is brought home in the final act when a broken Lacey Kincaid II, barely able to walk, returns home after spending several years in a German concentration camp—next to his tragic presence, as Brooks Atkinson, noted, "the Kincaid fortune looks like a very trivial thing." The play ends in a kind of rebirth with the Kincaids rejecting their past and committing themselves to defending the country they had so abused and taken advantage of.

The title for *The Land Is Bright* came from the poem, *Say Not the Struggle Nauth Availeth* by the Irish Victorian poet Arthur Hugh Clough. The pertinent line reads: "Look Westward, The Land Is Bright." Clough's poem was relatively obscure until April of 1941 when it was immortalized by Winston Churchill who used it in a powerful speech pleading for the United States to enter the war on the side of the Allies.

Churchill's advocacy of American intervention was fully supported by many Americans, including Max Gordon, the play's producer. Gordon, one of the most successful theater producers of his time, loved the intrigue of the political world and was never shy about using his own productions to advance his political agenda. Accordingly, he placed the stanza from Clough's poem in the play's program so that everyone who came to the theater would understand its meaning.

Gordon also decided to test run a production in Washington where, as Kaufman biographer Malcolm Goldstein notes, Gordon "could hobnob with friends in office and pay social calls at the White House." As it turned out, his hobnobbing paid off as we were invited to perform for the First Lady, Eleanor Roosevelt, as well as the Vice President of the United States, Henry Wallace.

After the performance, Eleanor Roosevelt wrote a review of the play. Throughout much of her husband's presidency, Ms. Roosevelt penned her own popular syndicated column, *My Day* in which the First Lady championed her various political and social causes. In the review, she expressed her enjoyment of the play, particularly with the depiction of the younger generation of Kincaids. Mrs. Roosevelt wrote: "In the evening a few of us were the guests of Mr. Max Gordon at his new play, *The Land Is Bright.* The play is well acted, and I came away with one great sense of satisfaction, for the youth of today are more serious and more purposeful than the youth portrayed in the first two acts of the play. The honesty of the younger generation, as it looks back on its ancestors, is like a breath of fresh air. It points the moral that the whole level of public responsibility and integrity has gone up over the period of the last 50 years."

And so, my life path again intersected with Mrs. Roosevelt. I doubt she recognized me as the little boy with the poem about his mother at the MGM/Loew's Screen and Voice Contest seven years earlier. But when she wrote of the "honesty of the younger generation as it looks back on its ancestors," I like to think that she was reflecting on my character, Timothy Kincaid.

My favorite line in the play—naturally my own line— brought a great laugh toward the end of every performance. It's set up by Timothy insisting that he doesn't want to go to school. When questioned, he explains that the class is studying United States history. "And tomorrow we come to the Robber Barons," he complains, "and Great Grandpa Kincaid was one of them!"

The family, of course, is properly mortified and tries to explain that it's not true. But Timothy responds fervently: "It is so true! It's in the history book. And a lot of the fellows won't speak to me because it says"—here Timothy picks up the history book to read the relevant passage: "'These despoilers of a continent were brigands who undermined the foundations of America.' And there's a picture of him"—meaning his great grandfather, Lacey Kincaid. The family again tells him that it's all "ridiculous" and that he shouldn't pay it any attention. That ends things for the moment.

But soon, everyone sits down for dinner at the dining table and conversation again turns to Lacey Kincaid. His son, Grant, now an elderly man, suddenly picks up his glass and proposes a toast to his father, "To the man who ran a pickax up into two hundred million dollars, a real American—Lacey Kincaid." Everyone raises their glasses to toast. It's a solemn moment of familial solidarity as they pay homage to their forebear. But, just as they all start to drink their expensive wine, I blurt out: "Great-grandpa was an old crook!"

With that, everyone choked on their drinks with a great deal of sputtering and spitting, and the audience loved it every time.

It was also the moment when I really learned about comedic timing—and I learned it from the master. During one of the dress rehearsals before taking the show to Washington, we did that scene. As usual, I could see George S. Kaufman and Edna Ferber sitting together in the audience watching attentively. Usually directors don't like the writers around, but Kaufman and Ferber had a very special rapport, and she was frequently there right at his side throughout the rehearsals and productions.

Kaufman, as always, was squinting at me through his thick horn-rimmed glasses, leaving me uncertain whether he was mad or just couldn't see. Anyway, after I delivered the line, he stopped the action and pointed right at me. I still remember his words: "Don't say it right away! Hold the line. Take a couple of beats. Let them start drinking and *then* say it."

The next time I did just that—holding the line for two beats—and it was magic. The whole table started spitting up their drinks as I waited until the toast was done and they were all actually drinking before abruptly announcing that "Great Grandpa was an old crook!" Edna Ferber also loved it. Afterwards, she told me if I did it like that when we opened on Broadway, I could have anything I wanted. Without holding for any beats, I told her I wanted a pet rabbit. So on opening night at the Music Box, I hit the line just right. I waited two beats and had all of them spitting up their drinks. After the show, Miss Ferber walked up four flights to the dressing room and entered with a big brown box, which she handed to me. I opened it, and there was a beautiful white rabbit inside. I was in heaven!

16

DANCING WITH THE STARS

By this time I had made a final transfer to New York City's Professional Children's School, which was designed for kids with jobs in entertainment. Throughout the years PCS has had many students from Milton Berle, Martin Landau and Joan Blondell, to more recent alumni such as Christian Slater, Macaulay Culkin and many more. PCS is still open today.

One day in the fall of 1941, a young girl named Patricia Poole showed up. The pretty young blonde with pig-tails sat right next to me in one of those adjoining desks.

Although younger than me, I immediately sized her up as a superior student, which meant that with a little tact, I could start copying her homework. At the time, this was the extent of my designs on Patricia Poole, having no idea, of course, that seventy years later we would be celebrating our fifty-fifth wedding anniversary.

Pat could dance before she could walk. She and her brother Robbie were the premier students of her mother, Helon Powell Poole, a true pioneer in the world of American dance. When Pat was born in 1931, Helon ran the biggest dance school in Charlotte, North Carolina, called The Poole School of Dancing and whenever the big name dancers traveled into the South, they would stop by to meet Helon.

Pat's mother was responsible for spreading new dance crazes, not just throughout Charlotte, but all across the country. Helon was a regularly featured writer in the most important dance magazine of the first half of the twentieth-century, titled *American Dance*. According to John Hook, author of *Shagging in the Carolinas*, Helon became America's principal spokesperson for the Big Apple, the Shag and the Swing in the 1930s. Hook, who has done remarkable research on the history of dance in the American South, marveled at Helon's accomplishments, claiming that Helon was "doing things that no other Southern gal could, or would, do."

He's right. Helon was a genuine innovator. Pat recalls a time in the mid-1930s when her mom drove off on her own to Columbia, South Carolina, just because she had heard there was a new dance circulating in the Black dance halls. She went to one of the auditoriums, sat up in the balcony, and watched as they worked on a new dance called, the Big Apple. She took detailed notes, choreographing all the steps. She then went home, showed it to her students, taught the steps on Charlotte's powerful WBT radio, and introduced it to a much larger audience in *American Dancer* magazine. Largely because of Helon's efforts, the Big Apple caught on everywhere. According to John Hook, Pat's mom was a key player as the Big Apple "exploded out of the South and across the nation and the Atlantic to Europe."

In fact, the Big Apple song and dance craze of 1937 was one of a number of factors that helped popularize New York City's moniker as the Big Apple. The nickname had been used in reference to New York City a number of times in the 1920s by sports writers, but it became far more widespread in the late 1930s. There is no doubt that Helon's promotion of the Big Apple dance played a small, but significant, part in making the nickname stick.

Helon was also the first to explain the choreography of the Swing in *American Dancer*. People all across the nation, who took part in the great Swing movement in dance and music, could learn the steps by reading Helon's articles. After all of his research, John Hook found it interesting that even some of Helon's relatives were unaware of her great influence on the dance world of the 1930s and 1940s.

Her best students were her children, Pat and her brother Robbie, who was three years older. With Helon working out their routines, the kids began dancing together in the late 1930s and soon became mainstays at all the dance exhibitions. Eventually Robbie and Pat appeared in *American Dancer*, billed as "The Youngest Exhibition Ball Room Dance Team in America."

Helon would also take her classes on the road. She brought her best students to competitions in all the big cities, including New York, Chicago and even London. She and her students did the Shag, the Big Apple and the Swing, and her teams won prizes everywhere. She also would attend the conventions for dance known as the Dance Masters of America held in different cities across the country. It was there that she first met a talented young dancer from Pittsburgh named Gene Kelly.

As a child, Pat remembers some of her mom's local celebrity. One memory from early in her childhood is seeing her mother on the big screen at the local movie theater where they played newsreels featuring dance exhibitions before a show. She recalls being amazed at seeing her mom's face so large up there on the screen.

In 1939, Helon brought her students to the World's Fair in New York City. They danced and twirled batons while leading the North Carolina Day parade. Pat, who was eight years old, was selected to pin a rose on the lapel of the North Carolina Governor, Clyde Roark Hoey. She had to stand on a chair to do it. The next day, the picture was on the front page of the *New York Times.*

Helon was never satisfied in North Carolina. Like my mother, she had bigger ambitions, including the chance to be around the great dance halls of New York City. She also recognized the talent in her own children and wanted them to have the opportunity to dance on the big stages—something unlikely to happen if she stayed in Charlotte.

But Helon's husband, Robert Poole, like my own father, was less interested in promoting the careers of his children. He wanted a stable family life and was satisfied with things in North Carolina. They were far from rich, but he made enough to support his family. Nevertheless, in 1941, Helon decided it was time to go. She packed up the kids and together with Pat's grandmother, headed to New York City. Although she separated from Robert, they stayed married. Pat was ten years old at the time and remembers her excitement about the move.

Still, the transition was difficult. At first, they all crammed into two small rooms in a hotel on Madison Avenue and 35th Street. Pat and Robbie enrolled in a nearby public school for a short time, but a few months later they again moved to another tiny apartment, also with just two rooms. Coincidentally the new place was on 67th Street, the very same street where I would soon be living. As it turned out, Pat and I actually continued living on the same street just a few blocks apart for years, and not once did we ever see each other out on the street.

At the time, there were five of them crammed into their apartment. But, to make matters still worse, Pat's grandfather just showed up at the door one day. Out of work and with no place to stay, Pat remembers thinking to herself, "Not another one."

The overcrowded living quarters made it difficult for Pat to do her schoolwork, and she was constantly worried about getting enough sleep with all the chatter going on with so many people crammed into just two rooms. As a result, to this day, Pat cherishes her privacy. When we raised our own kids, if they complained, she would remind them how lucky they were to each have their own room. Even now, Pat likes to set time aside when she locks the gate and enjoys just being alone for a few hours in the afternoon out in our backyard by the pool. It drives me crazy, because I like a big crowd around. No doubt growing up with everyone on top of each other, she learned to appreciate having a little space of her own. I'm sure that's true of many people raised in overcrowded city apartments, who turn to the suburbs for more space—even if it means a longer commute to work.

Helon found work dancing at the 52nd Street nightclubs. These were the bars where, in the 1940s, comics, singers and dancers of New York City congregated. The first time Helon met Jackie Gleason was at one of the clubs. Among her friends was a dancer named Sally Marh, the mother of comic legend, Lenny Bruce. It wasn't glamorous work, and she would always have to share a drink or two with the patrons between dance numbers, but she scraped together enough money for the family to survive.

Pat and Robbie took classes in the evening from New York's premier dance instructor, Alberto Gallo. They were grueling sessions—each night, Pat and Robbie rushed home from school, did their homework amidst the constant noise in the small, over-crowded apartment and then headed off to dance practice until late in the night.

Despite the grind and the overcrowding, Pat remembers her childhood in New York City as happy years. Like her mom, Pat loved dancing. She was a natural and dreamed about dancing on the big stage. One day that dream would be realized, but that was still a few years away from her arrival in the seat next to mine at New York's Professional Children's School.

17

THE SKIN OF OUR TEETH

Meanwhile, in 1942, I received a call to try out for the stage production of Thornton Wilder's Pulitzer Prize–winning play, *The Skin of Our Teeth*. It would be the first major Broadway production of a new, young and innovative director, Elia Kazan. Eventually recognized as one of the most prominent stage and film directors of the twentieth century, Kazan was especially known for his association with Lee Strasberg's Actors' Studio and the emergence of "method" acting—a style in which actors attempt to draw upon their own emotions in their portrayal of a character. If done well, "the method" can result in a performance that is more "real," and thus more believable.

Kazan later described method acting as less complicated than some have imagined. The technique, he said, "consists of recalling the circumstances...surrounding an intensely emotional experience in the actor's past." Lee Strasberg would have his actors take a moment "to remember the details" of that emotional experience just before their performance. Marlon Brando, with whom Kazan would work on numerous films, including the classic, *On the Waterfront*, became the most successful and popular representative of the method-acting style.

The Skin of Our Teeth starred Fredric March, his wife Florence Eldridge and Tallulah Bankhead—all practitioners of the older, classical model associated with the Barrymores. There was, however, an up-and-comer in the play named Montgomery Clift, who would eventually be cut more from the new style. At the time, Monty was in his early twenties and had recently finished working with the great team of Alfred Lunt and Lynn Fontanne. Kazan needed a teenager to play the role of a telegraph boy, and Fredric March recommended me for the part.

Although it won the Pulitzer Prize, *The Skin of Our Teeth* was a strange, if not downright bizarre, production. To be honest, I was fourteen years old when I first read the script, and I didn't have a clue as to what it all meant. And I wasn't alone.

One critic described the play as an "abstract allegory that portrays the difficulties of life through a series of scenes starting with Adam and Eve, through Noah's Ark and then finally a

Convention in Atlantic City, New Jersey." Well, that didn't help much. To further confound us, the play had a range of weird characters, including monsters and mammoths and dinosaurs. And the main character, Mr. Antrobus, was, through the course of the play, engaging in such eccentric endeavors as inventing the wheel and creating the alphabet.

If all that sounds strange, it was even more peculiar when performed live onstage. We took the play for tryouts in Washington, Baltimore, Philadelphia and New Haven, and we bombed everywhere. Nobody understood what it all meant, and the critics were savage.

In Washington, things got stranger still. I was in the middle of a scene with Tallulah Bankhead when suddenly these two ladies—and I shouldn't say this, but I remember so clearly that they were two tremendously fat women—came right out onstage, grabbed me by the shirt and dragged me off. I was stunned, and I said, "What's the matter?" They told me, "You're too young to be onstage." It turned out there was a law in Washington, D.C. that nobody under sixteen years old could go onstage professionally.

Laws protecting child actors were not unusual. They affected me at an early age. I was just six years old, and my mom couldn't get me roles on Broadway. I debuted in *Tapestry in Grey*, just a month after turning seven, which was the age limit. Laws protecting young actors were essentially child labor regulations, and a group called the Garry Society shielded children from abusive labor practices. In Hollywood, the Jackie Coogan Law forced the parents of a child actor to put ten percent of his income in an account they couldn't touch. Coogan had been a famous child star, playing with Charlie Chaplin in *The Kid* and many other roles. But when he became an adult, he discovered all his money was gone and he was broke. Years later, when my son, Vincent, worked on several television shows, a percentage of his earnings had to go directly into a trust account, which was turned over to him when he turned eighteen. There is no way to completely protect child actors against abusive or excessively greedy parents, but these laws certainly helped to ensure that situations like Jackie Coogan's were less common.

Anyway, these two women yanked me off the National Theatre stage, and the show came to an abrupt stop. After a short break, the curtain raised again and another actor, actually an older man, Stanley Prager, went on in my place. He looked silly playing the telegraph boy, especially after the audience had already seen me. But I'm not sure that it made much difference. *The Skin of Our Teeth* was such a strange play anyway—with actors periodically coming out of character and talking directly to the audience—they probably thought my being dragged off the stage was all part of the show. In fact, in the beginning of the play, Tallulah, who played Mr. Antrobus's maid, Sabina, stepped out of character and told the audience: "I hate this play."

The Skin of Our Teeth barely made it through the tryouts. Because it was written by Thornton Wilder, who two years earlier had penned the prize-winning play, *Our Town*, the theaters were generally full. But that didn't mean the audiences enjoyed it. In fact, some of the crowds literally booed us and walked out on the performance while the out-of-town critics brutalized the play. In the midst of all this, the actors began to grumble, and soon there was talk about getting off what seemed like a sinking ship.

Thornton Wilder, at the time, was serving as a captain in the United States Army. As previously mentioned, directors typically don't want writers hanging around too much, but this case was different. And so Kazan asked Wilder to come speak with us. Wilder agreed, and he showed up while we were in Baltimore.

Wilder spoke to us while in full military uniform. There were about forty of us present, and Wilder said: "I know that the critics don't understand my play. That doesn't bother me as long as you understand it. So I'm going to explain it to you now." He said the play was about the human spirit; that all people in all places and all times experience obstacles in life that threaten their happiness and even their survival. Nevertheless, said Wilder, we manage to get by—and we do so, "by the skin of our teeth." It was that simple. The play was the story of human persistence in the face of obstacles and crisis. Wilder also predicted that the catcalls and vicious criticism would end when we got to Broadway.

He was right. After bombing everywhere, we opened at the Plymouth Theater in New York on November 18, 1942, and suddenly the play was a smash hit. Furthermore, the critics were now writing great reviews. Howard Barnes of the *Herald Tribune* exclaimed: "Theater-going became a rare and electrifying experience" with Thornton Wilder's "daffy and illuminating" *The Skin of Our Teeth*. The play ran on Broadway for nearly a year.

I particularly enjoyed working with Monty Clift. He was eight years older than me and had also been a child actor on Broadway. That made it easy to talk with him. We stayed in touch for a while after the show, but then his film career took off, and he became one of the biggest draws in America. Ironically, his main rival, Marlon Brando, came from the same home town of Omaha, Nebraska. Sadly, Monty's life began spiraling downward as he reached his peak, and he died while still a very young man of 45.

The most interesting person in the cast was Tallulah Bankhead, who played the sultry maid, Sabina. From a powerful Alabama political family, Tallulah made them all blush back home with her public antics. Her reputation for promiscuous behavior was widespread, and Tallulah fueled the gossip columns with her constant comments and insinuations about whom she was sleeping with in Hollywood. On top of it, Tallulah was a genuine wit, which always added fuel to the fire. One of my favorite lines was when Tallulah, a tremendous baseball fan, famously pronounced there were only two real geniuses in human history: "Willie Mays and Willie Shakespeare."

I can actually tell you a little something firsthand about Tallulah's indifference to conventional standards. One day she said to me: "Dickie, I want to see you tomorrow in my dressing room before the show." So, I went to her dressing room, and there she was sitting on her chair in front of the mirror—stark naked! I did my best to act casual, as if it was nothing unusual. And Tallulah just started talking as if it was all perfectly normal. Referencing a point in the play when I pose a question to her, she said: "Dickie darling, when you ask me that question, you're asking it like you already know the answer. You're coming up at the end. Just do it a little more flat." I said, "Sure." That was it and I left. But for the remainder of the show, I kept thinking to myself, maybe I should mess up the line again so Tallulah would call me back to her dressing room!

During the run of *The Skin of Our Teeth* at the Plymouth Theater, there was a play called *Star and Garter*, across the street at the Music Box. It was pretty much a glorified burlesque. It was a big hit, and it starred the famous burlesque star Gypsy Rose Lee, the stripper I had unsuccessfully tried to see at the World's Fair. This time I was not to be denied.

Every night, I appeared in the first act of *The Skin of Our Teeth*. Afterwards, I had to wait for the curtain call at 11 p.m. That gave me about an hour and a half to kill. One night, a stagehand took me over to see the *Star and Garter* from backstage. I was just fourteen, and it seemed like great fun to me—with all those pretty girls, comedians, and, of course, Gypsy Rose Lee.

There was also a great animal act in the show performed by a fellow named Gil Maison and his roller-skating monkey. Maison put his chimp, Herman, on a stool while a group of dogs performed a variety of tricks onstage. Then every so often, Maison turned to the Chimp and yelled out: "Frank Buck!" With that, Herman went crazy—shaking his arms and legs all over the place. And what made it even more hilarious was that the audience knew Frank Buck was actually a famous guy who had made his name capturing animals.

I absolutely loved the act. So one night I made my way up to Gil's dressing room on the fourth floor of the Music Box to meet him. He must have liked me because he let me visit him every night while waiting for my curtain call across the street. He told me how he trained Herman and the dogs, who were all right there in the room with us.

One day, I whispered to him: "Mr. Maison, what would happen if right now I said 'Frank Buck.'" Gil shook his head and warned: "Don't ever do it." "Why not?" I asked. He looked at me with great seriousness and said: "Dickie, I don't want to go into it. Just don't ever, ever say it."

That was the wrong response. Now I couldn't stop thinking about it. One night while we were upstairs in his dressing room, the doorman yelled out: "Gil Maison, telephone." The phone was way down on the first floor. So Maison left, and there I was all alone with Herman and the dogs. I began staring at the chimpanzee. I was just fourteen years old and absolutely dying to know what could happen if I just said the words. Finally, I couldn't contain myself, and looking right at the chimp I whispered: "Frank Buck!"

What a mistake! Herman flew off his chair, and before I could make a move he had smashed the mirror, broken the window, and grabbed Gil's wardrobe, tearing all the clothes to pieces. Within seconds Herman had demolished the entire dressing room.

The dogs and I just stood there watching the rampage— and trying to stay the heck out of Herman's way. Eventually, he calmed down, and I crept down the stairs, out the backstage door into the alleyway and across the street. A few days later when I gathered the courage to go back, I was told by a stagehand that I wasn't welcome anymore.

As it turned out, Herman's destruction of Gil's dressing room didn't do any damage to their act. By the time *The Skin of Our Teeth* closed in September of 1943, Herman and Gil were in such huge demand that they also performed in a new show at the Plymouth, *The Naked Genius*. Thus, Gil Maison and his monkey were, perhaps, the only act in Broadway history to perform simultaneously in two theaters across the street from each other.

But with all of the interesting things that occurred during *The Skin of Our Teeth*, I was also exposed for the first time to a darker truth about life in America. I've always loved traveling, and through the years I've had the great fortune to see so many wonderful places across this country. But in 1941, we had not yet reached a point where all of America was living up to the promises on which our country was founded. I received a stark reminder of that fact one day on a southbound train.

One of the wonderful things about growing up in New York City is its diversity. Walk a few blocks, and you can eat Italian calamari, Jewish blintz, German sausage, the black eyed peas of a soul food stand, a Dominican empanada, a Polish pierogi and pretty much anything else you want. The convergence of all those great ethnic groups, with their distinct cultures, is at the heart of the great charm of New York City, and my whole life I've marveled at and enjoyed these wonderfully diverse traditions.

But we know there is a dark side to the story; a side where a wholesome diversity spirals down into the terrible racism that has plagued our country since its founding. When my grandparents, Vincent and Rose Acerno, moved into Kew Gardens, Queens, there was a deep and powerful undercurrent of racism against Italians. The Germans and the Irish had already been there a long time— the Germans for hundreds of years and the Irish at least since the Potato Famine of the 1840s drove them across the Atlantic to New York City. But the Italians were newcomers. Vincent and Rose were among the millions who stopped at Ellis Island in the 1890s, and their names are etched on the wall there. Vincent's parents would tell him about the thrill of standing on the transport ship and watching the Statue of Liberty come into view as they pulled into New York Harbor. Coming from the impoverished mountain village of Potenza, Italy, America really was the land of opportunity for my family.

Although I was aware of the ethnic tensions that persisted in my own childhood in Brooklyn and Manhattan, I never saw the truly ugly side of racism in this country until I worked on *The Skin of Our Teeth*. When we took the show on the road, the first performance was at the National Theatre in Washington, D.C. I was fourteen at the time, and I remember being excited about returning to the nation's capital. And, in fact, I did visit the White House, the Congress, and the Lincoln Memorial. It was also a unique time to be in Washington because we were fighting in World War II. And it's important to remember that sentiments about the war were very different than what we experienced with Vietnam or even the present wars in Iraq and Afghanistan, where the nation has been very much divided. In 1942, attitudes were different. The country was united and defeating the Nazi and Japanese war machines was something that just about everyone agreed on.

Anyway, the whole cast and crew of about forty people boarded the train at Penn Station in New York City. Everyone was there including the stars of the show, and we all sat in the same rail car. It certainly wasn't like today where big stars fly into the set on a private jet. Fredric March, Tallulah Bankhead, and Montgomery Clift were all onboard as we headed south to Washington.

The train made some stops along the way, first at Philadelphia and Wilmington. Then we pulled into Baltimore, Maryland. In Baltimore, a conductor started passing through the cars. I still remember his exact words: "All colored in the next car. Colored people in the next car."

We had four black actors in the show. I still remember their names: Earl Sydnor, Viola Dean, Eulabelle Moore, and Harry Clark. In fact, I had a slight crush on Viola Dean.

As soon as the Conductor made his announcement, the four of them just got up without protest and moved to a separate car. Nobody objected. Nobody said a single word. Nobody batted an eye. At fourteen, I had seen ethnic tensions in New York City, but never anything like this. It was really quite shocking, and I felt terrible for the actors who were forced to move. And the worst part, the most disturbing part, was that it all seemed perfectly natural to everyone, or at least that's how everyone acted.

While I'm certain that some people in the play didn't approve, nobody had the courage to express their disapproval. It makes me think of that old expression that evil triumphs when good people do nothing. On that train, nobody, including me, did anything. I wish I could say I stood up and protested or that I went to the other car to sit with those black actors, but I didn't, nor did anyone else. It would take braver souls, heroes like Rosa Parks, who just twelve years later heard those same words from a bus driver in Birmingham and decided that enough is enough and just refused to move to the back of the bus. One person standing up to evil can spark a revolution. We could have used Rosa on that train.

18

How to Beat the Races

My life as a student came to a crashing, and somewhat ignominious, halt not long after the close of *The Skin of Our Teeth*. In truth, it was extremely difficult for me to keep up with school assignments while working on so many different shows, both on the radio and in theater. But that's not an excuse. I also became caught up in a world that was incompatible with the discipline of schoolwork. In fact, it was my attempt to bring that world into the classroom that was the final straw.

The kids in our class at the Professional Children's School were required to write a composition about some subject of our choosing that had to do with how we had spent the summer. I knew a lot of the kids wrote about their families and things they did together. In fact, Pat was in the class and was ready with her essay. Since I generally cut corners on assignments, the teacher, Madame Motley, strongly suspecting this would again be the case, called me up onstage first to deliver my speech.

But Madame Motley had misjudged me—at least on that day. I actually did the assignment, and I had my composition ready and was looking forward to reading it as I walked up to the stage. It may say something about my state of mind at the time that I honestly thought I had chosen a good topic. So I proudly read the title of my essay: "How to Beat the Races."

With that, Madame Motley went nuts, screaming: "Get him off that stage!" Within minutes I was in the Principal's Office, and they had called my mother to the school. When she arrived, the Principal, Mrs. Nesbet, said to her: "Mrs. Van Patten, do you know what your son did today." My mother said, "No, what?" And she told her about my composition. Now my mother had constantly been after me about spending too much time at the track. But on that day, she surprised all of us. Instead of properly expressing her mortification at her son's behavior, she just started laughing. With that, Mrs. Nesbit let loose on her: "You're as bad as he is!" And the next thing I knew, I'd been expelled.

But I got my degree—although not for another sixty-five years. A while ago someone from the Professional Children's School found out I had never graduated, and they decided to give me the diploma. They had a very nice ceremony at the Beverly Hills High School, and the head of the PCS, James Dawson, made the presentation. It was a very nice event, but I'm not sure they realized that I'd been expelled from the school. Nobody ever mentioned it, and I had the impression they simply thought I quit. And I certainly wasn't going to bring it up. Anyway, I very much appreciated their gesture, and I hope they let me keep the diploma now that they know the real story.

19

Trouble at Home

While I was working on *The Skin of Our Teeth,* things got bad at home with Mom and Dad. Throughout the early years of my mother pushing me and Joyce into show business, my father was proud, supportive, and enthusiastic. But in time her ambitions took over my mother's life. All of her time was consumed with meeting people in the business, arranging tryouts, preparing us for rehearsals and always being on the hunt for the next big opportunity.

For me, that was fine. I enjoyed my life as a child actor. And, as I've said, I really owe everything I have to my mother and her determination. But the obsession with our careers began to take a toll on her marriage. My father began to miss his wife. He felt she was ignoring him, and no doubt he was right. When that kind of distance arises in a marriage, trouble is just around the corner.

As is often the case, it began at work. My father was selling furniture at Flint & Horner in Manhattan, where he met a young and attractive Italian girl, Eleanor Della-Gatta. They began having an affair, and my mother, completely absorbed in the theater world, was oblivious.

Then one day the girl's mother showed up at our house. She broke the news to my mother and said she wanted it stopped. Mom was stunned. At first, she didn't believe the woman. But that night she confronted my father, and he admitted it. A few days later, he moved out. Just like that, Mom's life was turned upside down.

Dad took an apartment in Richmond Hill. For a while, things really fell to pieces. I'd wake up in the middle of the night and hear Mom crying in her room. One day she asked me to go talk Dad into coming back. I didn't want to do it, but she was so distraught I couldn't say no.

I remember walking up the steps to his apartment, while she waited down on the street. I asked him to come home. I'm sure it was difficult for him as he tried to explain to me that it was impossible. I didn't really understand it all. I just wanted him to come back. But he wouldn't.

In a short time, Dad enlisted in the Marines. I guess he wanted to get away from it all. Many years later, after Mom died, he wrote Joyce and me a letter trying to explain the reason for his leaving: "Once you were safely launched in the theatre," he wrote to us, "I found the life we had imposed upon ourselves too one-dimensional. We lived, ate, [and] talked theatre. There was no room for anything else. We gradually grew apart."

It was a tough time. I was just fourteen, and my father was gone. It was even worse for Joyce. She was only nine years old, and she adored my father. Without him around, I think Joyce felt much more alone. She and I responded very differently to the whole process of being child actors. She felt the pressure a great deal more than I did and came to resent my mother's obsession with the entertainment world. At an early age, she had begun looking to Dad when things got tough for her.

Joyce also felt we were measured too much by our success. If we were working, we were treated one way; if we didn't get a job, it was something different. I didn't notice it as much, but Joyce was right; things did change depending on whether or not we were working.

Joyce rebelled. At sixteen, she left home, eloping with an older fellow, Tom King, an aspiring actor, who would later be a highly successful television executive for ABC. Joyce and Tom had a son, Casey, my nephew, who now, along with my three children, is my closest friend.

In retrospect, I think there was a parallel between Joyce and my father. Each decided at some point they'd had enough of a home where everything revolved around getting ahead in the entertainment world; where the woman who was their wife and mother was so driven along this path that she may have lost sight of more important things.

Joyce and Dad were alike in many other ways. He was a voracious reader, a sophisticated man who loved Shakespeare and reciting poetry. Joyce is much the same—highly intelligent and committed to acting as a craft, and not merely as a vehicle for advancement or gaining celebrity status. I think my sister is among the finest actors in the world, and, in many ways, what makes her so gifted is her attention to the art of acting, a quality she inherited in large part from my father.

Today we have very different views about our childhood in New York. For me, it was great; for her, it was a struggle. That's not to say she thought it was all bad. In fact, she loved acting and was more committed to the theater at a young age than I had been.

It would also be unfair to forget the pressures on my mother. I'm not sure we all fully appreciated just how hard she was working. I recently came across a revealing interview with Mom that appeared in March of 1944 in *The Dunkirk Evening Observer*, a newspaper in upstate New York. Journalist Jack Caver focused on Mom's unbelievably hectic schedule. "Mrs. Van Patten, a pretty brunette in her early thirties," Caver wrote, "is kept on the jump.... As it is, she is on the go from noon until midnight." In addition to the "usual meal, clothing and general welfare problems" of any other mother, Caver explained, Mom also had a series of other all-consuming obligations. "She spends as much time in a theater as her acting offspring," said Caver. "She has to keep a sharp eye on their varied and sometimes complicated professional affairs. She has about as much time for herself as a restaurant owner."

In addition to her frenetic lifestyle, something about her relationship with Dad also came through in the interview. Mom told Caver: "I will say this about having children on the stage: You have to have a husband who is able to understand that he sort of has to take a back seat. He is bound to be rejected a little from time to time." Caver then wrote that Mom's "worries on this score have been negligible for the past two years." That was because Dad was away in the Marines. But, of course, it wasn't true. In fact, it's sad for me to read this interview now. It's clear that Mom was both putting up a public front about what had actually happened in her marriage and, at the same time, expressing some anger and bitterness at the fact that in her eyes Dad had not been willing, as she put it, "to take a back seat."

But Joyce was still young at the time. Her enthusiasm for the stage never diminished, but her sense of an unhealthy obsession with success increased. One time, when Joyce was just thirteen, she took the train to Los Angeles to screen test for *Meet Me in Saint Louis* as Judy Garland's little sister. She didn't get the part. When she returned, our Grandfather Vincent said to her: "You know, we're all very disappointed in you." Joyce was devastated by that thoughtless comment.

Still, Joyce's attraction to the stage at an early age was profound. At the time of the interview with Caver, Joyce was playing in *Tomorrow the World*. Caver described Joyce, who was nine years old, as a "vivacious, inquisitive girl," who "knows that she wants to do nothing but act always, preferably on the stage." The portrait that Caver paints of my younger sister's infatuation with the theater is wonderful—and true. Mom told him that "Joyce started reading the critics when she was three and a half before she ever went on the stage." She even had a favorite critic—Ward Morehouse, who wrote for the *New York Sun*.

Mom also described Joyce's adamant refusal to take a day off from the show when she was sick. She explained to Caver that Joyce had "developed a slight temperature one evening back when everyone was having the flu and we tried to get her to go home. Well she put on a production number in the dressing room. The stage manager tried to explain to her that other players laid off when they were sick and that evening Judith Evelyn of *Angel Street* had gone home ill." But Joyce protested: "Yes, but she's a star. She can afford to. I'm just trying to become one and I can't afford to." Caver summed it up: "Joyce is stage struck."

And yet, it was more complicated than that. As she grew up in this single-parent home where one's work performance seemed to be the measure of things, Joyce grew increasingly disillusioned. For a long time, I couldn't quite understand why she would think such an exciting life could be a bad thing. And, at the same time, I think she may have wondered if I wasn't a little blind to what was really going on. But, as time passed in our lives, we've come to appreciate each other's view of that complicated childhood world a little more. I've certainly come to one definite conclusion: life is experienced differently by different people. Two people can have the exact same experience and walk away with very different feelings about it.

As suggested in Caver's interview, my mother never stopped loving my father. She never met anybody else and never really wanted to. She went to her death still loving him.

20

TOMORROW THE WORLD

Shortly after Dad left, Joyce landed a tremendous role in *Tomorrow the World*. It was a chilling play inspired by the nightmare in Nazi Germany. It focused on the indoctrination of German youth.

Opening on April 14, 1943, at the Ethel Barrymore Theater, *Tomorrow the World* lasted for 500 performances. Written by James Gow and Armand d'Usseau, the play told the story of a German-American, Michael Frame, played by Ralph Bellamy, whose brother died while living in Germany. The brother's son, Emile, is then sent to live with Michael in his Midwest home.

Michael Frame was a widower, with a Jewish girlfriend, Leona, played by Shirley Booth and a daughter, Patricia, played by Joyce. When the boy, Emile, arrived at the home, he stunned everyone by coming to dinner dressed in his Hitler Youth uniform. He had been so brainwashed by the Nazis that he believed he was still working covertly for the Third Reich. He began taking action against his uncle, especially when he learned that he was going to marry a Jew. When Patricia discovered him plotting against her father, he knocked her down the stairs, nearly killing her.

Joyce had a very big part in the play and really demonstrated the talent that has been so evident for all of her career. Writing of both Joyce and Skippy Homeier, who played Emile, Burton Rascoe of the *New York World-Telegram* exclaimed: "These two children are not only the spectacular hits of the newest surefire hit on Broadway they ARE the play; they make it. And this is no disparagement of Ralph Bellamy and Shirley Booth." Burns Mantle of the *Daily News* simply described Joyce as "exceptionally gifted."

But Joyce's biggest thrill came shortly after one of her performances, when she received an unexpected visit from a special fan. I happened to be backstage at the time and saw Judy Garland walk around the back and climb the stairs to Joyce's dressing room. This was four years after *The Wizard of Oz*, and Judy was already a legend. Seeing Judy Garland standing outside her dressing room, Joyce was stunned. Judy said to her: "I want to tell you what a wonderful performer you are." Joyce thanked her and Judy left. That's the kind of special moment you never forget.

There was also an unfortunate aspect to Joyce landing the role in *Tomorrow the World* that made her recognize just how harsh the entertainment business can be. Joyce was only a stand-in while the show was on the road. Patricia Frame was initially played by the director Elliott Nugent's daughter, Nancy. One day Nancy became sick, and Joyce filled in for her. Joyce was so exceptional they kept her in it—and dropped Nancy. It obviously wasn't Joyce's fault, but she was friends with Nancy and felt bad about it for a long time. It was a lesson in how unforgiving this business can be. I think Joyce learned that a lot earlier than I did.

Joyce was also more sensitive to the underside of the business. She saw that even on Broadway there was poverty. In most shows, there were kids from families who desperately needed the money. For some of these kids, there really wasn't much glamour at all since most of them didn't have starring roles or even speaking lines in the plays.

Still, *Tomorrow the World* was a real triumph for my sister, and we were all enormously proud of her. In addition to her own success, the play made an important statement about a serious subject. It was a disturbing reminder of how easily people can be deluded by demagoguery. Hitler was a monster who created other monsters—even out of innocent children like Emile. In 1944 we were at war with him, and *Tomorrow the World* was a reflection on the power of an evil man who knew how to play on fear and anxiety to make people believe the most terrible lies. My little sister helped bring a message of hope to thousands of people who saw in her character, Patricia Frame, a goodness that would never allow the evil delusions of a madman to triumph.

21

KIRK & THE BOYS

I've never been much of a rebel. Joyce was always more outspoken and ready to stand up to power if she believed she was right. Growing up, I was pretty much content doing what I was told.

But I had one night of rebellion, and Kirk Douglas was the instigator. I was sixteen, and we were in a show called *The Wind Is Ninety*. Kirk was about ten years older than me—to the day, as we happen to share the same birthday, December 9. He had just returned from the Navy where he fought against Japanese submarines in the Pacific theater.

The Wind Is Ninety was written by Ralph Nelson, a former Air Force captain, who would later become a prominent television and film director. In fact, our paths would cross numerous times throughout the years ahead, and Ralph would become a good friend. The production was also memorable because it was the first time I worked with my sister Joyce.

The play told the story of a family who had lost a son in the war. To help them through their grief, the ghost of a dead soldier from World War I appears. That was Kirk Douglas's character. The soldier's daughter was played by Joyce.

We played the Colonial Theatre in Boston before coming to Broadway. After the show, Kirk and a few other guys, Henry Bernard and Jim Dobson, were heading out to a midnight burlesque show at the Old Howard Theatre. I wanted to join them, but they said I was too young. In the show I played a Boy Scout, dressed in short pants and short sleeves, which made me look even younger. But I kept pressing them, and finally they agreed.

So, we went to the Old Howard on Scully Square, a real honky-tonk section, with all sorts of bars with lots of girls wearing spangled dresses. At the Old Howard Burlesque Theatre, Kirk and the others bought the tickets. They let me in without checking to see if I was underage.

The show was great. In addition to all the girls there was a great comic team, Stinky and Shorty. In fact, I still remember their full names, Shorty McAllister and Stinky Fields. They were well known in the burlesque houses.

At one point in the show, with all the chorus girls dancing onstage, Stinky and Shorty suddenly came out and said: "Hold it girls. You should be dancing with some men. Come on fellas. Come on up here and dance with the girls."

With that, Kirk and the others pushed me up onstage. The next thing I know I was dancing with a big, tall show girl, and in the middle of the dance for some crazy reason, I whispered to her: "Can I see you after the show?" She agreed and told me to wait at the stage door when it was over.

Proud as can be, I went back to our seats and told the guys that I was going out with the dancer after the show. They started laughing and poking fun at me, but when the show ended I met the girl in the alley behind the theater, and Kirk and the others left.

The girl's name was Sherry Everett. It was now about two o'clock in the morning, and we began walking along a street in what seemed to me as the wrong part of town. Soon we came to a tattoo parlor, and Sherry said to me: "Why don't you get tattooed?" I told her no, but she kept at me, "Come on get one. What, are you scared?" I said, "No. I'm not scared." And she said, "Well, go on and get tattooed." Finally, like a jerk, I agreed.

In those days, there were no electric needles. Instead, they took a regular needle, dipped it in paint and then cut. I picked out a design of a horseshoe that said: "Good Luck." The tattoo artist started cutting, and soon there was blood streaming down my arm. I've always become sick at the sight of blood, and Sherry kept taunting me: "What, are you scared?" And I kept bravely telling her: "No, I'm not scared."

Finally the ordeal ended, and I thought at least there will be some payoff—which to me in those days meant nothing more than that I was going to kiss this burlesque dancer. Before getting to her apartment, we stopped at a drugstore as she said she needed to pick up a few things. By the time we left, she'd bought pretty much everything they had. The bill, which I paid, came to $37, a lot of money in 1945.

Still, I was excited. I was almost home. In a few minutes we arrived at her hotel, the Crawford House on Parker Street. We went inside and walked up the stairs to her apartment on the second floor.

Sherry opened the door, looked inside, turned to me and then whispered in a panic: "Run! My husband is here! Quick! Get out of here! He'll kill you!" Without a thought I practically flew down the two flights and took off running back to my hotel. It wasn't until I told Kirk and the other guys what happened and they started laughing that I realized that Sherry had made a fool of me.

The worst part was the next day. I was playing a Boy Scout with short sleeves. When I arrived at the theater and took the bandage off, I had the tattoo on my arm. The Stage Manager looked at it and said, "You can't go on with that. You're playing a Boy Scout."

In the meantime my mother had arrived. When she saw the tattoo, she went ballistic. Joyce, who was there at the time, still remembers my mother literally throwing a shoe at me and screaming over and over again: "You've ruined your career!"

When the hysteria calmed down, the makeup people put some grease paint over the tattoo, and the show went on. But I ended up with a tattoo that I still have. It's a reminder of one crazy night at the Boston burlesque.

Things worked out a little better for Kirk. When we arrived on Broadway with *The Wind Is Ninety*, he received great reviews. More important, Lauren Bacall had suggested to Hal Wallis, a Hollywood producer, that he see Kirk in the play. Wallis came to a performance and ended up signing Kirk to a contract that launched his career in film.

The Wind Is Ninety struck a deep emotional chord in New York City. So many families had lost loved-ones in the war, and the play was a homage to those families. We opened in June of 1945 at the Booth Theater, and when the first performance ended, Ralph Nelson, the playwright, came onstage to give a rare curtain speech. With Ralph dressed in his army uniform, the whole crowd stood up and gave him a thunderous ovation. The war was still being fought, soldiers were still dying, and Ralph solemnly dedicated the play to "the next of kin of the country's casualties." While the play was a fantasy, its reception that night was a very real and cathartic moment for Americans suffering the terrible loss of their husbands, fathers and children. Joyce and I were proud to be a part of it.

22

THE MAGIC OF LUNT & FONTANNE

On occasion people ask who were the most talented actors I've ever worked with? I never hesitate: Alfred Lunt and Lynn Fontanne.

I'm not alone in that opinion. The great English actor, Lawrence Olivier paid the highest tribute saying: "Everything I know about acting I learned from Alfred Lunt." And one of those very few on the same rarified level of Olivier, Sir John Gielgud, described Lunt and Fontanne as "a perfect combination which we can never hope to see again." Olivier and Gielgud knew what they were talking about.

Onstage, Lunt and Fontanne were pure magic. I had the extraordinary privilege of working with them for four years in the hit comedy, *O Mistress Mine*—two years on Broadway at the Empire Theatre starting in 1946, and then on the road again in cities all across America.

The Lunts were unique; they acted in a way I'd never seen before, literally speaking over each other. While Alfred was talking, Lynn was talking too. Yet somehow they blended together perfectly. Ordinarily, it would be considered breaking the rules. With lesser actors, they would be accused of stepping on each other's lines. It's pretty simple; if two people talk at the same time, neither gets heard. But every single one of the millions who ever watched these two onstage knows just what I'm talking about. There was a kind of magic in the effortless way they wove their lines together like musicians playing different notes, but always in harmony.

And, of course, it only seemed effortless. Everything they did was planned and rehearsed a thousand times. The Lunts knew they had something special, but they also knew that all the talent in the world was no substitute for hard work. It was with the Lunts that I fully realized that it is only through relentless practice, rehearsing over and over again, that the best performances are created.

It is impossible to understate the impact of the return of Lunt and Fontanne to Broadway in 1946. It was simply the most anticipated American theater event at the close of World War II. Prior to leaving for England in 1942, the Lunts had been on the road with my friend, Monty Clift, in the Pulitzer Prize winning play, *There Shall Be No Night.* After Pearl Harbor, the play closed in the United States, but, a year later, the Lunts decided to bring it to England's Aldwych Theater, although Monty had, by then, moved on and couldn't join them.

When, three years later, the Lunts returned with their new play *O Mistress Mine,* every single young actor in New York City and beyond wanted to land the role of their son, Michael Brown. As Ward Morehouse later wrote in the *New York Sun,* there were seven parts, "but only three of them count." The buzz throughout the city's theater district was palpable, and I was fortunate to be there in the running. But to fully grasp the magnitude of their return, it is well worth taking a brief step backwards to see the fascinating events that led to this extraordinary moment.

* * *

Terence Rattigan was a former officer in the British Royal Army who, after fighting in World War I, embarked on a career as a London playwright. Rattigan had written a hit comedy in 1936, *French Without Tears,* and by the time of the war he had established himself as one of the principal London playwrights.

In 1941, he wrote a play that was a largely autobiographical examination of his own life. It was, in part, a self-criticism of what he believed to be his failure as a young man in living up to his own idealistic principles. Rattigan was a socialist. He was haunted by the fact that after finding success as a playwright he had compromised his socialist ideals, giving in to the irresistible lure of money. At a deeper level, Rattigan understood that life has a way of tempting us to betray our own values—the ideas that define who we are, and the ideals we consider most precious often become casualties in a battle with practical concerns and the enticing power of money to make our lives more comfortable.

And so, self-doubt and inner conflict led Rattigan to write a play where the central character was presented as a kind of "Hamlet" figure—a young man haunted by doubt and uncertainty as to what actions to take when confronted with the vagaries of life. That was the character of Michael Brown.

But this was England in 1942, and, as Rattigan wrote his play, London was being devastated by the relentless bombing raids of the German Luftwaffe. Confronted by the terrible reality of his country under siege, Rattigan decided that the public needed an escape from these horrors, even if only for a few hours at the theater. So he turned his story of inner conflict into a comedy. Michael Brown's internal struggle—in essence Rattigan's own personal torment—was presented as humorous rather than tragic. As it turned out, it was the right decision, not just for the British audience, but for the success of the play itself.

The play was originally titled, *Less Than Kind.* Michael Brown was the seventeen year old son of a British widow, Olivia Brown. His father had died while fighting in the war, and Michael was sent to boarding school in Canada at the age of thirteen. He studied there for four years, and the play begins with his return to England in the midst of the war.

While Michael was away, his mother began dating Sir John Fletcher, a conservative Minister in Churchill's War Cabinet. Michael, who had developed into a socialist while studying in Canada, is appalled to learn upon his return that his mother is now living, unmarried, with Sir John, who Michael views as a right-wing war-monger.

While Rattigan was writing his play, the Lunts were still performing *There Shall Be No Night* to sell-out crowds at the Aldwych Theater. In Jared Brown's *The Fabulous Lunts* he details their astonishment that in the midst of all the perils of war and the constant fear of attack, Londoners just kept coming to the theater. One evening, right in the middle of a performance, a bomb landed next the Aldwych. Lynn Fontanne later recounted for a friend: "A buzz bomb hit very near. I was on the stage and he [Alfred] was in the wings waiting for his cue when the smash came. I found myself somehow on the other side of the stage. The scenery was buckling like sails in a high wind, things were falling. I looked for Alfred. There he was pushing a canvas wall up with one hand and starting to make his entrance. Then I saw the fire curtain coming down and heard him shout in that metallic voice he gets when he is excited, 'Take it up! Take it!'

"Like a shot it went up, and then he turned to me and curious as it may seem, the precise line he had to speak in the script at that very moment was, 'Are you all right, darling?'"

The theater erupted with applause—and the play went on, even as the bombs continued exploding outside.

In the final scene of the play, Alfred delivered a soliloquy that again possessed an eerie, but uplifting relevance: "Listen, what you hear now," Lunt told the Londoners, "this terrible sound that fills the earth—it is the death-rattle of civilization. But choose to believe differently.... We have within ourselves the power to conquer bestiality not with our muscles and our swords, but with *the power of the light that is in our minds*."

Again, the audience stood for a huge ovation and, again, it was unsure if these were the actual lines in the play—which they were—or if Lunt was simply stepping out of character to address them about the perils outside that they had all just experienced. Whatever they thought, it was a stunning performance and lifted Lunt and Fontanne to even greater heights in the English imagination as heroes of the resistance.

Their London engagement at the Aldwych with *There Shall Be No Night*, ended tragically on June 30, 1944, when a bomb from the Luftwaffe struck the theater directly, killing a young British soldier who was purchasing a ticket at the box office. The Lunts, however, persisted, taking the play to the countryside, where the English people continued filling the theaters and responding to the world's two greatest actors with unbridled enthusiasm.

There Shall Be No Night closed its run in the summer of 1944. It had brought the Lunts an unprecedented stature, not just as great actors, but as great humanitarians. Alfred and Lynn understood the significance of what they were doing to boost English morale, and they wanted to continue to entertain the British people for as long as their nightmare endured.

And so they began looking for another play. It turned out that a friend of Terence Rattigan, composer Ivor Novello, learned the Lunts were on the hunt for new material and he arranged a meeting with Rattigan. As Geoffrey Wansell, Rattigan's biographer notes, Rattigan was absolutely elated that "the theatre's most famous acting couple" was interested in his play. The Lunts took a draft from the meeting, and a few days later, Alfred called Rattigan, telling him, that he and Lynn "would be proud to do your play." But, he had two conditions: first, that Alfred direct it and second that there be a few changes to the storyline.

Rattigan immediately agreed, although he soon learned that the changes Alfred envisioned were substantial. The play had been written principally for the characters of Michael Brown and his mother, Olivia. Lunt's role as Sir John Fletcher would have to be greatly expanded. Rattigan would later write to his own mother of Alfred's demands: "I didn't realize that he was asking me to write a new play." Still, Rattigan was pleased with Lunt's intervention, eventually conceding that Alfred had been correct: "In the end," he said, "I wrote a far better play because of his suggestions." When it was done, the changes were so significant that Rattigan felt it prudent to resubmit the play for a new copyright under a new name, *Love in Idleness.*

It was interesting for me to learn recently about the relationship between Lunt and the young English boy, Brian Nissen, who landed the part of Michael Brown. Rattigan wrote to his mother about Lunt's strict treatment of Brian: "The boy, poor little brat, is having a terrible time…. Alfred's way of rehearsing him is to take him over three lines in three hours, finally reducing him to tears and hysteria. It is hard to see whether he will be good or not, but I am willing to bet that if he survives the next two months he is going to become the best juvenile actor on the English stage." Many people have described Alfred's easy and amiable personality, but when it came to his profession, he was a perfectionist and could be as stern and demanding as any director I've ever known.

Love in Idleness opened on November 27, 1944, in Liverpool and the following week in Leeds. The critics were not kind. In both cities they concluded that the play "was not worthy of the Lunts' time and efforts." One particularly derisive critic was their close friend, playwright Noel Coward, who told them the play was terrible and continued trying, as Rattigan believed, to sabotage the production.

In the end, the critics and Coward were wrong. The play was wonderful and turned out to be the longest running production of Alfred and Lynn's fifty-year theater careers.

But much like *The Skin of Our Teeth*, the play was only saved when it reached the big city. On December 20, 1944, despite a terrible fog, Londoners came out to see the Lunts open the play at the Lyric Theater. They absolutely loved it—and the critics, while not entirely onboard, were much more accepting than their counterparts had been on the road. Alfred was grateful for their response and later wrote to his friend, William Le Massena, "We always loved playing in London but never more than now."

With the Lunts settled in the Lyric, the Allies were winning the war. The troops were marching toward Berlin, and the Lunts felt a whole new optimism among Londoners. Alfred recalled that earlier during a performance of *There Shall Be No Night*, Winston Churchill had sent a giant cigar backstage. Lunt held onto the cigar, as Jared Brown notes, keeping it carefully "preserved in cellophane, and he used it as a prop in *Love in Idleness.*" In the play Lunt spoke the line, "I left Number Ten [Downing Street, where Churchill, as Prime Minister, lived] only half an hour ago." Fontanne asked, "Was he nice about it?"—referring to Churchill, and Lunt then pulled out the old cigar from his pocket and replied with that inimitable Lunt timing: 'Very!'" The English crowds loved it, as they were all fully aware of Churchill's penchant for a good Cuban cigar.

One evening, while waiting for curtain call, Alfred and Lynn suddenly heard "cheering in the street." From backstage they watched as Winston Churchill walked "down the aisle to his seat in the front row, waving to the applauding audience." This was a victorious Churchill. The war was nearly won, and there was a general euphoria about this man who had led his people through England's most trying times.

Throughout the performance, Lunt recalled, Churchill just "sat there smoking" his cigar, with "everybody watching him more than us. When at the regular time I pulled out the cigar"—the one he had preserved in the cellophane wrapper—"such a cheering started as I'd never heard before by any stretch of the imagination. For five minutes...they cheered and cheered and Churchill got right up, turned around and stood there waving and waving back to them." It was for Alfred and Lynn an intoxicating moment.

The Lunts soon took the play on the "foxhole circuit." They played for victorious troops in France and Germany—even going as far as liberated Nuremberg where they performed for the American GIs. Lynn Fontanne had sent a letter of gratitude for being allowed to play for the troops, and she received a response from General George Patton: "I feel," wrote the General, "that you should not thank me but that I, on behalf of the Third Army, should thank you, Mr. Lunt and the others of your cast for the great pleasure which we derived from your unparalleled performances."

On August 8, 1945, with the war in Europe over and England safe, the Lunts came home to the United States on an American military transport. Arriving at La Guardia field in New York City, wearing U.S. Army uniforms with insignias reading, "Camp Show," Alfred and Lynn modestly rejected the idea that they had been heroes in Europe. Alfred spoke to the *New York Times* about their performances amidst the bombing: "You take your cue from the audience in that kind of situation. They are sitting there all through the storm, quiet, intense bending forward... readier with applause and laughs than any other audiences ever were. That's the opportunity of a lifetime for an actor."

Maybe so, but their humility aside, Alfred Lunt, Lynn Fontanne and the entire English cast and crew of *Love in Idleness* demonstrated true courage under the most difficult circumstances imaginable for any theatrical production. Everyone on Broadway was proud of its emissaries abroad, and when Alfred and Lynn brought Terence Rattigan's play, once again re-titled as *O Mistress Mine*, to Broadway, everyone awaited with tremendous anticipation. And when word got out that they would be looking for a new actor to play the coveted role of their son Michael Brown, every young actor in America was desperate to land the part. I know because I was one of them.

*   *   *

The Lunts were certainly taking the audition for Michael Brown very seriously. As veterans of the theater, they recognized that a role like Michael Brown "could elevate a young actor to stardom." Lynn Fontanne was particularly sensitive to the pitfalls. Discussing the difficulties in the audition process, she wrote to her friend: "It could easily turn out to be a disaster for the young actor who plays it. It could convince him at the start of his career that he knew all there was about acting, and he'd never learn another thing. There is a great responsibility in giving a sure-fire role to an unseasoned player. We must pick someone who will hold his head."

I remember going with Mom to the Shubert Theater for the tryouts. I was sixteen at the time, a relatively young age since Michael Brown was seventeen, and actors typically play characters who are younger than they are. But I was glad to be at the Shubert where I had first stepped on a Broadway stage ten years earlier in *Tapestry in Grey*. It seemed like there were thousands of young men there, although there were probably about forty or fifty.

Among them were at least two future stars, Marlon Brando and Roddy McDowell. It's ironic that Brando had just finished the Broadway production of a play called *I Remember Mama*, about a Norwegian immigrant family in which he played the oldest son, Nels, the same character I would play when the show was made into one of the earliest television situation comedies in 1949. Marlon had received high acclaim for his portrayal of Nels in *Mama*, and, according to Jared Brown, Alfred Lunt wanted him to take the part in *O Mistress Mine*. Brando was four years older than me and, therefore, three years older than the character, but, as mentioned, such an age difference is not at all uncommon.

The initial reading was onstage with Alfred Lunt. That alone was thrilling. There are people who today can tell their grandkids that, for a few minutes, they read a part with the great Alfred Lunt. We all came in through Shubert Alley and waited inside the stage door as one by one we were called in to read by John C. Wilson, the Lunts' renowned producer. Regardless of all my experience onstage, I still remember the thrill of that first reading. I can't say I was nervous. For some reason I felt very comfortable, with the role and immediately I knew that whether or not I actually got the part, this would be a fun audition. No doubt, Lunt's effortless style made it a little easier for all of us and may have helped to offset any nervousness that would be natural to feel in such an auspicious moment. I'm sure that as Marlon Brando rose to a stature similar to that of Lunt and Fontanne, there were many young actors who felt the same sense of awe working with him that he, no doubt, felt as a young man that day onstage with Alfred Lunt.

When all the readings were done, Alfred asked three of us to stay in the theater—Marlon, Roddy and myself. Wilson brought us to one of the dressing rooms, where we awaited the arrival of Lynn Fontanne. When I first saw Lynn she looked like a queen. She had a regal bearing that was stunning. As I told Jared Brown, when she came into the room, heads went up. Each of us read a scene with Alfred, while Lynn watched from the audience.

Although Marlon was better known at the time, I thought the real competition was Roddy. He had an English accent, which I believed was an asset for him. I later learned that the Lunts felt that since the character had spent so many of his formative years in Canada, too much of an English accent might not be credible, particularly with an American audience. After we finished reading, Alfred, Lynn and Wilson went outside to the lobby. Suddenly, I noticed that I was the only one still there. They must have sent Marlon and Roddy home while I was back in the dressing room. I began to get very excited. If they chose me, I would be working with the greatest stage actors of the time, and the wait while they were out in the lobby seemed like eternity.

After about twenty minutes, they came back inside. Alfred Lunt walked up and spoke to me. I remember his exact words: "We like you very much. We recently worked with another young boy named Montgomery Clift, who was wonderful, and we hope we can have the same result with you." He then asked if I would come out to their farm in Wisconsin to study the part with them.

I was ecstatic—and so was my mother. To be chosen for this part with these people was overwhelming. It was also tremendously flattering. Later I learned that Fontanne had written to her English friend Habetrot Dewhurst: "The American cast is on the whole an improvement on the English one…. The part of the boy is taken by a young American. He is really very wonderful. Only seventeen and a brilliant young actor. We are very pleased and excited about him." Such praise from a woman considered by many to be the greatest stage actress of her generation is something I will forever treasure.

Shortly after being selected, I packed my bags and boarded a train for Milwaukee where I was picked up and driven to Alfred and Lynn's beloved summer retreat, Ten Chimneys, in Genesee Depot, Wisconsin. Upon arrival I was struck by the rustic character of their life on the farm. It reminded me of the times I had thought, myself, about the life of a farmer. Ten Chimneys was full of animals, and every day Alfred was up with the roosters, tending to all the animals and working the farm. He talked as much about farming as theater. In an interview with the *Wisconsin State Journal* in 1947, Alfred explained his rigorous daily routine on the farm: "I get up about 4:30 or 5 o'clock. I don't milk—we have four cows—but I run the separator and bottle the milk…. I've got a pig pen out there—three pigs—that's more spic and span than this dressing room." Through the years I noticed that when the time for a break from the show neared, Alfred and Lynn became visibly excited about getting back to their beloved Ten Chimneys.

Today, Ten Chimneys is a museum. Even though it's located far from Broadway, there are many travelers and theater enthusiasts who stop in to see the home of American theater's first couple. Sadly, there are not many of us around anymore who saw the Lunts onstage, and each year the number is dwindling. This year I scheduled a trip to speak at Ten Chimneys, but my plans were interrupted by heart surgery. Hopefully, I'll get back there soon.

In 1945, I spent three weeks living on the farm and working with the Lunts on *O Mistress Mine*. I stayed in the bedroom reserved for their close friend Noel Coward. Each day we rehearsed the play for several hours in their living room. Later I went swimming in their pool, and in the evening Alfred, who was a master chef, cooked us dinner. When I think back on those weeks at Ten Chimneys, I'm astonished at how fortunate I was. Imagine a sixteen year old actor today being invited to live with and rehearse every day with someone like Anthony Hopkins, Kevin Spacey or Meryl Streep. I learned more about acting in those three weeks than I ever imagined possible. They taught me their technique of overlapping lines, and after intense practice sessions I began to get the hang of it. It was all about timing the lines so that it appeared we were talking at the very same time, but never in a way that disrupted the clarity of the words.

After taking the play on a short road trip in the winter of 1945, *O Mistress Mine* opened in New York at the Empire Theater on January 23, 1946. Although I generally don't get nervous before a performance, I remember being anxious that first night on Broadway as every single critic in the city came out to see the Lunts triumphant return. I think I also felt more of a responsibility than ever before. This was a special moment for both Broadway and for the Lunts, and a great deal was riding on my performance. If I did poorly, it would ruin this wonderful moment. Fortunately, it all went well.

"They came like a whirlwind to the Empire last night," wrote Lewis Nichols in the *New York Times*. "The theater is cheerful again. The Lunts are back." John Chapman of the *Daily News* exclaimed, "The most celebrated married couple in the modern history of the stage returned from the war in Britain in a comedy which permitted them to make unmarried love to each other." And Vernon Rice of the *Post* simply declared: "Good old-fashioned magic returned to the theatre last night.... Alfred Lunt and Lynn Fontanne are home again."

And, thankfully, they liked me as well. Ward Morehouse wrote, "Dick Van Patten plays the rebellious Michael, the adolescent Hamlet, and he moves right along with the stars. He has force and a sense of comedy values and his scenes with Lunt are enormously amusing." In the *Times*, Nichols reminded his readers of my history onstage as a child and acknowledged that I had moved on: "Dick Van Patten, who used to be Dickie as a child actor now has grown into fierce young manhood. He is serious and intense: some of the best passages are where the minister knows the boy as a viper and the widow knows him not at all."

My performance aside, Nichols was right that Rattigan's play was particularly good when Sir John sees through Michael's high-minded posturing. A number of times Michael would spout off quotations from the writings of the contemporary British socialist, Harold Laski, and Sir John would scoff at his pretentions. But, Olivia, being his mother, was blind to her son's conceit. Much of this dialogue was part of the rewriting that Rattigan had done at Alfred's insistence, expanding Lunt's character and, in the process, improving the play.

The review I enjoyed most came from Robert Garland, the renowned critic of the *New York Journal American*, who wrote that

"Dick Van Patten…brings a boyish likability to a priggish, puritanical part." I liked that because it's always a challenge for an actor to make a villain appealing. And while Michael Brown was not quite a villain, he was, at least for most of the play, pompous and insufferable. Yet, the Lunts had stressed to me that the audience must find something to like in his character, or they will find it hard to join in the laugh. I had made a conscious effort to strike that balance and was delighted to see that Garland had noticed.

This was, by far, the high point of my stage career. In a little over ten years, and with the relentless support of my mother, I was now playing on the biggest stage with the greatest stars. Looking back I don't think anything can compare with the electricity of that first night and then the enormous satisfaction—and no small relief—in reading the wonderful reviews the next day. Montgomery Clift had called me after I first won the part and assured me there was nothing like working with the Lunts. He was right. And this was no ordinary part. One columnist noted that it was the longest juvenile role up to that time on Broadway. Michael Brown's part took up ninety side sheets—meaning a full ninety pages in the play book. It was a role that could really spark a career and, as Lynn Fontanne anticipated, such situations inevitably bring new opportunities and hard decisions that have to be made.

It was interesting that John Chapman in his review in the *Daily News* captured a bit of the dilemma. He started with an extremely flattering review, but ended with an admonition: "There is an uncommonly good performance by an ex-kid actor named Dick Van Patten, who last season was playing child stuff and called himself Dickie. Mr. Van Patten is growing up fast and growing up very well in the theatre, and I hope to goodness, he stays here and does not flit off to the movies."

The Lunts had the same concern. It greatly increased, when shortly after the opening, I was contacted by several Hollywood studios—Warner Brothers, MGM, and Twentieth Century Fox—each offering me a standard seven-year deal to get into the movies. But there were strings attached. Basically, they said I could go to Hollywood, and they would pay me for six months while I worked. But they were under no obligation to actually use me. If, for any reason, they weren't satisfied after six months was up, they could just let me go. Those were the terms.

It would, thus, be taking a risk and, frankly, I wasn't sure what to do. At the time, I did recall the advice Tallulah Bankhead gave me when I considered leaving *The Skin of Our Teeth* to try out for the role opposite my sister, Joyce, in *Tomorrow the World*: "Don't ever leave a hit for something uncertain," Tallulah advised.

The Lunts also played a key role in my decision. They called both my parents in to talk in their offices and expressed their strong opposition to any such move. What's interesting now is that I still remember Alfred using the same word the critic John Chapman has used, "Don't let him "flit" his career away in Hollywood." Alfred told my parents: "Dickie has a future here on Broadway."

In any event, I also remembered Monty Clift's congratulatory call when he told me how much he had learned working with these legendary stage actors, and I knew that I still had a great deal more to learn from them. Most important, I felt indebted to them. After all, they had placed their confidence and trust in me. In the end, my parents and I decided that I should stay.

At times I've wondered what life would have been like had I tried my hand at motion pictures. It turned out to be a blessing in disguise that Marlon Brando had lost the audition with the Lunts. Within a year Brando exploded into stardom with his extraordinary portrayal of Stanley Kowalski in Tennessee Williams's *A Streetcar Named Desire*. The play, directed by Elia Kazan, opened on Broadway on December 3, 1947, and is often credited as the beginning of the ascendancy of the method school of acting.

There were other contemporaries among the actors circulating in New York City at the time who made the transition to film and had great success, but I was still very young—barely seventeen when *O Mistress Mine* opened at the Empire—and this rare opportunity to work with and learn from the Lunts was not something to be squandered. Perhaps my career would have been different, but I have no regrets at all.

The Lunts were the hardest workers I'd ever known. About every three weeks, Alfred would entirely change the play's blocking just to keep it fresh. In other words, Alfred was conscious of the role of physical movement in a play and believed it should be altered before it became stale. Think of a fellow driving to work every day, taking the same route. Then one day he changes the route, and somehow there's something new and fresh about it. The change affects his mood and, therefore, his behavior.

Lunt understood that the same principle was true in theater. Let's say that I had a line to deliver while sitting on the couch. The next week Alfred would change it to where I was saying the same line while walking across the stage. As we did this, I started to notice that the lines really did come out differently. With each change, there was renewed energy that enhanced the performance. Throughout the duration of the play, Lunt just kept changing the blocking and keeping the play fresh. I have never seen anybody else work that way, and I found it amazing that such a simple thing could have such a profound effect.

Throughout the long run on Broadway, I was happy. It was a time when I was in that strange phase between being a teenager and an adult. I was also beginning to enjoy a bit of the fast life, and, for that, there's no place on earth more exciting than New York City.

23

COMING OF AGE IN THE BIG APPLE

In addition to playing the part of Michael Brown, my unofficial role during the years of *O Mistress Mine* was as Alfred Lunt's personal talent scout. Whether in New York or on the road, I would head out to see the local shows and return to Lunt with a review. If I said the show was good, he would come and watch it with me. Once, we were playing in Detroit, and I saw a comedian, Irving Harmon, at a burlesque show at the Avenue Theatre who was terrific. Harmon had tremendously long legs, and he would somehow wrap them around his body and twist himself up like a giant pretzel. Then he'd sit down as though everything was perfectly normal. It looked so silly that the whole place was hysterical. I told Alfred, and the two of us went back the next day, and he loved it as much as me.

Many years later I ran into Irving Harmon. He was a friend of Sammy Smith, an ex-burlesque comic whom I was working with in a 1974 Broadway show titled *Thieves.* One day Harmon came to a rehearsal, and Sammy introduced me to him. Although he had aged greatly, I immediately recognized him as the comic from Detroit. When I told him how much Alfred Lunt had enjoyed his performance, he became incredibly moved and excited. "You mean Alfred Lunt was out there watching me? My God, why didn't you come backstage—if I had only known!" Harmon's reaction showed just how revered Lunt was among entertainers. This old fellow was genuinely touched by the fact that he had made Alfred Lunt laugh. I went away wishing I had brought Lunt backstage to see him.

Part of the reason Lunt was so revered was because of his own willingness to learn from other actors and comedians. In the early days of his career, Milton Berle recalled seeing the same guy in his audience night after night. This fellow came so often that Milton started to assume he was some kind of oddball. Then one night the fellow came backstage. He introduced himself as Alfred Lunt. He wanted to tell Milton how much he had learned watching him. It turned out Alfred was about to do a show with some burlesque humor in it, and he wanted to watch this young comic who was being so highly touted. Milton was floored by it, as well as genuinely humbled.

Alfred, of course, also loved high culture, and we would occasionally see the big theater stars together. Once we went with Lynn Fontanne to see John Gielgud at the Plymouth Theater performing in Oscar Wilde's *The Importance of Being Earnest*. The Lunts laughed at Wilde's wit and Gielgud's wonderful performance. In fact, Lynn later wrote to the play's producer Binkie Beaumont telling him how much she and Alfred enjoyed the play, saying that Gielgud "made me laugh louder and longer than I have laughed in the theatre for years."

* * *

It was around this time that I ran into a young kid who had his sights firmly fixed on the big time in show business. At first, he tried his hand at acting, but his real talents lay elsewhere. Soon we became fast friends and for a while enjoyed a lot of crazy stuff together. In the end, we were both lucky to come through it in one piece.

I, of course, had no idea whatsoever that this brash, intense young daredevil would become one of the greatest motion picture producers of the twentieth century. For those who might think I'm stretching it a bit, just ask yourself: who else can count among their credits *The Godfathers* I and II, *Love Story*, *Rosemary's Baby* and *Chinatown*?

Bob Evans was a fifteen year old kid—about two years younger than me—when I first noticed him hanging around the radio stations. In his autobiography, *The Kid Stays In The Picture*, he recalls the time when, as he put it, "my new best pal was Dickie Van Patten." While I couldn't have predicted his astonishing future career, I did instantly recognize that Bob was a real character.

At first he kind of tagged along after me. He seemed impressed with my status, and years later he generously wrote that at the time we met, "Dickie Van Patten was the top juvenile actor in New York." Soon I realized we had a lot in common, and for a couple of years we really were, as he says, "best pals."

Bob was absolutely the most determined young man I ever knew. If he decided he wanted something, no matter how crazy— or dangerous—he wouldn't stop until he had it or was knocked cold in the pursuit. One time that was literally the case. We were on the shore at Long Beach, and we started a friendly sparring match. Even though it was "friendly" we were still tagging each other a good bit when we noticed this old, short, fat guy with an overcoat, completely out of place on the beach, watching us fight.

I guess he saw that same determined insanity in Bob's eyes that a lot of studio heads and directors would dread over the next fifty years, and so he asked: "You guys box?"

We said, "No." But the old guy just ignored our response and said to Bob: "You look pretty good. I'm running some amateur fights tonight. Why don't you come, and I'll set you up with one of them."

Bob was intrigued, but he told the guy, "Look we're actors. I don't know how to box." That's when I knew I had him: "Ten bucks says you're afraid," I blurted out without missing a beat. That settled it. So later that night we were in the locker room at the Long Beach Stadium on the Boardwalk with Bob in some old gym shorts and me lacing up a pair of boxing gloves the old man had left for him.

Bob was in the last fight—number sixteen on the card. The beauty of going last—at least the beauty for me—was that we got to watch them all—one bruised, battered and bloodied loser after another limping all the way back to the dressing room—not always under their own power.

Finally the time came for the final fight. Bob describes it best in his memoirs: "Entering the ring with Dickie behind me, I saw for the first time the guy I was to fight. This animal with no teeth wasn't looking to get into flicks."

That was certainly true. And I have to admit I was enjoying the view as much as Bob was, wondering what in the world he was doing in there. But the power of ten bucks and a dare was more than he could handle. So it continued.

The fight went for three rounds. As Bob calculated it that was just "six minutes to stay alive." At first he held up pretty well, making it through the first round with no major damage. Then as he tells it: "Gong! Round two. The animal came out charging again." Bob actually landed a pretty good right, and he made it into the third round. But then he threw another right and suddenly—lights out. Bob hit the canvas so hard I thought he was never getting back up. He was unconscious as I dragged him to the dressing room. At least he was still breathing when we laid him on the bench. A few minutes later he woke up, and I dropped a ten dollar bill on his stomach. A deal's a deal. The old man also gave Bob a wristwatch. They couldn't pay him money because he was an amateur, but his blood was worth something.

There were three "obsessions" that, according to Bob, he and I shared: "danger, women, and gambling." I need to clarify that a bit. First, Robert Evans was an absolute magnet for women—and I'm talking about when he was still fifteen! Walking down the street with Bob was a guarantee of female company whether you were "obsessed" or not.

One day Bob and I were on Fifth Avenue and spotted a stunning young lady walking opposite us. He said to me, "That's Lana Turner." This was at the height of her popularity. Bob then said, "I'm going to go talk to her." I told him: "You're crazy." I bet him ten bucks he couldn't get a date with her. I wasn't stupid. I knew how good he was with women, but, this was Lana Turner. A few days later, he showed up at the Empire with his new date. When she wasn't looking I gave him the ten bucks.

Bob also dated Grace Kelly. A few years later, he and Grace came to see me in *Mister Roberts* and afterwards, we went out to Ruby Foos on 52nd Street for dinner. Grace was one of those young women who had it all; beauty, intelligence and a wonderfully charming personality. If anyone was to become a real-life princess, it should have been Grace. In 1982, I went to Monte Carlo on a celebrity tennis tournament and met her again, now as the Princess of Monaco. We had a wonderful time chatting about Bob Evans and the old days in New York City.

I also remember that trip because my son Nels won the celebrity tennis tournament. His doubles partner was O.J. Simpson. I got to know O.J. a little from the various celebrity events. He was always nice to be around. And I can attest to his inclination for women. Once at a celebrity tournament in the Bahamas, I was awakened at around 1 a.m. by a knock at my hotel door. I got up, opened the door and there were two beautiful girls standing in the hallway. They asked, "Is O.J. in here?" I politely told them he wasn't. It's hard to imagine that the guy those girls were looking for, and the good-natured fellow we played tennis with, would be accused of murdering two young people in cold blood. I didn't follow the case very carefully, but it did seem they had a lot of evidence against him. It ended up a tragedy for all involved.

As for Bob Evans, he wasn't just obsessed with women, they were obsessed with him. I've never seen anything like it, and after eighty years, I'm guessing I never will again.

As for Bob's claim that we were obsessed with danger, he gives me too much credit. My real obsession was getting him to indulge his own amazing appetite for putting it on the line. One day he was hanging around the NBC Studio where we broadcast, *Young Widder Brown*. When I finished my part, I went out in the stairwell and had a cigarette with the other kids. At the time, smoking didn't have the kind of taboo that's attached to it today. Bob was also there in the stairwell—the ambitious kid who would do just about anything to be the center of attention. Knowing that made me think. How could I get him to entertain us? I looked down the middle of the stairwell—it was a straight drop from the third floor to the bottom. So I said to Bob: "A buck says you can't hang by your fingers for five minutes."

Bob couldn't resist a challenge. Before I knew it he had lowered himself from the stairwell and began hanging with his feet dangling in the open air. If he fell, he was dead. I started counting. Bob held on for dear life. "I hung, and hung," he later wrote. "I shut my eyes and counted off the seconds, trying to block out the pain."

When three minutes were up, we all grabbed him and pulled him to safety. I'm sure it was just in time. Looking back, it's hard to believe we could have done something so incredibly stupid. But we were young and reckless—and Bob Evans, as Hollywood would soon find out, was one of a kind.

* * *

While working with the Lunts, I moved out of our apartment at the Des Artistes, on 67th Street in Manhattan, where I had lived with my Mom and Joyce for the past several years. I was nineteen and dating a woman, Lois Woodson, who happened to be a friend of my mother's. That made things awkward at home so Lois and I moved in with her friend, an actress named Norma Anderson and Norma's boyfriend, also a struggling actor, named Burt Lancaster.

The four of us lived together in an apartment on 55th Street. Burt was about ten years older than me and working in a play called *The Sound of Hunting*. The play bombed, but Burt received excellent reviews, which helped launch his career.

Burt was a quiet and reserved guy, though very nice. While living together we pretty much went our own ways. He did tell me that he was an acrobat. In fact he had just returned from performing a circus act on a USO tour. It was there he met Norma, and when I moved in, Norma was pregnant. Later I recall them telling the newspapers they had adopted a child. In those days it was a way to avoid any kind of scandal. Soon afterward, they moved to Hollywood.

My coming of age in New York also involved the acquisition that was most important to me. I had spent a good portion of my youth at a racetrack, and now I was going to see it all from a new vantage point.

109

24

PENETRATOR

Early in my run with the Lunts, I became the youngest racehorse owner in America. That had been one of my dreams, and now that I was making $750 a week, an enormous sum in those days, I decided it was time to buy my own horse. With my mother's reluctant acquiescence, I took a train to Lexington, Kentucky, where all the big horse auctions were held.

I saw a yearling colt at the auction—a beautiful bay, meaning he was a rich, dark brown color. He was Jersey bred and best of all, he only cost $900. His name was Penetrator. We took him from the auction and shipped him by train to the stables at the Aqueduct in Ozone Park, Queens, where it cost $8 a day to keep him.

My father was also excited about my owning a horse. He came to my first race at Jamaica racetrack. Proud that his son had a horse in the race, he said to me: "I don't care who is in the race, I'm betting on Penetrator." But I knew the horses far better than Dad, and Penetrator didn't have a chance. So I argued with him: "Forget about Penetrator, play the seven." That was a horse named Mist O Gold. But my father was adamant. He wouldn't change his bet. He said he just couldn't bet against his own son's horse.

Mist O Gold won, and my father missed an excellent payday. I couldn't wager myself because you're not allowed to bet against your own horse. But I would have liked to see Dad win a few bucks, even if it did mean betting against his son's horse.

Penetrator nearly brought me a touch of immortality. There had been racing at Monmouth Park in New Jersey from the 1870s until it was shut down twenty years later in the 1890s. Then, just after I bought Penetrator, the racetrack opened again. The first races were held on July 19, 1946, and we entered. I was lucky to have a jockey named Ronnie Nash, who was one of the top riders. I remember being the youngest guy in the owners' box as they went through the ceremonies commemorating the reopening of the track after fifty-three years.

When the ceremonies finished, they started the first race of the day. This was Penetrator's race, and I couldn't believe my eyes. As they took off, he was out among the leaders. As they came into the stretch, I was all excited. But there was another horse, Blind Path, also in the mix. In the homestretch it was just the two of them—a photo finish! But, we lost. The next day, even the *New York Times* covered the opening race, noting that Blind Path "got on the inside going into the stretch and withstood a challenge by Penetrator."

About five years ago, I went back to Monmouth Park. I hadn't been there in over fifty years. I saw above the entrance a big picture of that very first race run at the new Monmouth Park. I looked up, and there's my Penetrator—getting beat by a nose.

To make it even worse, at the bottom of the photo, it named the jockey, the owner, and the trainer of the winner in big black print. Penetrator and I could have been immortalized.

25

SIDESHOWS

I've mentioned scouting for Alfred Lunt, but I also scoured the streets of New York to satisfy my own penchant for oddities, often by heading over to Hubert's Museum on 42nd Street where they frequently featured a variety of freak shows. I can still remember the names of all the stars at the Hubert: Robert Mervin, the boy with two faces; Betty Lou Williams, the girl with four legs; Francesco Lentini, the man with three legs; Coo Coo, the bird lady; and, of course, Zip and Pip, advertised by the Hubert's barker as "the human pinheads, whose heads were no larger than the size of my fist."

One day at the Hubert, they announced a coming attraction: "Albert/Alberta—the world's only living hermaphrodite on exhibition today." That was just the thing to get my juices flowing. I was performing before thousands of people every night at the Empire with Alfred Lunt and Lynn Fontanne, yet after hearing that announcement all I could think about was that upcoming freak show with a half man/half-woman.

The big day finally came. I watched as Albert/Alberta stepped onstage and announced: "Ladies and Gentlemen, I'm half man; and I'm half woman. As you can see on this side, I have the lovely complexion of a woman. And over here, I have a beard." He/She spoke with a thick French accent: "Over here, you see I have no breasts. Over here, I have these beautiful breasts. I'm a very feminine woman."

I was amazed. I went straight back to the Empire that night, knocked on Lunt's dressing room door and exclaimed: "Mr. Lunt, you won't believe what I just saw at the Hubert—a half man/half woman." I kept going on and on, and Alfred Lunt kept listening intently, just saying: "Hmm. Hmm. Yes. Yes." I knew I had him hooked for the next show.

But things didn't go as planned. A few days later, I went to a double feature at the New Amsterdam Theatre. I should mention here that my father had always told me there might come a time when a man would make an advance toward me. I remember his exact words: "If you are ever in a place like a movie theatre, and somebody sits next to you and you feel their hand on your body, just say in a very loud and clear voice: 'Stop what you are doing. Stop what you are doing immediately.'" He assured me the person would stop, but he stressed that I had to say it loud and clear.

Sitting in the New Amsterdam, I noticed the balcony was empty. Suddenly a man came in and sat right next to me. It sounds like a cliché, but he was actually wearing a trench coat. I thought it was creepy. Sure enough, a moment later, I felt his hand on my knee. With that, I remembered what my father told me and was just about to say very loud: "Stop what you are doing" when I glanced over at him—and it was Albert/Alberta!

I was stunned. I just couldn't bring myself to yell at this great celebrity. Instead, I got up and left. The worst part was that I was totally disillusioned. The great hermaphrodite, Albert/Alberta, was a fake. I went back to Alfred Lunt, and he had a big, long laugh at my expense.

I also saw the great boxing legend, Jack Johnson, at the Hubert Museum. The first black heavyweight champion, Johnson's rise to the title set promoters on a desperate search for a white contender. When no one could touch him in the ring, they coaxed Jim Jeffries out of retirement, calling him "the great white hope." Their fight in 1910 was one of the biggest sensations in boxing history. And to the disappointment of the promoters, and many others, Johnson demolished him.

Jack Johnson was no ordinary champ. He was truly great—in fact, one of the greatest heavyweight fighters in boxing history. But he also refused to play the role of a submissive black, grateful for being allowed to participate in a white-dominated business. On the contrary, Johnson was a supremely confident, even arrogant, man who, at a time when Jim Crow was the law of the land, refused to bow to the prevailing racism. For that, Johnson paid an enormous price, both professionally and personally.

Johnson came out onstage at the Hubert wearing a brown suit with a white shirt and tie and his trademark navy-blue beret. Self-assured and well spoken, he pointed to a picture on the wall of himself lying on the canvas in Havana, Cuba, after losing to Jess Willard in 1915. At the time of the fight, Johnson was under indictment for a Mann Act violation, accused of bringing a woman across state lines for illicit purposes. He was literally a fugitive, exiled from his country and on the run, and also under enormous personal and financial pressure.

Johnson told us that he took a dive for a cash payoff. He wanted us—and the world—to believe that Willard had not actually beaten him. Taking a pointer, he directed it at the picture of himself lying on the canvass. "If this were a true knockout," he explained, "I wouldn't be shading my eyes from the sun." And it's true, in this famous picture of Johnson on the canvas, his hands are raised in the air as if shielding his eyes from the brutal Havana sun.

Shortly after I saw him, Johnson died in a car crash in North Carolina. No one will ever know for sure whether he took a dive or legitimately lost the fight. Today most of the experts are against him. Some twenty years later in 1966, a film of the fight was discovered that seemed to show that Willard won. Either way, Johnson was one of the most charismatic men of the century, a legend both in and out of the ring, and it was fascinating and a little bit sad, to see him at the close of his extraordinary life working for fifty bucks a week at the Hubert trying to undo a wrong committed so long ago. On the other hand, there was also something uplifting about a man who, against all odds, kept on fighting right to the bitter end.

26

MAMA: A BRAVE NEW WORLD

The national tour of *O Mistress Mine* closed in the summer of 1948. The play had been a tremendous success and helped to establish my reputation as a comic actor. As I looked ahead, I had no idea that my immediate future would see another turn to a new medium that would become one of the most important developments not only in entertainment, but in every aspect of life. Television had arrived in America.

To appreciate the stunning suddenness of the transition, it's worth considering that when we entered World War II in 1941, there were just 7000 television sets in the entire United States. Most of these sets were owned by very wealthy people. Just eight years later, when *I Remember Mama* first aired in 1949, the number had grown to about 3.5 million sets. But even with this tremendous increase, televisions were still largely a phenomenon of the cities—nearly all of them were located in New York, Chicago, Los Angeles and other major urban centers.

But that was about to change. And it did so just as *I Remember Mama* took to the airways. By the time of *Mama's* final performance in 1957, there were nearly 60 million television sets nationwide. Not only did television explode, but it exploded throughout the duration of our show.

Mama was originally planned for radio. When I went to audition at CBS studios on Madison Avenue, it never crossed my mind that this would be a television program. At that point there were no situation comedies on television—the first was *The Goldbergs*, which debuted just six months before *Mama* in January of 1949. Most of the programming consisted of news and variety shows, often the latter would have a comedian, like Jack Benny, hosting. But the idea of a television sit-com was the furthest thing from our minds, and I recall being skeptical when told that the format was being changed from radio to television.

It turned out to be a brilliant decision. *I Remember Mama*, which was eventually known as simply *Mama*, was a groundbreaking show that helped push the brand-new medium of television forward. But at the time, I certainly wasn't thinking about that. Television was untested, and we were all uncertain how this would turn out.

The *Mama* story was adapted from a best-selling novel, *Mama's Bank Account*, written by Kathryn Forbes, about a Norwegian immigrant family who settled in San Francisco in the early years of the century. The actual time in which the first show took place was 1915, thus World War I was already underway in Europe, but the United States had not yet entered the conflict.

The show told a series of stories about an idyllic family, as it was later recalled by one of the children, Katrin, who was wonderfully played by my good friend, Rosemary Rice. Although the family life was idyllic, there was always a constant struggle with the small salary that the father, Lars Hansen, played by Judson Laire, was able to eke out in his job as a carpenter. Many of the storylines dealt with Mama's imaginative ways to stretch their small income and make ends meet.

Before being tested for television, *I Remember Mama* had been a big hit on Broadway in 1944. Ironically, as earlier mentioned, the very first actor to play Nels Hansen, the eldest son, was Marlon Brando. In fact, it was Brando's debut on Broadway and helped move him into the spotlight. His success in the role contributed to the reason why the Lunts were so interested in him for the role of Michael Brown in *O Mistress Mine*.

Thus, Marlon had played Nels in *I Remember Mama* before we both auditioned for the Lunts, while I played Nels after finishing with the Lunts. Of course, it worked out much better for Marlon, since he soon landed the role in *Streetcar* that launched him into arguably the greatest acting career in the history of American film.

But the role of Nels didn't fall so easily to me. In fact, I lost out at first—something that would also happen years later with *Eight Is Enough*. The part first went to Jackie Ayers, a child actor whom I knew from The Professional Children's School. I still recall the producer using those polite, but gut-wrenching words that every actor has heard: "You were very good, but we're going in a different direction."

They rehearsed for a couple of days with Jackie when suddenly they called and asked me to come back. I believe the change was prompted by Ralph Nelson, whom I had worked with in *The Wind Is Ninety* and was now a producer and the principal director of *Mama*. I returned, but I did feel sorry for Jackie. He was a friend, and I know how tough it can be to lose a part— especially after you think you already have it.

Once we started shooting, I immediately learned something about this new medium: it was powerful. I had already been well known as a model, a child actor, an adolescent star who worked on Broadway with the Lunts, and an actor with major roles in hundreds of radio programs. But all of that paled next to television. Even at the height of my career with the Lunts, I could walk into a restaurant, have a quiet meal with friends, and never be recognized. All that changed overnight. Suddenly everywhere I went people were coming up, asking me if I was that guy Nels on TV.

I was also among the very few people who immediately transitioned from a large role on Broadway to a large role on television—and the difference was truly dramatic. I had been in front of large crowds since I was five years old, but I never felt like a celebrity. With television, that also changed—both for good and for bad. It made me recognize not just that my life was changing, but that the whole nature of American entertainment was in transition.

Getting ready for the premiere of *Mama* was a difficult task for everyone. Besides *The Goldbergs* who had started just a few months earlier, there was no precedent for the kind of live episodic television that we were shooting. Worthington Minor, a CBS executive—and also the father of Peter Minor, the boy from *On Borrowed Time*—was involved both with *Mama* and *The Goldbergs* and described the uncharted waters of live television: "It was all new and terrifyingly complex. Since until now no one had ever tried to do it before, nobody really knew how to do anything. An 'old hand' was somebody who'd worked on the show last week." Minor was right. Nearly everybody involved with the show, including me, had the majority of their experience in theater and radio.

I Remember Mama opened on July 1, 1949. It was an immediate hit. Within a short time millions of people were tuning in every Friday night to watch the travails of this family of Norwegian immigrants. Until the show closed in 1957, we performed 500 episodes. I remember Ralph Nelson joking to me during the last show, "If I've told you once, I've told you 500 times...." During those eight years, I grew from a young man to an adult. I married and had all three of my children before the final performance of *Mama*.

As with Tom Bradford in *Eight Is Enough*, when you perform a role for that long, particularly a part that changes with each performance—unlike those long-running plays where the story is always the same—it's hard not to develop a sentimental attachment to the fictional character. For me, Nels Hansen was almost real.

Like all the characters, he was the original brainchild of Kathryn Forbes. But Nels also became a creation of the principal writer Frank Gabrielson and, ultimately, my own interpretation and personality added to the mix—all of which created the young man who came each week, with his family, into the homes of millions of Americans.

During the years on *Mama*, the producers would bring in different people to play mine or Rosemary's friends. Often these would be recurring roles. Three young actors who played for varying periods would later become film legends: James Dean, Paul Newman and Jack Lemmon.

The one most involved was James Dean, and we became good friends for a while. He was a couple of years younger than me and seemed to like to tag along all the time. Often that meant going to the Forrest Hotel for a game of poker. Jimmy never played, but he was content to sit behind me and get us cigarettes and cokes and hang out all night just watching the game.

In 1952, I was going to be away from the show for a few weeks. I suggested to Ralph Nelson that James take over as Nels while I was gone. Ralph agreed, and for several weeks James Dean played my part on *I Remember Mama*. I've noticed that in accounts of James Dean's life, this fact is usually downplayed. But, the truth is that his first national exposure came playing Nels in *Mama*.

Although I wasn't there at the time, Rosemary Rice remembers it well. It was clear to her and to others that James really wasn't suited for the part. There was always something a little dark about James's personality, very unlike Nels, an upbeat, happy member of an idyllic family. Later, when asked about the short-lived change in Nels, Rosemary would pay me a wonderful compliment, saying that "Dick Van Patten was irreplaceable." I don't know whether that's true, but I can say that there was a special magic among all the cast members that was, indeed, irreplaceable.

Of all the stars who appeared on the show, including Paul Newman, James Dean, Jason Robards and Jack Lemmon, Jimmy was the last I would have expected to become a star, much less an iconic figure in American culture. But, looking back, it's also not so surprising that he would come to symbolize a kind of disaffected element of American youth. He was brilliant in *Rebel Without a Cause* and his role was, of course, far more tailored to his particular personality than Nels Hansen.

Like millions of Americans, I was deeply saddened by James's premature death in a car crash in 1955. I still think of him as that interesting young kid who used to tag along to my poker games and who took over my spot for a few weeks on the show. But, of course, he became much more than that, and I'm proud to have worked with and gotten to know him in the days before he really entered our consciousness as the ultimate American rebel.

* * *

Live television was very different than the recorded shows we watch today. Sid Caesar, one of my all-time favorite comics and among the earliest stars of television with his 1950 show, *The Sid Caesar Hour*, said it best: "People today have no idea what live television means." It meant "flying by the seat of your pants." There were "no cue cards, Teleprompters, no second chances and no net. You only had one chance and that's it. If a fly landed on your nose, you squinted and you kept walking and talking, or you incorporated the fly into the scene."

A few incidents on *Mama* illustrate Sid's point. Each of the *Mama* episodes consisted of five scenes. If you were finished after an early scene, you could go home. There was no reshooting and no curtain calls. One night, believing he was done, Judson Laire took off for home before the show ended. He forgot he was in the fifth scene! So there we were, the whole family, but no Papa—while Judson was calmly riding away in his taxi. His calm didn't last. Suddenly he realized he was in the final scene, and in a tremendous panic he had the taxi driver turn around and speed back to the studio. He didn't make it.

And we didn't know what to do. Millions of people were watching live. So, Ralph Nelson came to the rescue. He got down on his hands and knees behind the set. And whenever we came to one of Papa's lines, we ran to the back door and talked as if he were in the backyard. Ralph would answer as if he were Papa, but from a place where no one could see him. It looked ridiculous. I remember Peggy Wood was very upset, but Ralph kept saying: "Don't worry, no one will notice it." But of course, they did. The next morning I was listening to the popular *The Dorothy and Dick Show* on the radio, and all they talked about was the screwup last night on *Mama*.

In another episode, a young Jack Lemmon knocked on the door for his date with Katrin. Rosemary answered and said: "Oh won't you come in." She was then supposed to say: "I haven't a single solitary thing planned." Instead, she got the words all jumbled and said: "Oh won't you come in, I haven't a thinkle sing planned solitary."

The moment she said it, she broke out laughing and couldn't say her next lines. And so the cameraman, not knowing what to do, turned his camera on me. But by then I was also laughing so hard, I couldn't stop. The two of us just stood there in front of millions of viewers laughing uncontrollably. So the panicked cameraman again switched the camera to Peggy Wood just in time to catch her yelling out: "Get those Goddamn brats off the stage!" The next day, of course, the incident was the talk of the town.

But the honor for the most embarrassing early live TV moment is certainly reserved for Philip Loeb, the father in *The Goldbergs*. In one of their episodes, there was a scene in which several of the men were taking a sauna with their towels wrapped around them. But Phil hadn't done such a good job in wrapping his towel, at least the part covering his genitalia. So now there were millions of men, women and children all over the country staring at Phil's testicles. Live television could be tough!

Peggy was only half wrong in calling Rosemary and me "brats." The truth is I often didn't follow the rules and occasionally that got me into some real jams. One day while rehearsing, a pair of very serious looking guys—Rosemary thought they looked like a couple of Humphrey Bogarts, all dressed with long trench coats and dark felt fedoras—came right into our rehearsal flashing their police badges. The next thing I knew, they had grabbed me and dragged me off to the Long Island City Department of Corrections. It turned out I had ignored a few parking tickets—well, not really a few; it was more like fity.

It happened to be an interesting time to land in lockup, as all the other prisoners were very impressed with their newest inmate. Not me, but a fellow named Willie Sutton! Anyway, they gave me a shirt to wear that had the letters, D.O.C., which, like an idiot, I thought was a nickname. I figured that in prison everyone gets a nickname and mine was Doc. I found out later it means Department of Corrections. When I was on the way out, all the prisoners gave me their wives and girlfriends' phone numbers to call. So I made the calls, and with every single one I got the same response: "He can sit there, for all I care."

Fortunately, our producer, Carol Irwin, had clout. Friendly with a well-known Manhattan judge, Carol reached out for assistance. Showtime was approaching, and I was stuck in the city lockup. The judge agreed to help, but it came with a price. He wanted a small part in an episode. So to get me out of jail, Carol arranged to have the judge come in and do a cameo playing a local judge in the show. It was a small price to pay.

Friday nights after each performance, the *Mama* cast and crew would head out to a restaurant, usually the House of Chan. I never went. In my twenties at the time, I preferred the fights at the Garden and later a burlesque show. They kept after me, but I continued to politely decline. Finally Carol decided that if I wouldn't go out with them, they'd come out with me. So that night the whole cast and crew of *Mama* headed to the fights and a burlesque theater in Newark, New Jersey.

At the time, I was dating Rita Moreno. Recently arrived in New York City with her mother from Puerto Rico, Rita was still an unknown, aspiring actress. Perhaps we got along because her mom, like mine, was determined that her child would become a star. Her efforts paid off a few years later when Rita won great acclaim for her unforgettable role as Anita in *West Side Story*.

The downside to dating Rita was that her mom always insisted on coming out with us. On that night I also arranged a date for Rosemary with a questionable character I knew as "Midtown Murray." I won't say "Midtown" was a thief, but he used to show up with a box full of expensive Patek Philippe watches and swear he got them legitimately. So I took a bunch and sold them to the folks on the show. Judson and Rosemary each bought one for $250.

Most of them, especially Peggy and Rosemary, were less than pleased with the brutality of the fights. But that was nothing next to the fiasco at the midnight show in Newark. In every burlesque there's a stripper who removes her clothes to the rhythm of a song played by a live band. But this time it was a little different. The stripper that night was the famous Blaze Starr, who had a notorious affair with Louisiana governor, Earl Long. Their story was the basis for the 1980 film, *Blaze*, with Paul Newman and Lolita Davidovich.

That night, Blaze decided to do a "strip-on." This meant she started out buck-naked and then put her clothes on—one piece at a time. So when the curtain opened, there was this woman standing there completely naked on the stage. The *Mama* cast was mortified. Rita's mother was also fuming. I still remember Rosemary putting her hands in front of her eyes so she couldn't see the naked woman. Carol was also livid. Only Ralph Nelson thought it was funny, and his laughing made things worse for me.

That was the last time they ever joined me after the show. It was also the end of my relationship with Rita Moreno. Her mother wasn't about to have her girl running around to cheap burlesque houses with Dick Van Patten.

* * *

For several years our principal competition was *The Goldbergs*. For a time, both shows were filmed at the Liederkranz Hall on 55th Street—*Mama* on Friday night and *The Goldbergs* on Monday night. Using the same studio caused some tension, particularly between Peggy Wood and Gertrude Berg, who were always fighting over little things, like who got the bigger dressing room. I guess it was natural since each was the matriarch of a major television series competing for ratings.

Still, everyone respected Gertrude Berg. She not only starred as the matriarch of *The Goldbergs*, but she was its creator and writer. Also, *The Goldbergs* had been on the radio for twenty years, beginning in 1929. Throughout the life of the show, Gertrude had grown into an important figure, both in the Jewish community and in the entire entertainment world. Not afraid to air her political views, particularly her support for President Roosevelt, Gertrude was willing to run the risk of sparking negative responses and alienating some producers and sponsors.

In his biography of Berg, Glenn Smith Jr., recounts an episode of *The Goldbergs* inspired by the atrocious "Kristallnacht" when Nazi thugs smashed the windows of Jewish shops across Germany. In the show, someone throws a rock through the window of *The Goldbergs* home during Passover service, and Molly has to comfort the children. She also insists on continuing with the service. It reminded me of the mob outside the home of Martin Gunther in *The American Way* shouting "Slacker" at the German-American family. Berg's principles would be tested again during the blacklisting controversy that swirled around Philip Loeb, who played Jake Goldberg, the father in the show.

Everyone was aware of Loeb's entanglement in the political mess involving the congressional investigation into entertainers. Both Elia Kazan and Lee J. Cobb had testified before the House Committee for Un-American Activities that Loeb had been a communist. Then in September of 1950, a report came out in a journal also charging Loeb with communist ties. He denied it, but General Foods, which owned CBS, began to pressure Gertrude Berg to fire him. She refused. But shortly afterwards, Loeb resigned, reportedly receiving a substantial settlement. A few years later, Phil committed suicide, taking an overdose of sleeping pills in the Taft Hotel in New York City. Loeb is considered by many to be a casualty of blacklisting.

My sister Joyce was convinced not only that Phil Loeb was blacklisted, but that there was a widespread practice that ruined many careers. Consequently, Joyce became politically active around that time in an effort to prevent blacklisting. It was then that she met Martin Balsam, who was also very outspoken on the subject. Eventually she married Marty, and they had a daughter, Talia Balsam, who grew up to have a wonderful acting career, with many appearances in movies and popular television shows.

Beyond her politics, Gertrude was an entertainer who clearly saw the possibilities of television. As Smith points out, she wanted to follow Ed Sullivan and Milton Berle into the new medium. Sullivan was hosting *Toast of the Town*, the precursor to his famous *The Ed Sullivan Show* and Berle had his *Texaco Star Theater*, each of which were tremendously popular variety shows. Like the producer of *Mama*, Carol Irwin, Berg thought television was ripe for what Smith calls an "episodic video stage play with continuing story lines and an established set of related characters" —in short, a situation comedy/drama.

* * *

Of the 500 live broadcasts of *Mama* the most popular by far was "The Night the Animals Talked." It was a wonderful Christmas story, first airing in December of 1950. After the show, there was so much positive fan mail that Carol and Ralph decided to do it over again each year at Christmas time. It was beautifully conceived and written by Frank Gabrielson, the marvelous writer who as much as anyone deserves credit for the tremendous success of the show.

"The Night the Animals Talked" began with Mama telling a story to young Dagmar about an old-time Christmas back in Norway. The story dissolves back to a Norwegian home with all the same characters as the Hansen family in San Francisco, but also with a cow named Hilda and a goat named Olaf. Television critics Christopher Denis and Michael Denis describe the "touching, beautiful scene wherein Papa tells little Dagmar how the animals were given the gift of speech only for a few hours each Christmas Eve as a heavenly reward for their protection and devotion to the Christ Child in the stable in Bethlehem."

But in the episode, there are thieves outside the home who plan to steal from the house when everyone is asleep. Before they can complete their scheme, the little girl, played by Robin Morgan, gets up at midnight and sneaks outside to try to hear the animals talk. She urges the goat and cow: "It's midnight. It's when Jesus was born…. Say something."

The thieves are hiding, and they decide to answer, projecting their voices so that the child thinks it's the animals talking. As they speak with her, they trick her into going back to the house and getting the family's "silver" as a gift for the Lord Jesus. But Papa and Nels catch the thieves, while, themselves, pretending to be the animals talking. Instead of turning them over to the Sheriff, however, the family decides to invite them into their home for the Christmas celebration.

"The Night the Animals Talked" was a deeply Christian show. Christopher and Michael Denis describe it as an episode "with powerful religious overtones," but which were "readily acceptable to mass audiences in those days." It even ended on a spiritual note when it appeared that perhaps the final words in the barn really were spoken by Hilda and Olaf, the cow and the goat. Little Dagmar queries her father about the voices she heard: "If it was not you and it was not Nels then who was it? I wonder." The episode was scored with the religious hymn: "Oh Come all ye Faithful."

No doubt, this beautiful Christmas tale attracted such a tremendous audience due to its affirmation of faith and its celebration of the birth of Jesus. But it was also a parable that taught universal lessons—the importance of timeless values such as caring for others, and, in the case of the two thieves, the power of forgiveness.

Another well-known episode and one of my very favorites was "Katrin's Wedding," featuring Rosemary Rice. Katrin had always dreamed of a big wedding, but plans quickly changed when her fiancé, Phil, had to suddenly leave for France to fight in World War I. Mama expressed her anxiety about the war that rings true even today: "When I read in the papers the things that happen in France!" she exclaimed to Papa with great sadness.

Katrin and Phil decided to have the wedding immediately in the Hansen's small San Francisco home. There was a moment of drama when Katrin, while waiting upstairs, became anxious and frightened about leaving the comfort of her home and family on Steiner Street.

Mama, as always, comforted her. One thing about Mama's lessons was that they never avoided the truth. Mama told Katrin that after coming to America from Norway, she never saw her own mother again—something that must ring true for many first-generation immigrants. But, she further explained, the distance never stopped her from loving her mother, nor did it mean she would never feel close to her again. It was a moving scene, and Rosemary and Peggy played it beautifully.

During Katrin's wedding, there was a scene that reminds me of Sid Caesar's description of the dangers of live television. With family and friends waiting downstairs—and with Dagmar playing "Here Comes the Bride" on the family piano—Katrin and the bridesmaids started down the stairs. Just as the first bridesmaid reached the bottom step, she lost her balance and stumbled. About to fall, she quickly reached out for the handrail and managed to catch herself, preventing a disastrous tumble to the ground on live television. The young actress regained her composure and continued leading the wedding procession so quickly, that it was hardly noticeable. As Sid said, on live television in front of millions of people, there were no second chances. Like that bridesmaid, we often had to recover and improvise in order to avoid calamity. Fortunately, we had such a wonderful group of actors that we always seemed to land on our feet.

Mama was symbolic of a wholesome American family. Its enormous and continuing success was due to many factors. Kathryn Forbes, the author of *Mama's Bank Account*, was asked in a 1956 interview: "Why has *Mama* been so popular...while other family-type programs have come and gone?" Kathryn noted that the show had always "retained the basic theme of the story—a child's dream of 'mama.'" She explained that her "only idea" in writing the novel "was to show that my grandmother was a wonderful person. I never realized how universal that theme is." Peggy Wood would make a similar observation: "Each week as I get into the role, I'm reminded of my own mother. She's the secret of my portrayal of Mama."

While I can certainly understand the very personal perspectives of both Kathryn and Peggy, there was also a more "universal" appeal to motherhood that drove the show and its ratings forward and upward for eight years. Our ability to convey that appeal was due in great part to our writers and directors. In fact, I believe that any show is only as good as its scripts and direction. We were fortunate to have brilliant writers in Frank Gabrielson and his staff, as well as an equally outstanding director in Ralph Nelson. Peggy Wood, speaking of both Frank and Ralph, correctly noted that "we had a feeling of security in them." Both men had many other great accomplishments. Frank was a performer and writer on Broadway and television since the early 1930s while Ralph would go on to direct such hit films as *Requiem for a Heavyweight* and *Lilies of the Field*.

In their book *Favorite Families of TV*, Christopher and Michael Denis begin with *Mama*. They rightly claim that in spite of all the technical and other difficulties of coping with the beginnings of television, the show had "heart"—"enough to carry this simple sweet show to glory during its eight-season run." I couldn't agree more. Mama came along as television was just getting underway. Its tremendous popularity helped set the stage for so many other shows—including *Eight Is Enough*—that through the years have tried to convey a similarly positive and healthy image of family life in America. I was proud to have been a part of it.

Watching the birdie in Manhattan around 1934.
(Photo from Dick Van Patten's collection)

Joyce and me around 1937 at ages four and nine.
(Photo from Dick Van Patten's collection)

Broadway took a hard stand against the Nazis in 1937. Here I am as Isaac, in Max Reinhardt's *The Eternal Road*, a spectacular retelling of the Old Testament as set against the backdrop of a European dictator's persecution of the Jews.

(Photo from Dick Van Patten's collection)

That's me in the center as the telegraph boy (age 14) with Tallulah Bankhead (right) and Florence Eldridge (left) in Thornton Wilder's 1942 Pulitzer Prize–winning play, *The Skin of Our Teeth*, directed by young Elia Kazan. (Photo from Dick Van Patten's collection)

The audition to play the Lunts' onstage son, Michael, in Terence Rattigan's *O Mistress Mine*, brought out every aspiring actor in New York City. I had the great fortune of landing the part. Here I am as Michael Brown, alongside Alfred Lunt (seated), as Sir John Fletcher and Lynn Fontanne (far right) as Olivia Brown.

(Photo from Dick Van Patten's collection)

This magical Christmas story, "The Night the Animals Talked," from my first TV series *I Remember Mama,* was so popular we performed it every holiday season. From left to right are Judson Laire (Papa), Rosemary Rice (Katrin), me (Nels) and Peggy Wood (Mama); in front is Judy Sanford (Hedvig, Mama's niece). (Photo © CBS/Landov)

The whole cast of *I Remember Mama* showed up for my happiest day, April 24, 1954, when Pat and I married in the Actors' Chapel in Manhattan's Saint Malachy's Church. That's me and my beautiful bride, Pat, sharing the day with "Mama" (**Peggy Wood**). (Photo from Dick Van Patten's collection)

Pat and I admired the Reagans and were delighted to lend a hand to Nancy's "Just Say No" campaign against drug abuse. Here we are with President Reagan and Nancy after a White House celebrity tennis tournament. (Photo courtesy of Ronald Reagan Library)

Farrah joins us at home in the early '70s just prior to her rise into the celebrity stratosphere. Top row: Bill Sheppard, Farrah, and Pat; seated: me, Mom and Vincent. (Photo courtesy of Bill Sheppard)

Pat and I were deeply touched by these beautiful children of Ethiopia. Their wonderful smiles in the face of such great poverty left me with a brand-new understanding of courage. (Photo from Dick Van Patten's collection)

Surrounded by family and friends, I received the great honor of a star on the Hollywood Walk of Fame in November of 1985. Front row, left to right: Nels, Pat, me, Jimmy and Vincent. Second row: Left to right: my nephew, Casey, half-brothers, Tim and Byron Van Patten. Milton Berle can be seen in the back together with various cast members from *Eight Is Enough*. (Photo from Dick Van Patten's collection)

27

MISTER ROBERTS

In the 1940s, it was rare for television actors in New York City to do additional work in the theater, especially during production. Today, it would be impossible. With the intense filming schedules of a typical television series, actors are far too busy to take theater work. Also, the center of television production is now in Hollywood, making it impossible for an actor to work on a TV set during the day, run off to Broadway at night and then return to the TV show the following morning.

In 1949, however, my schedule on *Mama* included rehearsals five days a week and then a live telecast on Friday night at 8 p.m. That made it possible to work both on TV and on Broadway at the same time. Life would certainly be hectic, but it could be done.

I remember when Henry Fonda returned to Broadway in 1948 after ten years away working in films. While auditioning for *Mama*, I heard of a new play directed by Joshua Logan, my old friend from *On Borrowed Time*, that dealt with the exploits of the crew of a World War II cargo ship, the USS *Reluctant*, and its tyrannical commander, Captain Morton. The leading character was the 2nd Lieutenant, Doug Roberts, who sided with the crew while doing his best to protect them from the Captain's wrath. At the same time, Roberts desperately wanted a transfer to a warship so he could "get in the fight" before it was over. Although it had some extremely powerfully dramatic moments, the play, adapted by Logan and Thomas Heggen from Heggen's novel *Mister Roberts*, was a comedy, with most of the humor centering on the character and crazy antics of the ship's Morale and Laundry Officer, Ensign Frank Pulver.

Mister Roberts opened on February 14, 1948, at the Alvin Theater with Fonda as Mister Roberts, William Harrigan playing the captain, and David Wayne as Ensign Pulver. It was an immediate smash hit. At the 1948 Tonys, *Mister Roberts* ran away with the awards, winning Best Play, Fonda winning Best Actor, Logan Best Director and David Wayne receiving a nomination for his portrayal of Pulver. That same year, Logan and Heggens won the Pulizer Prize for Drama. *Mister Roberts* had struck a chord in the aftermath of the war, and it would be rewarded with a Broadway run of 1,157 shows, lasting nearly three years.

In 1950, David Wayne decided to leave the show. I thought about auditioning for the part, and my mother called our agent, Maynard Morris. But Morris, who was also one of the producers of the show, told her categorically that I was too young. It's worth remembering that David Wayne, whom I'd be trying to replace, had played my father in *The American Way* and was fifteen years older than me.

As always, my Mom was undeterred. She insisted that we just show up at the theater during the auditions. I was less enthusiastic after hearing Morris's assessment. After all, he was one of the show's producers, but I went along. I remember arriving at the Alvin and immediately Josh Logan spotted me and asked what I was doing there. I said I wanted to audition for Pulver. Logan agreed, and so with Morris, my own agent who had told me not to come sitting in the audience watching the auditions, I gave it my best. It turned out Logan liked my portrayal and didn't think the age difference was important. His view prevailed, and I landed the part.

As I began thinking about taking on the role of Ensign Pulver, I was thrilled at the prospect of working with Henry Fonda. He was one of the truly great actors of the day, and *Mister Roberts* was already his biggest Broadway success.

At the same time, like everyone in the business, I was conscious of the enormous stress Henry was under in his personal life. His wife, Frances, had just committed suicide a few weeks before I was scheduled to work with him.

It was well known that Henry's marriage to Frances had been failing. In fact, he had been dating another woman, Susan Blanchard, whom he later married, for quite some time, and I recall seeing her come to the set on occasion during the final six months of the show. Frances had struggled for years with a psychiatric condition for which she had been repeatedly institutionalized. A few months before I joined *Mister Roberts*, she was moved to a sanatorium in New York's Hudson Valley. On April 14, 1950, she wrote out a suicide note and killed herself. She was just forty-two years old.

Word spread quickly. Billy Hammerstein began to rehearse the understudy, Marshall Jamison, for that night's performance. But in the late afternoon, Henry came to the theater and spoke with the producer, Leland Hayward—who ironically was the previous owner of my present home in Sherman Oaks, which was the setting for his daughter Brooke's best-selling book, *Haywire*. Henry told him: "I'm going on. It's the only way I can get through the evening." Like Lou Costello ten years earlier when his son died, Henry Fonda was going to put the enormous weight of the day's tragedy aside for at least a few hours. Later Hammerstein said Fonda's performance that night was no different than any other night.

I thought Henry showed real bravery. Lou Costello with his son's death, the Lunts with bombs hitting the theater, and Henry Fonda in the wake of his wife's suicide were, to me, all examples of great professional courage. Entertainers are frequently criticized —and often with justification—for behavior that is less than respectable. But in these difficult circumstances, certain performers have demonstrated that show business also has many people who are not only good, decent and admirable, but are capable of great fortitude in moments of crisis. The next time we are tempted to dismiss all entertainers because of the ghoulish antics of a few, we should remember that there are people like Costello, the Lunts and Fonda who stand as examples of what is decent and honorable in our business.

Henry had two children at the time, Jane and Peter. They were often backstage in his dressing room at the Alvin Theater. We began to develop a friendship. On matinee days, when Henry would go out to dinner after the show, he'd leave me to babysit Jane and Peter at the theater. They were delightful kids. At the time, of course, I had no idea of the public controversies that would one day ignite around Jane during the Vietnam War. To me she was just a sweet kid—and so was her brother.

Henry used to tell me I reminded him of a young Jimmy Cagney, which is interesting because later Cagney would play the captain in the movie version of *Mister Roberts.* As great as Cagney was in that role, for me, one of the finest actors I've ever worked with was William Harrigan, who played the captain on Broadway. I'll always remember him yelling at me during one scene, with that deep contempt in his voice: "You college son of a bitch. I grew up waiting on you pansies."

I really looked up to Harrigan, who was married to Josh Logan's sister, Ella. We talked a lot in the dressing room, and I told him about my time with Logan in *On Borrowed Time.* Most of all, he was a good friend and a great actor.

I was just twenty-one years old during *Mister Roberts* and still a bit of a troublemaker. One incident hit the newspapers, causing me some embarrassment. It involved a charge that I'd sideswiped another car on the Crossbay Boulevard in Ozone Park.

My license was already suspended from prior traffic violations, and I was now confronted with a third-degree assault, which could have landed me in jail. I was with my cousin, Donald Citro, at the time of the incident, and the driver of the other car had felt intimidated by us. He was certainly justified and now was angry and frankly wanted nothing more than to see me rotting in a jail cell. A court date was set for August 15, 1950, before Judge Henry Soffer. As the date approached, I was getting really nervous that the judge would look at my history of traffic violations and send me off to prison. That would be catastrophic since I was playing in both *Mama* and *Mister Roberts*.

In the end, things worked out—although I admit it was not my finest hour. After the court date, the newspaper reported: "Actor Dickie Van Patten Forgives, Is Forgiven." It continued: "All charges…were withdrawn" and further noted that "the case was dismissed yesterday when all parties shook hands." They reported happily that "Van Patten…is back playing 'Ensign Pulver' in *Mr. Roberts* after a summer vacation."

But the newspapers didn't have the whole story. What they and no one else knew was that the case was really settled on the courthouse steps before we ever went inside. As I've said, this was not a shining moment for me. But the truth is I paid the other driver three hundred bucks for him to drop the charges. I was desperate. I didn't mind the prospect of some time in jail, but I might have lost my parts in *Mama* and *Mister Roberts*. That's not an excuse, just an explanation of what was going through my head. Maybe the most amazing thing is that I clearly remember paying the money directly to the guy and his attorney. Anyway, it's been just about sixty years now, and I guess it's time to clear the air.

28

COMMAND PERFORMANCE

In the years immediately following the Second World War, the biggest radio show in America was the *U.S. Steel Hour*. The show, debuting on September 9, 1945, was also known as the *Theater Guild of the Air* and played for over ten million listeners a week. It was initially a forum for bringing theater productions to a radio audience, and soon expanded to include Hollywood films.

I was fortunate to have a role in one of the first broadcasts in 1947, which was a rendition of the play, *Kiss and Tell* with Elizabeth Taylor. Performances for the *Theater Guild of the Air* were held at the Belasco Theater in front of thousands of people with the actors dressed in formal attire. Seats were placed on the stage, and typically there were two microphones. When your lines came, you got up and walked to the mike just as the other person was sitting down.

I had a wonderful friendship and working relationship with Doris Quinlin, an Associate Producer on *Mama*, who was also casting director for *Theater Guild of the Air*. As a result, each time a big production was set to play she contacted me if there was an appropriate role. In addition to Liz Taylor, I did shows with Gloria Swanson, Van Johnson, Orson Welles and many more.

But the biggest thrill came in 1951, when the *U.S. Steel Hour* presented a radio version of the hit film *Father of the Bride* starring Spencer Tracy and Elizabeth Taylor. As often happened, the radio production utilized the same actors that appeared in the film. But Doris was looking out for me. Although I wasn't in the movie, she called and asked me to play the part of Elizabeth Taylor's younger brother. More important, it was going to be a "command performance" in Washington for President Harry Truman. Needless to say, I was thrilled.

I still recall the train ride from New York's Grand Central Station with Spencer Tracy, Liz Taylor and the rest of the cast. We stayed that night at the Willard Hotel across from the White House, and the next day we went to Constitution Hall for the performance.

Constitution Hall, located on 1776 D Street, was the equivalent of the Kennedy Center for the Performing Arts today. Home to the National Symphony Orchestra, it was built by the

Daughters of the American Revolution in 1929, and nearly all performances for the President took place there.

I don't know exactly how it came about, but apparently President Truman enjoyed the movie, *Father of the Bride*. Perhaps it was because his own daughter, Margaret, a young actress and singer, was approaching the marrying age. Years later, I met Margaret at the Saratoga Playhouse when I was closing in *Will Success Spoil Rock Hunter*, and she was opening in *The Happy Time*. I stayed there an extra day, watched and very much enjoyed her performance.

On June 25, 1951, I joined the stellar cast for our command performance before the President. Constitution Hall was a big place with nearly four thousand seats, and it was thrilling to see the President in the theater.

Afterwards we all got to meet and speak with President Truman. In fact, a newsreel was made of our meeting titled *President Truman Meets The Father of the Bride*. The reel can still be seen as a special feature of the rereleased version of the 1950 movie. Most of the reel shows the President talking with Spencer Tracy, Liz Taylor and Joan Bennett, but if you watch close, you'll see a young guy moving stealthily behind the President like a pickpocket sizing up his mark. That's me!

Looking back, I can't help but think how my mother must have felt. In less than twenty years since she first started looking for modeling agencies, her son was now performing for the President of the United States. I hope that gave her great joy and satisfaction.

29

DREAM GIRL

One night, a young freelance theater critic, Herb Worth, brought his fiancée to a performance of *Mister Roberts*. This was before I joined the production, and David Wayne was still playing Pulver. For some reason they sat way up in the balcony, and his date, a young dancer named Patricia Poole, had trouble hearing the show.

Still she thought it must have been very funny because everyone up front was laughing so hard. So she decided to go back and see it again—only this time she went by herself. By now, I was in the show, and Pat Poole, in a better seat, laughed from beginning to end. But she especially liked the new Ensign Pulver, whom she recognized as her old classmate—the crazy one who used to copy her homework and got thrown out for reading his essay on how to beat the races.

Pat Poole had been working hard as a dancer in the years since her family arrived in New York City, always dreaming of dancing on the big stages. She got her chance at age sixteen, when she joined the ballet company for the summer of 1947 at Radio City Music Hall. Most people have heard of the famous Rockettes and their leggy production numbers, but Radio City also has a ballet group, meaning dancers who worked on point—i.e., on their toes—not that they dance only ballet. In fact, most of the acts for the ballet troupe were ballroom style, and the girls were among the very best dancers in the world. They were less famous but at least as prestigious in the dance community as the Rockettes.

It was at this point that Pat made the most difficult decision of her life. She had been dancing with her brother Robbie throughout her entire childhood. As kids, they were billed as "The World's Youngest Exhibition Ballroom Team," and they were terrific together. Tremendously talented, Pat and Robbie had several signature numbers, their favorite being their dance to the tune of *Jealousy*. They were hits at all the competitions.

But there comes a point in every life when each person has to make their own decision as to what it is they're shooting for. What are their dreams and their aspirations? We all do it—or should. And it isn't selfishness; it's a part of understanding who we are as individuals. One thing we know about life is that we're happiest and most productive when doing what we truly love and moving toward some goal that is our dream.

For Pat, that dream simply was not as a dance partner. As she grew older, she came to better understand that realizing her potential meant going it alone. She was right. Her mother knew she was right, and Robbie understood it too. So, in one of the most painful moments of her young life, Pat decided it was time to end the dance partnership.

To her surprise, Robbie understood perfectly. I believe he was relieved. Shortly afterward, Robbie returned to North Carolina. There he finished college, married a wonderful girl, Barbara, and raised a family in Lynchburg, Virginia. Robbie was happiest there. Had he wished to continue in the dance world, he could have stayed in New York, and doors would have opened for him, just as they did for Pat. But, like his father, Robbie never shared Helon's intense aspirations. Pat was much more like her mother. I believe Robbie was released from a burden. Ending the partnership allowed him to return to his roots and live a wonderfully happy life with Barbara and their four terrific children.

Pat remained close to Robbie throughout their entire lives. Their childhood had built a bond between them that was enduring, and they continued to share the memories of their years on the dance floor. In 1999, Robbie collapsed of a heart attack. He died instantly. We went to the funeral in Charlotte, North Carolina. I don't think I've ever seen my wife so sad. Robbie was her childhood confidant. It was Robbie who understood, better than anyone, the difficulties Pat endured as a child and the hard work she undertook in her quest to be a great dancer. When Pat had to say goodbye to Robbie, there was a part of her that went with him. I've never expressed it as fully as I have here, but his death was a great sorrow in Pat's life, and a terrible loss for all of us.

* * *

At seventeen, Pat graduated from the Professional Children's School and soon joined Radio City Music Hall's Corps de Ballet full-time. For several years, she danced in all the great Radio City productions, including the famous Christmas and Easter shows.

Then one day Pat had her own brush with greatness. She heard about auditions for a new theatrical production, *Courtin' Time*, in which the producers were trying to create another

Oklahoma, which had just finished its hugely successful run at the 44th Street Theater in 1948. The lead in *Courtin' Time* was Lloyd Nolan, a great actor, and very popular at the time.

But the show's real attraction was the choreographer—none other than George Balanchine. By this time, Balanchine was already widely considered the greatest choreographer in the history of American dance. When Pat heard about Balanchine's involvement, she was desperate to have a shot at the audition.

But the producers at Radio City didn't want their dancers heading out on auditions. They were afraid of losing them, especially the girls in the Ballet Corps, who were among the most talented dancers in New York City. So they cleverly arranged their own rehearsals at the exact time they knew the Broadway shows were having their auditions. Despite this, Pat had managed to get to the first one when the field was winnowed from around 500 to 100 dancers. The next audition, however, landed right at the time of a Radio City Ballet Corps rehearsal, and Pat couldn't go.

But Pat outsmarted them. She wrote a letter directly to Balanchine and left it at the stage door asking if she could skip the second audition and come to the finals. She was pleasantly surprised when they agreed.

For the final audition each of the girls had to dance on point. One by one they moved across the stage, on their toes, doing turns as they went. Pat was toward the back of the line. When her time came, she took off dancing and turning until arriving at the end of the stage. There she looked out and saw Balanchine standing in the aisle. He was pointing right at her, as if to say, "That one."

She was absolutely thrilled. Nothing could compare to receiving that kind of recognition from one of the greatest figures in dance history. Later that night, she told her mother all about it. To have her daughter singled out by Balanchine was a great thrill for Helon as well, who rightly saw it as vindication for the difficult decision she had made years before to give her children a shot at dancing on the big stage in New York City.

Pat joined *Courtin' Time*. She got to know Balanchine pretty well, and he impressed her as a real gentleman. Although supremely self-confident, he was never dismissive of others and never allowed his great stature to interfere with his decency as a person. Pat recalls a special moment while they were on the road. After a rehearsal, Balanchine said to Pat, "Well, I'm going across the street to have a coffee. Would you like to come?"

So they went together for coffee, and while at the table, one of the singers in the show rushed up all excited: "Oh, Mr. Balanchine, Mr. Balanchine, I want to introduce my friend. This is Anna." Balanchine politely responded, "How do you do?" Then, realizing that Pat had been ignored, Balanchine turned to Pat, and without missing a beat, said to the couple: "And, I would like for you to meet my mother." Pat was all of twenty at the time, and could have passed for sixteen. Everyone laughed. But his inclusion of Pat in the conversation and his sensitivity to the feelings of those around him, were a reflection of his strong character.

Balanchine directed his dancers in a uniquely relaxed manner. Most other choreographers were forever screaming at the dancers. But Balanchine spoke softly. Pat recalls his pensive style: "He was the first choreographer I'd worked with," she says, "who was quiet. You'd see him thinking, and he would blink his eyes in a certain way, and then he'd get up and show you very softly how to do it correctly."

Her description reminds me of a similar change I'd seen on Broadway. Elia Kazan was the very first director I worked with who wouldn't shout. When he had some instruction for an actor, he would give it in a soft, calm, relaxed manner. No doubt, his personal style had a great deal to do with his training in "the method" style, where reaching inward was as important as projecting outward. Perhaps Pat was seeing a similar transition with new theories of dance.

Another of Pat's fascinating encounters during *Courtin' Time* had little to do with dancing. Just as *Courtin' Time* was preparing for its Broadway run, the United States was still in the thick of the Korean War. After the initial success of General Douglas MacArthur's invasion at the Korean Port of Inchon, the Chinese entered the conflict, and the war bogged down. As a result, a well-publicized feud began between MacArthur and President Harry Truman, leading to the General's dismissal in April of 1951. He then returned home, his first trip to the mainland in fourteen years, where he received one of the biggest welcomes in history. I still recall the ticker-tape parade in New York City, which was the largest ever. MacArthur finished his tour of America with an address to a joint session of Congress where he famously ended with his bittersweet lament that "old soldiers never die, they just fade away."

A few weeks later he decided to take in a Broadway show. Pat recalls the excitement at the end of the performance as everyone lined up in a semicircle onstage to shake hands with this legendary five-star general who had defeated Japan in World War II and ruled over the Japanese Islands for years after the war. Now he was back home taking in a Broadway play like everyone else. Pat still vividly recalls shaking his hand with a degree of amazement at the presence of this bigger-than-life figure.

Notwithstanding Balanchine's marvelous choreography and a boost from the former Supreme Allied Commander, *Courtin' Time* lasted only a week on Broadway. Regrettably, they lost their star, Lloyd Nolan, who developed problems with his vocal chords and was unable to sing. Once he was replaced, the show never gained much traction.

Still, Pat's brief association with George Balanchine made it worthwhile. And it was a testament to her tremendous talent. Balanchine wanted dancers with the ability to express his vision. Only a few had that unique talent, and my future wife was among them. I've always been so proud of her marvelous accomplishments onstage—and so grateful that, along the way, she chose to spend her lifetime with me.

* * *

From *Courtin' Time*, Pat went immediately into *Two on the Aisle*, starring Bert Lahr, the famous Cowardly Lion in *The Wizard of Oz*. From there she worked in a number of other venues, including a stint dancing on *The Steve Allen Show*. She was quickly making herself a reputation as one of the best young dancers in New York City when she heard about tryouts for a dance company established to work with the new comic sensation, Jackie Gleason. The head of the company was June Taylor, the sister of Gleason's future wife, Marilyn, who was a dancer in the group and remains a good friend of ours today. Soon these dancers would become famous the world over as The June Taylor Dancers.

Jackie Gleason had now worked his way up through the clubs in New York City—where Helon first worked with him—to "B" films in Hollywood, and then to his big break in 1949 when he landed the lead on *The Life of Riley*. I have a strong memory of the show—and of Gleason—because it began the same year as *I Remember Mama*. But I also remember him because I truly believe he was among a very elite group of great entertainers. Milton Berle, Lou Costello and Jimmy Durante were other comics who come to mind. But Gleason had one advantage over most everyone; he was also a great dramatic actor, with such timeless roles as Minnesota Fats in *The Hustler* and Maish Rennick in

Requiem for a Heavyweight, directed by my friend, Ralph Nelson, who felt the same about Gleason's prodigious talents.

In 1950, Jackie began hosting *Dumont's Cavalcade of Stars* on the Dumont channel, which later moved to CBS and was renamed *The Jackie Gleason Show*. Gleason always loved the old Busby Berkeley musicals extravaganzas of the 1930s with their elaborate dance routines, and he worked similar numbers into his variety show. His penchant for these spectacular numbers caused him to rely more and more on his own June Taylor Dancers, which were becoming a central feature of his programs.

By 1952, Gleason had already developed many of television's unforgettable characters: Reginald Van Gleason, Rudy the Repairman, Joe the Bartender and, of course, Ralph Kramden, the ever-scheming, loud-mouthed but lovable Brooklyn bus-driver. As the show's popularity soared, he increased the number of June Taylor Dancers to sixteen, and Pat set out to land one of the new spots.

Gleason, with a style all his own, turned the audition itself into a spectacle. He arranged for *Life* magazine to cover it and once June had narrowed the field to about fifty qualified girls, Gleason had them all paraded down Broadway to his suite at the Park Central Hotel—with *Life* magazine photographers snapping away as they went. Once inside, each girl had to walk, one at a time, in front of Jackie, who would tell them: "Pull your skirt up to your knee"—this was obviously before the days of harassment lawsuits!

Pat was chosen. She worked on the *Jackie Gleason Show* for two years beginning in 1952 and was featured in a number of the routines choreographed by June Taylor. Recently my kids and I watched one from 1953 in which Pat was featured on an old reel, and we all just marveled at her amazing talent.

In 1953, Gleason chose six of his dancers to go to Europe during the summer break. Pat wasn't among them. Annoyed at not being selected, Pat decided to break off and form her own dance act. She contacted a choreographer from the *Steve Allen Show* who worked up a series of dance routines for her. But before things got underway, Pat's godmother, Marie Spataro, decided to take a trip to Europe and asked Pat to come along.

Before leaving, Pat mentioned to Gleason that she was also going to Europe for the summer with her godmother. He took her aside and, in typical Gleason fashion, handed her a note and said good-bye. When he left, she opened it, and there was a $50 bill inside with a message that read: "Have your first drink in Europe on me." Pat still has the note.

Pat then sailed for Europe and had a wonderful time with her godmother. She also had the last laugh on Jackie because when she returned on the U.S.S. *Constitution,* the New York paparazzi showed up at the dock in Manhattan. As she came off the cruise liner, they photographed her, and the next day her picture was on the front page of the *New York Daily News.*

After arriving home, Pat's mother received a phone call and yelled out to her: "It's Gleason on the phone!" So she took the phone, and Jackie invited her to his place in the Adirondacks in upstate New York: "I have this house," he said, "and everybody comes up for the weekends. They usually spend the night, and we have a party, and it's a lot of fun. Would you like to come?" By now, Pat and I were dating, but I was away doing summer stock, so Pat took my sister Joyce, and the two rode up to Gleason's house on the train.

At the party, Gleason's producer, Jack Philbin, told her they wanted her back for the next season. Philbin was surprised when Pat told him: "I'm not coming back." She explained she was putting together her own act and was planning to take it on the road. He took it with a certain degree of disbelief and even umbrage that she would have the temerity to dare to leave this hugely successful show and strike out on her own. She still remembers Philbin looking down his nose at her and scoffing: "Well, get her!" But Philbin didn't know my wife, and she went off to better things on the Broadway stage—and elsewhere.

Many years later, I met Jackie at a Morton's Steak House in Chicago. He invited me to his table. I remember his booming voice: "Sit down and have a drink, Dick." I told him I didn't drink and was about to order a coke when he commanded: "Nobody sits with me and doesn't drink!" So I ordered something and nursed it while we talked. He remembered Pat, and we talked about the old days in New York.

* * *

When Pat saw me in *Mister Roberts,* she was still dancing at Radio City. Later when she joined the Gleason show, she and the other June Taylor Dancers rehearsed in the afternoon at New York's Grand Central Station, the same place we rehearsed *Mama* in the morning.

One day I was watching the dancers come in and spotted the prettiest girl I'd ever seen. I remarked to Ralph Nelson: "Look at that girl. She's so beautiful, I could marry her tomorrow." Ralph laughed and said, "What kind of nonsense is that? You don't even know her."

So I approached her to strike up some conversation, and she looked at me and said: "Don't you remember me? I'm Pat Poole, and we used to sit next to each other at the Professional Children's School?" Suddenly, I remembered the pretty blond girl whose homework I copied. She told me she had seen me in *Mr. Roberts* and really enjoyed the show. I was ecstatic.

Immediately I began thinking of ways to connect with this bombshell. I discussed it with Ralph Nelson, and he came up with a plan. Ralph suggested we put a small dance number into one of the *Mama* episodes. He would then call Gleason and ask him to send her over to teach me the dance. I thought it was a great idea, and so Ralph called Gleason, told him what we wanted, and specified that it had to be the young girl named Pat.

It worked like a charm. The next day, Pat came to our rehearsal to teach me The Turkey Trot. We worked on it every day for a week. Then I invited her to come see the show, which was broadcast live on Friday night. I was delighted when she agreed to come, but she showed up with her fiancé. Rosemary Rice, who played Katrin in *Mama*, came to the rescue. She suggested that she host a small party for the people in the show and invite Pat. But she would stress to her that she should come alone.

Rosemary came through. Later that night, Pat showed up at Rosemary's apartment on East 55th Street. It wasn't really a party, just me, Ralph and Rosemary, and, at first, Pat thought it was all very strange and was about to leave. But Rosemary coaxed her into staying, and we ended up having a great time. At the end of the night, I finally told Pat that I wanted to start seeing her. She reminded me she was engaged, but I just ignored that and kept at her. After a while, she relented, and for a time Pat was dating both of us.

I knew that could only last for a while. Pat was working all day, then going out with Herb and afterwards heading back out again with me for a midnight show. But I had a good plan. I realized that the best way to get to Pat was through her mom, and the best way to get to Helon was to buy her ice cream. So every night while Pat was out with Herb, I'd come around the apartment plying Helon with quarts of ice cream. It worked. In short order, Helon was on my side.

* * *

In the meantime, things had become complicated for Pat on a professional level. Agnes DeMille, the great choreographer and niece of film giant Cecil B. DeMille, contacted her about the possibility of taking a lead dance role in a revival of *Oklahoma* as it went on the road. She would be the central ballet dancer to Florence Henderson's beautiful singing. One of the biggest hits in Broadway history, *Oklahoma*, written by Rodgers & Hammerstein, had run from 1942 through 1948 and was now headed for the road after its revival at the City Center Theater.

At the same time, Pat had an opportunity to dance in another Rodgers and Hammerstein production, *Me and Juliet*, which was already running on Broadway. The stage manager had asked her to come see the show, so she and my mother went to a performance. She enjoyed it immensely and took the job, dancing in the chorus with a talented young dancer named Shirley MacLaine.

Shortly after Pat and I began dating, she separated with Herb. I had fallen in love with her, and for the first time in my life I began to think seriously about marriage. Still, I had enjoyed my independence for quite a number of years, and I knew that if I married her those days would end. At the same time, I realized Pat was the one for me, and by the beginning of 1954, I had made up my mind that I couldn't live without her.

Around that time, I became close friends with Maxie Rosenbloom, a great boxer who had been the light heavyweight champion of the world in the 1930s. Maxie and I met at a place called A Bird In Hand on 51st and Broadway, where all the actors and theater people would hang out after the shows. I remember Steve McQueen was there every night. He wasn't a star yet, and I still recall that he had big bags under his eyes that distracted from his natural good looks. I've always thought he must have had surgery, because he was so handsome in the movies.

Maxie lived in the Piccadilly Hotel on West 45th Street. He was a legend in New York City, not only as a great boxer, but as a stand-up comic. Maxie did a hilarious routine, and I'm sure that the boxing legend, Jake LaMotta, who also became famous for his comedy act, took his cue from Maxie.

Pat loved Maxie. We used to hang out together every night. I remember Maxie telling me: "You'd better marry that girl." Pat, who really didn't know much about boxing, was especially impressed one night when we went to see a fight at Eastern Parkway Arena, and Maxie came with us.

When we arrived, the three of us got out of the car and started walking toward the stadium. Suddenly a crowd gathered around. Within moments we were being mobbed. By the time we were about a block from the arena, there was a huge throng of people on all sides of us, chanting, "Maxie! Maxie! Maxie! Maxie!" As we entered, the fans inside went crazy as soon as they saw him. I'd been on television, radio and Broadway, but none of that even remotely compared to the adulation that these fans had for this truly unique boxing legend. It was an exciting night—and Pat still recalls her astonishment that her friend was so revered.

Like so many of the old timers from New York, Maxie's gone now. I guess that makes it safe for me to tell another story I'm not so proud of. Maxie was a big horse player, and we often went to Belmont Park together. One afternoon, after the sixth race, Maxie had to leave. He gave me $100 and told me to bet it evenly on a horse in each of the two remaining races. I remember that the horses were numbers 4 and 7.

When he left, I looked at his choices and thought neither one had much of a chance. So I got the bright idea of pocketing the money rather than placing the bets and losing. If Maxie did get lucky on one of them, I'd just pay him. It was a terrible thing to do, but I was young and reckless, and the idea that this was a betrayal of his trust never really entered my mind.

Well, I got exactly what I deserved! Maxie's horses won both races. Had I bet the money, he would have made $1,600. Instead, I walked out of the track with his $100 and wondering what the heck I was going to tell the former light-heavyweight champ of the world the next morning at breakfast when he'd come looking for his cash.

Desperate, I had another bright idea. It was still early enough to make a bet on a baseball game. It was particularly stupid because I didn't know anything about baseball. Also, I didn't have enough money to make a bet that would recoup Maxie's losses. But there was a sports bookie I knew, Zip Russo, over on 51st and Broadway who would take the bet over the phone with the understanding that I'd be good for it if I lost. So I called and bet $1,600 I didn't have on the Yankees. It was a six to five pick-em, which meant I would get back even money, and so I had to bet a lot. If I lost, of course, I'd be in a real jam.

But someone was looking out for me that night. The Yankees won by 16 runs. I've never seen such a walk over. I went to the bookie, got the cash, and the next morning met and paid

Maxie, acting like nothing had ever happened. But I do thank God he never knew what I did. I just congratulated him on his two great picks and never mentioned how much grief those two horses had really caused me.

The great thing about Maxie is that he really loved Pat. As I mentioned, he kept telling me: "You've got to marry that one, Dick." Maxie was right. Still, I took my time and nearly lost my chance. I found out later Pat was getting tired of waiting. By the spring of 1954, she had expected me to ask her already. One day we had to go to the wedding of one of her friends, a dancer named Joan Donavan. Pat later told me if I hadn't asked her on that very day, she was moving on. At the same time, I also realized that if I didn't take the plunge I could lose the best girl I'd ever known. So I picked her up in my '49 Oldsmobile convertible at her apartment on West 67th Street. When she got in the car I just sat there for a moment with the car parked. I don't know why, maybe because of the wedding, but it just suddenly came out: "Well, I was thinking that maybe we should get married."

And just as matter of fact, Pat responded, "Oh, well, when would you want to do that?"

I was looking straight ahead in the car and so was she.

"Well, I was thinking that Easter is coming up, and I thought that April 25…." And she said: "I would like to have a family." So I responded, "Well, I was thinking I would like to have a family."

And that was the end of it. I turned the engine on, and we drove to the wedding without saying a single word.

But when we arrived at the reception, I just couldn't contain myself. I told everyone, "We're engaged!" In retrospect, it was in very bad taste, stealing a bit of the thunder from Joan's wedding.

From that inauspicious proposal, Pat and I have enjoyed fifty-five wonderful and romantic years that just keep getting better. We were married on April 25, 1954, in a small church, Saint Malachy's in what was appropriately called, The Actors' Chapel. The whole cast and crew of *Mama* was there, as well as many of the June Taylor Dancers. My grandfather, Vincent, was my best man, and Pat's best friend, Dolores Dawson, was her maid of honor. She was stunning in her white wedding dress, and it was the happiest day of my life.

30

Every So Often!

Not long after our wedding, while on break from *Mama*, I took a role in a summer stock production of Edward Chodorov's psychological comedy, *Oh Men, Oh Women*. It was an interesting play that dealt in a humorous way with the lighter side of psychoanalysis. It was especially fun because my sister, Joyce, also had a part as Myra Hagerman, an attractive young woman engaged to the psychiatrist, who was played by Richard Kendrick. On the eve of their wedding, I show up, playing a troubled neurotic named Grant Cobble, who manages to make a mess of things.

We opened at the Pocono Playhouse in East Stroudsburg, Pennsylvania on August 3, 1955. I only mention this performance because of a review written in a local paper, *The Daily Record* by Leonard Randolph, the paper's theater critic. Every actor has their own way of dealing with the inevitable negative critiques that come crashing down on us throughout our careers. There are, of course, those once in a generation performers, like the Lunts, who routinely, and justifiably, are met with acclaim pretty much every time they perform. The rest of us take the good with the bad.

But every so often we get lucky. Who knows why, but sometimes a particular performance just happens to strikes a certain critic just the right way at just the right time and that can make it all worthwhile. Well Leonard Randolph of East Stroudsburg, Pennsylvania, was that guy for me.

Randolph's review of *Oh Men, Oh Women*, had the auspicious title of "Superior Acting By Dick Van Patten Lifts *Oh Men, Oh Women* To Enjoyable Heights." Randolph really wasn't crazy about the play itself, which he described as "a rather weak-minded piece of writing." Still, he thought it "quite funny and highly enjoyable." Why? Mr. Randolph explains in a section with the preposterous subtitle of: "Superhuman Humor." Randolph wrote: "The principal reason for this is Dick Van Patten's side-splitting performance…. What Van Patten does with the part of Grant Cobble is uproarious caricature which is so far superior to the role itself that it becomes very nearly superhuman in stature." Randolph continued: "using a constricted, high-pitched voice with amazing skill, the actor lifts the play by its heels and shakes it frantically for all the humor he can rattle from it."

Well, that one goes up on the wall! We actors are a thick-skinned lot—or at least we better be. Generally, we get critiqued a bit too harshly. But on occasion, it balances out when we get more than we deserve. And *every so often*, we just might have the perfect guy sitting out there in the crowd. I had him that night in the Poconos. While it's been some fifty-three years, I still get a kick out of Leonard Randolph's overly-generous review. And it reminds me of how fortunate I am to be in a profession where the greatest accomplishment is to help people forget their troubles and just have a good—even a "superhuman"—laugh.

31

SLIPPING AWAY

Mama finally wound down in the summer of 1957, and for the first time in my life, I didn't have a job. With a wife and three young kids to support, pretty much all the money we had was gone. Worse still, for the first time in my thirty years working in New York City, the phone stopped ringing.

I thought maybe I had been typecast after eight years as Nels on *Mama*. Later we would hear about people getting typecast on television and it having terrible repercussions on their careers. George Reeves, who played Superman, was the most famous— although somewhat exaggerated. It has often been said that his role in *From Here to Eternity*, with my old friend Montgomery Clift, was reduced or removed from the film after people in the first viewing starting yelling out, "It's Superman" in the theaters. The film's writer and producer denied that there was any diminution of Reeves's role. Still, Reeves's typecasting was widely perceived, and many people believed that the depression preceding his final suicide was worsened by the fact that everyone saw him as Superman, and he couldn't get other work.

When I first took the role of Nels on television, I was astonished at the power of instant recognition. At first I thought it was great, a real sign of success. But at the same time, the public was getting used to me as that particular character. For eight years and 500 episodes, everyone who watched television thought of Dick Van Patten and Nels Hansen as one and the same. The show had ended, but not my association with Nels in the public eye. Suddenly I realized that being so well recognized had a downside.

But there was more to my troubles than simply being typecast. The truth is that my enjoyment of the track had developed into a problem. By the fall of 1957, just months after the close of *I Remember Mama*, I was flat broke. What little money we had I was increasingly throwing away at the track in some crazy hope I could turn my bad luck around with one big win. That led to one of the most devastating mistakes of my life.

When Pat and I were married, we received a series of war bonds from my family. My grandfather gave us $2,000, and my mother and father also gave them to us. In total they would have been worth $5,000 when they matured. In October of 1957, with no money left, I started harassing Pat to cash in the bonds so I could bet them on a "sure thing" at the track. There was a marvelous horse that year named Gallant Man who had won all the big races and was now coming to Belmont Park. His jockey was none other than the great Willie Shoemaker, one of the legends of the sport.

Pat refused. But I kept at it, harassing her every day to cash the bonds. It was the last bit of money we had in all the world. Also, to cash them in prematurely would be to take a tremendous loss as they were not even close to maturing. At the time, they were only worth $3,750.

But by this point, I had pretty much lost touch with reality. A gambler always believes—and I mean <u>believes</u>—that he's only one bet away from turning it all around. For me, that "one bet" was Gallant Man. That horse was going to be my salvation.

I continued pressing Pat relentlessly. All week I kept after her. There was no way this horse could lose. I kept repeating it. It was a sure thing. All our problems will end, if only we put the wedding bonds on Gallant Man.

She finally relented. I suppose a person can only take so much before it just doesn't seem worth the fight. It's a miracle she didn't walk out on me, and I'll always love her for not turning her back on me when I hit rock bottom. It's easy to stand by someone when things are great; the test of real commitment is what you're willing to endure when things are falling apart.

On the day of the race, Pat turned over the bonds. I cashed them at the Bank of America and headed straight for the track.

It was a beautiful afternoon. There had been several races on the card, but I resisted the temptation to play around and waited for Gallant Man. He was a three-year-old chestnut colt. It was a fast track, and that would suit him well. The odds were even money. At the $50 window, I had to place 74 tickets, which took forever and held up the line. I placed the entire $3,750, all the war bonds we received at our wedding, on Gallant Man.

The gate opened, and they were off. I stood by myself at the head of the stretch. As they came out of the gate, Gallant Man was still far back in the pack. But I wasn't concerned because that's how he ran. He always came from behind. Then when he took the lead no one could catch him. He would later be voted Horse of the Year by *Thoroughbred* magazine.

But on that day, the stars were not aligned. In an amazing turnaround, a horse named Dedicate came barreling out of the pack. They hit the stretch, and Dedicate and Gallant Man were neck and neck on the rail. When they crossed the finish line, I couldn't tell who had won. It seemed from my angle to be a photo finish.

It wasn't. Dedicate had pulled ahead at the line by a full quarter length. The principal horse-racing magazine was—and still is—*Blood Sport*. In the November, 1957 issue, there's a picture of Dedicate edging past Gallant Man for the biggest upset of the year. I stood there at the track for what seemed an eternity. All our money was gone.

32

FLITTING OFF

Things had pretty much dried up in New York. The phones had stopped ringing, and I was dead broke after the Gallant Man fiasco. And so twelve years after the Lunts warned me against "flitting off to Hollywood," and twenty-three years after my Grandmother Florence and I stood outside Stan Laurel's office, I finally decided to give California another try. With a family to feed and no prospects on the East Coast, I gathered up the brood and headed west.

Miraculously, I landed a part in *Rawhide* with Clint Eastwood. *Rawhide* was a great western series that launched Clint's career. He played the gritty young cowboy, Rowdy Yates. Eric Fleming was also excellent as the head cattle-driver, Gil Favor. Only a few years after Rawhide, Fleming became one of the few actors to actually die while working on a television set. It happened in Peru where he drowned while filming a scene for the series, *High Jungle.*

The *Rawhide* story line involved Favor and Yates leading a team of cattle to a point where they needed to cross the land of a wealthy rancher, played by Brian Dunleavy. I was the rancher's son, Matt Reston. At first, the old rancher seemed polite enough to Rowdy and Gil, but soon they found out about his mistreatment of his Indian workers, flogging them for minor infractions. And as a sub-plot, the rancher was ashamed of his son, who he believed to be weak-kneed and cowardly. He dreaded the idea that one day this boy would inherit his ranching empire.

Thus, my character started out as a kind of hapless guy, whose father was ashamed of him. The father's shame was evident one day as he watched Matt trying to tame a wild bronc— repeatedly getting thrown from the unruly horse. Rowdy offered to help, but stubbornly, Matt declined and kept looking foolish as his father watched him with disgust.

Interestingly, all those western fellows, including Clint, naturally assumed a guy from New York with a career on the Broadway stage wouldn't know a thing about horses. But, for better or worse, I'd been around horses every day of my life—and not just to gamble. I'd learned to ride when I was seven years old, and my earliest dreams were of being a jockey. The truth is I could handle horses far better than any of them.

So when the time came to fall off the horse, I did it myself—over and over again, just as it was called for in the script. Later that day a fellow came up to me and asked for a word. I didn't realize at the time that this guy was a prominent Hollywood stuntman. He told me that I shouldn't have done those stunts myself. He explained that every time an actor did his own stunt, a stunt man loses work. Suddenly I felt terrible about it, and since then I've always been conscious, not only of the stuntmen, but of the many, many people on a movie or television set who are working hard to make a living. Often their ability to earn money depends on the rest of us. Every so often, we still see some prima donna star bullying people on the crew. I cringe each time I hear about it. When it happens, it creates justified public anger at our profession. We are all lucky to be part of this business, and every star on every show, movie or play should be thankful to the hundreds of people who work so hard just to make them look good.

I still remember the wonderful final scene in which I did finally stand up to my father. Just as he was about to hang an innocent Indian, I came to the rescue, and in doing so, grew into my own as a man. In the last shot, I was up on the horse, and Rowdy and Gil asked if I wanted to ride with them. I remember my response, because it kind of summed up where I was in my own personal life at the time. I looked down at Eastwood and Fleming and said: "No Thanks, Mr. Favor. I'd rather be on my own for a while." I then turned the horse and rode off. It was a turning point for me—a time when I would also head off for a while. I packed up my family, and we moved back to New York. It would be another decade before making one last try in Hollywood.

But, before we left, we had a terrible scare—one that seemed to sum up the entire trip. My mother had suggested I contact Burt Lancaster. After all, he and I had shared an apartment back in New York, and now he was a big movie star. Since the days on 55th Street, Burt had moved up quickly, playing memorable roles in *From Here to Eternity* and *Gunfight at the O.K. Corral*, with Kirk Douglas. The following year he would win the Academy Award for his performance in *Elmer Gantry*.

So I called him on the phone, and he invited us to his big house up in the hills in Bel Air. He told us to bring swim clothes as they had a beautiful pool in the yard.

When we arrived, his wife, Norma, met us and brought us to their pool. We talked about New York as we waited for Burt to come outside and join us. Suddenly, right in the middle of our conversation, Norma screamed: "Oh My God!" Before I knew what was happening, she jumped up from her chair and dove into the pool. Norma, like Burt, had been an acrobat in the circus, and she was in the water before I could even react. Then I saw Nels, who was five years old, under the water, drowning. I rushed to the poolside, where Norma had already pulled Nels up and was giving him mouth to mouth resuscitation. Pat and I were terrified as we watched her work on Nels, who, at first, was unresponsive. His face had turned a deep blue. Those few seconds seemed like hours. Suddenly Nels coughed, and water came bursting out of his mouth as he literally came back to life.

Norma had saved my son's life. Pat and I are forever grateful for her amazing reaction and calm in what was a moment of life or death. We gathered the kids and called it a day, never even seeing Burt. No doubt, he learned about it later from Norma, but as it turned out we left town shortly afterwards, and I never saw them again. It was time for us to go.

33

CRASH

After five months in Los Angeles in 1958, we headed back to the Big Apple. Had I been a young man it might have been different. After all, in my short time in L.A. I did land a guest spot on *Rawhide*. Perhaps with a little persistence, I might have made a go of it.

But I was also feeling my age. It was a hard fact that I was now thirty years old with a wife and three young kids to support. This was not the time to try to jumpstart a career that may have required a long time knocking on doors. Of course, there wasn't much for us back in New York either, but at least it was home.

As we packed for the trip, we were dead broke. All of us piled into my Olds convertible, and we took off on the long trip back. As always, the journey was, itself, an adventure, especially as our money literally dipped to zero. I tried to get some help from family members, but they thought I would just gamble anything they sent. The truth is we didn't even have enough to pay for the gas.

That's when I got creative. We pulled into Albuquerque, New Mexico, and I went into a small store to buy something. All I had was a Diner's Club credit card. Crazy as it sounds, at the time there was some kind of law against selling alcohol to Native Americans. I remember there was a Native American fellow outside the store. He actually offered to give me a few bucks if I would buy him some booze. So I put a $2 pint bottle of whiskey on the Diner's card, and he gave me $5 in cash. After he paid me, I noticed there was a whole crowd of his friends gathered outside the store, and they all wanted whiskey and offered the same deal. So I kept going in and out of the store, making a few bucks each time. The store owner knew what I was doing, but he sold it to me anyway. I kept putting the purchases on my Diner's Club card, and after about a half hour I had accumulated enough cash to pay for the trip home.

After the failure of Hollywood and the difficult trip home, we arrived back in New York just in time for another blow to strike. On December 13, 1959, my grandfather, Vincent, died. I've already described his terrible death from exposure after falling in the snow. His loss could not have come at a worse time. My mother was devastated. We were all worried about how she would handle it, and our worst fears were realized. The viewing was held at a funeral home in Rego Park, on Woodhaven Boulevard. Afterwards, we went to the cemetery on Queens Boulevard. All along I was concerned about Mom's emotional state. Together with her children, Vincent was the closest person in the world to her. They had always shared a special bond. He was immensely proud of her, and especially proud of what she had accomplished with her children's careers. While my father eventually stepped away from it all, Vincent embraced it. He never missed an opening night, and he was deeply involved in her life—even more so in the fifteen years since my father left.

Just when we thought we were going to make it through the whole process without incident, Mom broke down uncontrollably. As Vincent's body was being lowered into the ground, she literally ran toward the grave and tried to jump in. My Aunt Katherine and I rushed to grab her right at the edge of the grave before she could fall. Aunt Katherine actually slapped her several times across the face to bring her back to her senses. It worked. Mom regained her composure, and the body was buried. It was a terrible ordeal.

* * *

I continued looking for work, but it was slow in coming. I was grateful to Larry Hagman, not yet famous as Barbara Eden's husband in *I Dream of Jeannie*, for giving me a part in a 1961 summer tour with David Wayne of *The Golden Fleecing*. But that ended shortly, and without money coming in, we made the difficult decision that Pat should look for work. After all, she was one of the best dancers in New York City. She immediately landed a job on a show playing at the Jones Beach Theater called *Hit the Deck*, with music by Guy Lombardo. She did so well that in August of 1960, there was a photo in the *New York Daily News* of Pat and a group of naval recruits at the Jones Beach Marine Theater. One of the highlights for Pat was meeting a terrific young actor on the rise named Elliot Gould, who was her dance partner in the chorus.

In 1961, I did manage to score a recurring role on a popular soap opera, *Young Doctor Malone*. I played Larry Renfrew, the sinister brother-in-law of Doctor David Malone, who was married to Gig Houseman, played by Diana Hyland, who would later be my wife in the initial episodes of *Eight Is Enough*. Interestingly, my character Larry shared my own biggest vice, horse betting. But, in fairness, Larry was far worse than me since he played the horses with stolen insurance money. Eventually, Larry falls—or is pushed—off a building and dies, thus ending my soap opera career. I did have some forewarning. Before his demise, producer Dick Holland invited me for a drink in a nearby tavern. At the bar, he broke the news: "Dick, I feel awful about it, but I'm just going to have to kill Larry Renfrew. He's so heavy. We can't do anything more with him."

I'm not sure I agreed that Larry's problem was being too "heavy," but it was the first time—and the last—that I was ever told they were going to kill off my character. In today's episodic television, it's a little more common. It's also more common in soap operas, where people are constantly coming in and out. Larry's death actually warranted an article in the *New York Post*, "Dr. Malone Faces Death in Family." Pete Williams wrote: "the sentence was pronounced soberly, albeit in a midtown bar." He revealed that Larry was scheduled to fall from the top of a tall building and that "Van Patten was inclined to think that Larry Renfrew deserves what he's getting."

Deserve it or not, death for Larry Renfrew meant unemployment for me. That was bad enough, but things got even worse. One night while playing poker in my friend Andy Meyerhoffer's basement in Woodhaven, we were robbed. Andy had one of those finished basements where you had to enter through stairs leading up into the backyard. We used to play poker there pretty often. I mentioned to another actor I'd worked with on *Young Doctor Malone*, Dort Clark, that I played cards every Wednesday night and asked if he wanted to join us. He said he'd love to. That turned out to be a mistake.

That night we were in the middle of the game, and suddenly two guys burst in with guns. They started yelling: "Everybody up against the wall!" We all did what they said—except Dort. He thought it was a gag. He said to me: "Dickie, what is this, a joke? Come on, Dickie, I know you. This is a joke." And he just wouldn't get up. In the meantime, I'm standing against the wall, and some thug has a pistol to my head. I still remember it was a big gold-plated gun. My knees were wobbly. It's the only time in my life I ever felt like that. It was a terrible sensation. For a moment, I thought these guys were going to kill us. They didn't wear any masks, which made me think they didn't plan on leaving any witnesses.

They took several thousand dollars off the table, but none of our jewelry. I had a watch and a diamond ring, but they left it and just took the cash. They kept yelling, "Give us the money!" I remember when they went through Dort's pockets, thinking it was strange when they pulled out a needle. But I later found out he was diabetic.

As quick as they came, they were gone. After recovering our composure, we decided not to call the police. I don't know whether or not that was a mistake, but my feeling was that if these fellows weren't afraid to show us their faces, they must be connected to other people we didn't want to mess around with. Nobody had been hurt, and it was better, we decided, to just let it go. We discontinued the game, and I'm sure poor Dort thought twice before accepting any more invitations to a friendly poker game.

34

FLEETING FAME

Shortly after the poker robbery, I somehow managed a trip to Florida. I don't recall exactly why, but I'm sure I was following up some lead for work. Whatever the reason, I did scrape together a few bucks and headed out to the Hialeah Racetrack near Miami. Suddenly, I looked over and saw Rocky Marciano in the next box.

Rocky was one of my biggest heroes. He'd been heavyweight champ in the mid-1950s while I was still working on *Mama*, and I used to love seeing him fight at the Garden. And like so many fans, I was glad when he retired undefeated—still the only heavyweight champion to do so.

After a while someone introduced us. I was in awe of the "Rock" and was even more delighted when his trainer asked me: "Dick, could you drive Rocky back to the Fontainebleau Hotel?" I immediately agreed.

I was ecstatic driving the champ. I put the top down and went cruising along, reminiscing with the great Rocky Marciano about his many fights. For me it didn't get any better. When we arrived at the Fontainebleau Hotel, I parked the car, got out and walked with Rocky into the lobby.

In the hotel foyer, I noticed a guy shining shoes. I didn't recognize him at first, but later realized it was Beau Jack, the former two-time lightweight world champion. Rocky must have seen him too. We walked by, and nobody said anything. But as we got closer to the elevator, Marciano turned to me, and he said, "Go give him $100. Tell him it's from the champ." I said, "Okay," figuring Rocky would reimburse me later. Fortunately, I had won that day so I pulled a hundred from my wallet—my last hundred—walked over and gave it to Beau. I told him: "This is from the Champ." Beau looked up at me, and I still remember his exact words: "Thank you, boss, thank you."

That shook me up a little. By now I knew who he was, which meant I knew he was no ordinary ex-fighter down on his luck. Beau had been the world champ—two times. One of the most prolific fighters at Madison Square Garden. I'd seen him numerous times and joined with thousands of fans in rooting him on. Beau was one of a trio of great lightweights in the 1940s, along with Bob

Montgomery and Ike Williams. Their battles for the title were among the most exciting rivalries in all of sports. All three men are now in the Boxing Hall of Fame.

Many will remember the famous War Bonds Fight at the Garden. Both Beau and Bob Montgomery had been privates in the U.S. Army, and they each refused to take any money for the fight. Tickets were only given to those who purchased war bonds. In fact, there were many wealthy people who bought the bonds and then left the tickets for servicemen. The War Bonds Fight was a great way to raise money to support the troops. In the end, they took in $35 million—the biggest gate in boxing history! I always thought of Beau Jack and Bob Montgomery as great patriots.

But when I reflect on Beau Jack shining shoes at the Fontainebleau, it's impossible not to be struck by the great irony— the tragic irony—of a man who started and ended his life shining shoes for tips, but somehow along the way rose to great heights; rose to the very pinnacle of his profession and enjoyed all the acclaim, advantages and adulation of a world champion.

Not everyone was aware of Beau's amazing journey to success. As a teenager in the 1920s, he shone shoes at the Augusta National Golf Club where the Master's is played. I later learned that he picked up money on the side through a truly diabolical practice called "Battle Royales." This was a perverse tournament run for the amusement of wealthy white men who arranged boxing matches by putting six blindfolded black men in a small arena where they fought until there was only one standing. Beau later described these macabre spectacles, noting that, at the time, participating in the bloodbaths was the only way to put food on the table.

Beau's situation—and talent—came to the attention of a particular Augusta Club member, Bobby Jones. Jones was already an American legend, like Ruth was to Baseball or Dempsey to Boxing. Bobby Jones raised a collection for Beau at Augusta and sent him north to New York City where he would not just learn how to fight, but would electrify the boxing world and be elected to the Boxing Hall of Fame.

So how does a man like that end up back where he started, shining shoes? It was troubling to see, and I certainly didn't have any answers. I've always known how easy it is to lose money— even large sums. God knows I've lost my share. But this was different. Beau was the world champ. Someone must have taken it out from under him. My greatest hero, Joe Louis, lost it all. He also ended up at a hotel, but at least he was reasonably compensated. I was friends with the great actor, George Raft, who was close with Joe Louis, and George told me they paid Joe $750 a week plus room and board at Caesar's Palace in Vegas, just to greet people as they arrived. That's nothing compared to what he used to make. But Beau Jack was shining shoes.

I went back over to Rocky. He was by the elevator, still holding court. I didn't ask him for the money, but I waited, assuming he was going to reimburse me. He never did. He just said good-bye and that was that. I've since heard that Rocky was a little tight; that he didn't trust banks and always insisted on being paid in cash, which he kept in his house. He grew up in a poor family and those old fears die hard.

Later I was happy to hear that Beau Jack's situation had improved. Eventually he started lobbying for a pension plan for boxers so they could avoid ending up like him at the Fontainebleau. I was a little annoyed at Rocky at the time, but in retrospect I'm glad he didn't pay me back. It was my best-spent hundred dollars that day—or any other day.

35

TOUGH CHOICES

There soon came a point in the early 1960s when there simply wasn't enough money coming in to pay the bills. I came to the reluctant realization that I had to do something about it. I couldn't just watch my family living from hand to mouth, especially knowing that our predicament had been partly brought about by my gambling problem.

For the first time in my life, I decided to look for a job outside the entertainment world. This was the toughest decision of my life. I'd been working steadily since I was three years old in modeling, theater, radio and television, and now I had to accept that, at least for a time, that old life was being put on hold.

I settled on real estate. I'm not sure why. It may have been nothing more than the fact that I had liked Murray Adams, the fellow who sold me my own home in Bellerose. So I swallowed my pride and walked down to his office on Jamaica Avenue in Queens and told him I wanted to work for him.

He was receptive and explained to me about the test to get a real estate agent's license. He never once made me feel uncomfortable for needing the job. Murray lent me a bunch of books, and for the first time in my life, I studied hard for several weeks. Soon I took the test and passed, receiving a New York City real estate agent's license. I brought the license home to show Pat. Later she told my nephew, Casey, that she was never so proud of me. She understood how tough it was for me to do this. I had to swallow my pride to keep the family going, but nothing was more important to me than that.

The truth is my life story was not a rags to riches tale. I never really knew what it was like to be without money. Even as a child throughout the Great Depression, I was working steadily as a model and actor. That kind of steady work and hectic schedule did impress on me a very strong work ethic. I've always juggled multiple jobs, and I seemed to always have the energy needed to keep at it. Even today, at eighty years of age, I'm not happy unless I'm working.

Still, I never knew what it was like to be desperate. There was always another job or a show waiting around the bend. I've known many celebrities who remember a time in their youth, often their entire youth, when they were dirt poor, but a fire burned inside them driving their pursuit of success and pushing them to rise up out of impoverishment. Often, these people suffered indignities along the way, but they managed to persevere. That's what makes their success so compelling.

But I never felt like that. For the first time in my life, I had to look myself square in the mirror and really feel the overwhelming pressure of being without money—having little prospects, but great responsibilities. Perhaps it wasn't as bad as I imagined, but I certainly felt a great weight on my shoulders the day I first walked down the street to the Adams Realty Agency. It was a moment of truth for me. Swallowing my pride and taking a job as a real estate agent was the most difficult thing I've ever done. Pat knew that and, perhaps, that's why she felt proud of me at that moment.

Ironically, I ended up enjoying my new job. I found a way to channel the same energy I possessed as an actor into my work as a real estate agent. Quickly, I was selling houses to everyone in Queens. I discovered I had the same enthusiasm for selling a home that I had found for so many other things in my life. Pat still recalls me waking up in the middle of the night practically yelling out: "I've just thought of the perfect house for so and so!" I loved to try and figure out what people wanted and then match their wishes to a home. I've always been a good listener, and I listened carefully to the dreams of the people who came in to buy a house. I found myself obsessing over their dreams, just as I had obsessed over a racehorse or learning a script.

There was, of course, an occasional indignity. I remember one time at Jones Beach some guy made a snide comment to Pat about my fall from star status in the entertainment world. But that was the exception. All in all, those were wonderful years, and I was lucky to have had the support of a wife who made it all possible. Most of all, and much to my surprise, I was happy.

* * *

A great part of that happiness, no doubt, resulted from the fact that it was during those real estate years that Pat and I raised our three children. Growing up in Bellerose, Queens, they didn't think of their father as a radio, theater or television star. For them, Dad worked with Mr. Adams at the realty office, and they never had, or expected, any of the privileges that sometimes spoil the children of celebrities. We had enough money to enjoy a good middle-class lifestyle, but nothing more.

I also think I was free to spend more time with the kids than would have been possible if I had stayed in Hollywood. Those years in real estate allowed me to have more of the family life that my own father had wanted, the absence of which may have prompted his moving out and looking for it elsewhere.

While I've played parts in family shows my whole life, most notably as a father of eight children, the truth is I had no idea whatsoever of the joys—and responsibilities—of fatherhood until having my own family. During the run of *Mama*, Pat and I had three beautiful boys beginning in 1955. We named the first child "Nels," after my character on *Mama* who had brought us such good fortune. A year later, Jimmy, came along and a year after that, Vincent.

Around the same time, we also took in Joyce's three-year-old son, Casey, while she was filming on location in Europe. As it happened, Casey was staying at a very nice boarding house, and Pat and I would take him with us on the weekends. One Sunday afternoon as we were driving him back, he began crying and saying he didn't want to leave. After we dropped him off and were pulling away, Pat and I looked at each other, stopped the car, turned around and went back for him. We ended up holding on to Casey through a good deal of his youth, and I've always thought of him as a fourth son.

I think most parents will agree there is nothing to compare with the experience of watching your children grow. Along the way, you also learn a great deal about yourself—and your spouse. I didn't marry Pat because I thought she would be a good mother, but I sure did get lucky on that score. I could tell from the very first time I saw her holding our first baby that he was in good hands. She was a natural. As for myself, I also discovered the joys of fatherhood. I probably haven't expressed it as much as I should, but I'll never forget that feeling of awe and wonder with the birth of each of my children. I also immediately understood the meaning of unconditional love. Sometimes we hear on the news about a parent standing by a child who has committed some horrible, even unspeakable crime. The whole world is understandably enraged at that person, and yet the parent stands there for him, often all alone. That's unconditional love; it begins at birth and it never ends.

Through the years, I've also learned that being a father is a marathon, not a sprint. Learning the job is not a magic trick you perform once or twice and then think you've got the hang of it. In fact, every single day, there's some new and often unexpected challenge—and they just keep you guessing. And no matter how old your kids get, they are always still your kids, and the concern you felt for their well-being on the day they were born continues until the day you die.

I was like my own father in that I wanted to be a part of my children's world—in fact, maybe too much so. Sometimes they jokingly remind me how the kids in the neighborhood would come by and ask Pat if Mr. Van Patten could come out and play! And there were many times when I piled the whole neighborhood into our old yellow Oldsmobile—including some who stuffed themselves in the trunk—and headed off for a day at Jones Beach.

As a father, I came to cherish the wonder in a child's eyes. That's not just a platitude, all parents know what it's like to see their children marvel at things that seem to them so mysterious and awesome. For years I told the boys there was a special "money tree" up at Alley Pond Park. At night I would go alone and tie dollars to the branches and place coins by the trunk. The next day, I'd get the whole gang together, drive to the park and watch as the kids ran like crazy to that special place. I still recall the amazement and delight on their faces as they discovered the coins and dollars I had left the night before.

All our kids were athletic, and I encouraged them to play tennis and other sports. Nels and Vincent loved the more traditional games, while Jimmy preferred doing acrobatic stunts on the horizontal bars and juggling tennis balls. As a child, Jimmy also shared my love of magic, and even today he can make silverware disappear at the dinner table. Later he became an exceptional swimmer and surfer—and loved to bring my grandchildren Duke and Vincent, the children of Vincent and the wonderful actress Betsy Russell, surfing in the Pacific. Today Duke rides the big waves at Malibu while young Vincent heats up the local golf courses.

Like my father, I believed in the old adage, "healthy body, healthy mind"—especially when it involved physical exercise in the great outdoors. Often in the middle of winter, I would round the kids up, and we'd head off to Forrest Park for a workout. That meant shoveling the snow off the three-wall handball court and playing a brisk game until we were all sweating in the freezing cold.

My love for cold weather exercise later developed into a family tradition on the West Coast. Every New Year's Day for many years now, our family and friends gather together and head out for a dip with the Venice Beach Penguin Swim Club. In 2007,

I had the honor of being named King Penguin of the Year, which meant a photo op with my personal hero, Norky, the seven-foot penguin. Since we began, we've had quite an array of notables joining us to inaugurate the New Year with a brisk swim in the freezing Pacific, including Farrah Fawcett, Christopher Atkins, Debbie Gibson and Jerry Paris.

I always loved the competition of one-on-one sports and so I introduced the kids to the most competitive of all them all, boxing. Nels, who was the most interested in all forms of athletics, recalls the many Friday nights we spent down at Sunnyside Gardens watching the up-and-comers in the Golden Gloves. He still talks about a devastating young man we watched named George Foreman in his first professional fight. It was particularly memorable as it came just after the 1968 Olympics when Foreman stunned the world with his show of patriotism, walking around the ring with an American flag after winning the Gold. Later in his life, Big George would strike a blow for all of us senior citizens when he accomplished the seemingly impossible task of winning the heavyweight championship at age 45!

Nels speaks fondly of those Friday-night fights, not just because we had such a good time out together, but because there were lessons to be learned from those fierce competitors in the ring. "I learned about hard work," Nels recalls, "because most of these fighters came from nowhere." I think my son may have understood just how true that was even before I did. Nearly every one of those guys in the ring were fighting their way out of difficult circumstances. For many, they had only one path out: hard work. Some made it, and others didn't, but, as Nels recognized, there were no slackers in those rings. Everyone was working hard in pursuit of some dream. I think Nels took the lessons he learned from those fighters and has passed them on to the thousands of people he's coached in thirty years as one of the finest teaching professionals in the tennis world.

Casey, of course, brought his own unique personality to the mix. Even as a child, Casey, like his mother Joyce, was thoughtful and curious about the world, always with a book in his hands. I recall when he was just six, he went on a big trip to the 1960 Summer Olympics in Rome with Joyce and her husband, the actor Martin Balsam. On returning, he told me about a young fighter he saw named Cassius Clay, who would, of course, go on to greatness as Muhammad Ali. I always loved Ali. Years later, I was at a fight in Las Vegas when I noticed him sitting in the first row and thought it was strange that he kept turning his head and looking ominously back at me. When the fight ended, I was even more concerned as he got up from his seat and headed straight for mine. So I just stood there not knowing what to expect, when the Champ put his tremendous hand on my shoulder, leaned over and whispered in my ear: "I've been watching you a long time." I was thrilled!

Nels, Jimmy, Vincent and Casey have now grown into wonderful, sensitive and accomplished adults. They are also my closest friends. I feel so very fortunate to have all of them still living nearby so we can continue to share this amazing journey. In recent years I've felt their presence more than ever. I think it's probably fair to say they are all more concerned about my health than I am. Nels and his beautiful wife Nancy Valen, a former *Baywatch* actress, who for twenty years has been like a daughter to Pat and me, are a constant support since my two strokes and open heart surgery. Vincent and his lovely wife, Eileen Davidson, a legendary soap opera star—and their newest arrival, Jesse, who, at age two reminds me just how wondrous this life can be—are also a constant source of joy. And Casey, Pat King and their two children, Bridgit and Christopher have always been a treasured part of our family.

And Jimmy, an eligible bachelor, has been there with me during some of my most memorable moments. A few years ago, we had the great fortune of sharing the stage lights. Together with the great Frank Gorshin, Jimmy and I toured over a hundred cities across America in Neil Simon's *The Sunshine Boys*. In a difficult role, Jimmy showed his marvelous acting skills. But more important to me, we had the time to really get to know each other as we made our way through a million motels and pit-stops all across this wonderful country. It was a special time for both of us that created memories I will always cherish.

* * *

While working as a real estate agent I continued looking for roles. One of the advantages of real estate is that the schedule is flexible. I always had time to audition or even take a part, from time to time. There was no clock to punch and no boss checking to see that I put in a certain number of hours. I worked on commission, and if I sold a house, it gave me time to try my hand at another audition.

I was hoping that things might turn around in December of 1963 when I landed a role in a comedy, *Have I Got a Girl for You*. It was a humorous story of a Jewish family torn by the familiar conflict between getting ahead financially and maintaining their high principles. Before the show even started, I had a nice piece written by William Raidy in the *Long Island Press* in which Raidy reviewed my thirty years in the theater. But the show, which played at the Music Box, didn't last long or open any substantial doors.

The same year, I also took a part in a ninety-minute special, *Men in White* produced by David Susskind, which aired live on ABC. I seemed to always have problems with doctor skits. I did one with Lee J. Cobb and Richard Carlson that was a disaster. We were playing surgeons, and at one point Cobb says: "We must operate." Because it was filmed live, we had to run off the set and put on rubber gloves and then get back for the next scene. When the camera turned to us again, we were all standing there with our hands, now covered with rubber gloves, held up in the air like we were about to begin the operation.

But when Carlson, Cobb and I rushed over to the table for the rubber gloves, I couldn't get mine on. It was hot, and I kept trying to put my fingers in and they kept slipping out. Time was running out, so I just ran back for the scene with the gloves only half on. So as we were all standing like doctors about to perform surgery the camera moved from Lee J. Cobb to Richard Carlson, and then to me. And I'm standing there with my hands held up in the air like I'm about to operate, but the white-gloved fingers were drooping down on my hands. It looked absurd.

Afterwards David Susskind said to me, "What the hell happened there? This is ridiculous. Can't you get the gloves on?"

I said, "No." So David, who was pretty piqued at this, realized what was wrong. He pointed to a bottle on the table I hadn't seen and said to me, "Put the damn talcum powder on your hands."

Worse was an episode of *As the World Turns* where I also played a doctor. The moment came when I was supposed to listen to the patient's heart with my stethoscope. I had it around my neck, but forgot to put it in my ears. So I placed the stethoscope on the patient's chest and started listening intently—without anything in my ears. The other actor, Mark Rydell, who went on to be a big director, was looking at me funny. Then he just started laughing and shaking his head while I'm telling the patient, "Your heartbeat sounds very good. Yes, it sounds very good." I remember wondering why the heck Mark was laughing.

36

THE ROAD BACK

In 1968, I landed a small role in a film, *Charly*, a moving drama about a mentally handicapped man who becomes highly intelligent after an operation. The results, however, are temporary, and he discovers that he will soon regress to his former condition.

I suppose the psychological torment he endures must be similar to what happens in the early stages of Alzheimer's, when a patient knows that he will, in time, begin to lose his way. I think all Americans were brought closer to those feelings as we admired the way President Reagan confronted the onset of his illness. Nothing was more courageous than the beautiful farewell letter he wrote to the country in which he recognized that he was slowly slipping away.

That was the dilemma of Charly Gordon, marvelously played by Cliff Robertson. I had known Cliff years before when he was my understudy on *Mister Roberts,* and now he had developed into a powerful performer and deservedly won the Academy Award for his portrayal of Charly Gordon. While my own role as one of the doctors was very minor, it was, at the time, a welcome opportunity to get back into entertainment. It was also my first film. With all of the work I had done on television, radio and the stage, I had never had a part in a movie.

Shortly after filming *Charly*, I landed a role in a Broadway play by two authors named Renee Taylor and Joseph Bologna called *Lovers and Other Strangers*. It was a well-conceived and written comedy involving a series of storylines centering around an upcoming wedding.

The play, which opened at the Brooks Atkinson in September of 1969, was very much reflective of the changing times. As the legitimacy of marriage as an institution was being increasingly questioned, *Lovers and Other Strangers* highlighted what was both good and bad about marriage. The strongest performance was by the veteran character actor, Richard Castellano, who played the groom's father.

At the wedding of one of Castellano's sons, it becomes known that his other son is in the process of getting a divorce. Castellano's character, Frank, spends more time obsessing on how this could have occurred. Throughout the play he continuously interrogates his son: "Okay, what happened?" His questions assume there must have been some precipitating incident. He believes that once it was revealed, he could then help resolve it—even to the point of suggesting that his son consider taking a mistress.

But hearing only vague responses from his son about how the enjoyment or "fun" of his marriage had been lost, he becomes utterly confused—unable to understand that for many in the younger generation of the 1960s, a marriage had to be about more than just getting by for the sake of convention. The divide between Frank and his son reflected what became known as the "generation gap"—a phenomenon that played such a powerful role in the social turbulence of the 1960s.

My character, Hal, the father of the bride, is more flexible—although not in a particularly attractive way. Hal tries desperately to strike a balance between his own marriage of thirty years and his relationship with his long-term mistress. His inability to take action, either breaking up his failed marriage or cutting off his affair, represented the hypocrisy so prevalent in many relationships when they begin to stagnate and men—at least, typically men—begin looking outside the marriage for ways to find fulfillment.

But *Lovers* was not a wholesale attack on marriage. For that reason, I believe, it became a success—although not so much as a play. We closed after just seventy performances, but the next year it was made into a motion picture in which Castellano starred, along with Diane Keaton and Cloris Leachman. Gig Young, who had just won the Academy Award for his supporting role in *They Shoot Horses Don't They*, took my role as Hal. The movie did much better than the play, and the song played during the wedding scene, *For All We Know*, became a classic, winning the Academy Award and prompting *The Carpenters* to sing a version that became a best-selling record.

Lovers and Other Strangers was my first play on Broadway in five years, and it did crack open a little bit of a door for me to get moving on the road back. A few months later, I took a small part in a drawing-room comedy, *But Seriously,* at the Henry Miller Theater on Broadway. Opening in March of 1969 and starring Tom Poston and Bethel Leslie, it lasted just a few days, when, as *The New Yorker* wrote, the play "closed wisely after its fourth performance."

One positive note was a stand-out performance by a young actor playing the couple's son, named Richard Dreyfuss. I wasn't the only one who noticed him. The same critic who panned the play also noted that Richard had come "within an ace of stealing the show." He also had a kind word for me, saying he "enjoyed Dick Van Patten as the hearty and pompous neighbor."

During rehearsals for *But Seriously*, my nephew Casey came to the set with me nearly every day. He was interested in making his way as an actor, and I was glad to see him hanging around with Richard, who advised him to hone his acting skills by doing as much live theater as possible. I certainly agreed with that.

37

THREE'S A CHARM!

Later in 1969, I received a call from Wayne Carson, an acting friend who had worked on *Mister Roberts* and now was the stage manager for a show called *Adaptation/Next* at the Greenwich Mews Theater starring Jimmy Coco and produced by Elaine May. *Next* was a one-act comedy written by Terrence McNally about a hapless, middle-aged, overweight divorcé who mistakenly finds himself at the draft board, where the strict female Sergeant Thech tries to enlist him. The repartee between them is wonderful.

Jimmy Coco was getting very hot at the time, soon to win a Tony for his role in Neil Simon's *The Last of the Red Hot Lovers* and in the winter of 1969, Jimmy wanted to leave the show. Also, the production was going to Los Angeles for several months, and Coco wasn't interested in doing it on the West Coast.

I auditioned for the part, and Elaine May selected me as Jimmy's replacement to finish up the New York run and then go to Los Angeles. At the time I thought I'd be away for just a few months and then come back to New York and the real estate business.

Coincidentally, at the very same time, Connie Stevens was looking for a young boy to play her son in a show she was prepping for television. She had heard about my son, Vincent, who was 12 years old at the time. Connie came to see him for an audition in New York City. She loved him and decided he should come to Los Angeles to film the pilot.

So with two reasons to once again think about Hollywood, Pat and I decided that we would all head west—at least temporarily. The time constraints were more pressing for Vincent, so he and Pat took a plane, which left me, Jimmy, Nels and Casey to drive out.

By now, I thought I had the gambling thing pretty much under control. But with several weeks to kill on the road, I decided to do something a little out of the ordinary: take a cross-country tour of America's race tracks. I've known hard-core fans who tour the baseball parks—zigzagging from state to state, catching games in all the famous venues, so I decided to do the same with the tracks. I sat down at the kitchen table in Bellerose making a list of all the tracks in the country and then mapping out our circuitous route west.

We almost lost everything in Ohio. Stopping at the Beulah Park racetrack in Grove City, I quickly lost a series of races. Suddenly we didn't have enough money to keep going. By this time, Jimmy and Casey had returned to the car and sat there wondering if they were going to sleep in the racetrack parking lot. Nels stayed with me as I put all the remaining money on the final race. The two of us watched as our horse came roaring down the stretch with a tremendous upset. We ended up pulling away with more than when we arrived.

I'm sure all this sounds reminiscent of the Gallant Man fiasco when the urge to bet was threatening to destroy my life and my family. But by this time, things had changed. The grip that gambling and the races had over me in the late 1950s had diminished greatly. I certainly realized that gambling addictions don't just go away. I also realized it would be a constant presence in my life, and I would have to be vigilant to ensure that it never controlled me again. It might make a nice story if I could say I just walked away from the horses and the poker tables and never looked back. But it would be dishonest. The truth is I found a middle ground; a place between addiction and abstinence. I understand there are many good people who say that can't happen, or that it's not the right way to beat a habit. And I don't dispute them. But I will say, as I've said about so many things in life, that every one of us is different. We're all unique. And what works for one of us may not work for someone else.

Moderation has worked for me. That's as much as I can say. I still go to the racetrack with an excitement I've felt my whole life. I love the grass, the track, the horses, the jockeys, the stables, and, most of all, the people. And each time I look out at the infield, it takes me back to my childhood watching my grandfather sitting up there on the high stool next to his big blackboard on the beautiful grounds of Saratoga.

What's changed is that I won't bet the house. In fact, I don't really bet that much at all. It's true there will never be that wild, insane rush gamblers feel when they put it all on the line. There's a natural high that comes from living on the edge. I felt it that day in 1957 when I lost the wedding bonds. But the price was too high. It nearly cost me my family—and that was the most frightening thing I've ever experienced.

It's different now. And it was already changing by 1969, even though I did drag the kids along on that crazy zigzag through America's racetracks. I suppose I'll always feel the impulse to put something down on a horse, but it's as much a social event as anything else. Out at Santa Anita or Del Mar, I enjoy the company of my good friends, Mel Brooks, Tim Conway and Jack Klugman, not to mention the more colorful characters like Jimmy the Hat, Fat Eddie, and many more. For better or worse, the horses have been an important part of my life, and, while I'm figuring out whether it's all been good or bad, I'll be out at the track still looking for the big win—but doing so on a much smaller bet.

Yet that's not to say my trip out West was a model of maturity. Nearly every day, I'd stop at a motel with a pool. And while I'm not so proud of it now, I had the kids put on their bathing suits and jump in for a swim as if we were motel guests. I figured no one would think a grown man with three kids would do something so stupid—and I was right. While I feel a little ashamed of it now, we did enjoy great pools all the way to the West Coast.

The road trip continued through a dozen different tracks. And along the way, we stopped in Arizona to see the Grand Canyon. I still had a vivid memory of this natural marvel from my trip with Florence in 1935, and I wanted my kids to enjoy it too. Finally we arrived in Los Angeles on Halloween Day, October 31, 1969. And we're still here.

* * *

Just as we were getting comfortable in our new home on the Queens Road cul-de-sac in Hollywood, a big family moved in next door. As we watched them unpack, we could see that there were a lot of them. Pat and I went over to meet the family. The parents introduced themselves as Joe and Katherine Jackson, and then we met all of their kids, including their eleven-year-old, Michael.

They had just moved from Gary, Indiana. The kids played together in a band, which already had some local success back home, but now they had gotten a recording contract and were making a push for the big time. I thought nothing of it, but I was happy to have a bunch of kids next door. The transition had been difficult for our boys, especially Nels, who had to leave all their friends back in New York and now at least there were some new kids on the block.

Quickly the Jacksons became like family. The kids played sports together and hung out all the time. Every day I could hear them practicing their music in the garage. Michael became especially attached to Pat. He came by every day to see the kids. If the kids weren't home yet, he was so nice that he would always agree to help out if Pat was working hard in the house.

Years later, Michael and Pat just missed running into each other in Las Vegas, and Michael thoughtfully left a note for Pat who arrived after he left. In it, he remembered the time he spent with her on Queens Road. Pat still has the note: "Mrs. Van Patten: It's Michael here. I truly love you and miss you. Please say hello to the kids. I miss cleaning your house."

As our families grew close, I could see that the Jacksons were well-behaved, polite and fun-loving kids. Pat and I believed they were a fine family, although later revelations by some of the children paint a somewhat different picture.

I remember one time when I did something really stupid. Deciding it was time for all the boys to learn a little something about the great outdoors, I piled the Van Patten and Jackson broods into the station wagon for a camping trip. Now Hollywood may not seem like a rural place to most people, but compared to New York City it's like living in the Australian outback. In fact, there are a series of mountain ranges that surround Los Angeles—the famous Hollywood sign is on one of these, and there are many more.

Like my father, I believed in living healthy, which for him meant going to the park in the middle of the winter and shoveling the snow off the handball court and then playing until your body temperature rose to the point that you'd be sweating even though it was below zero. That ruggedness was something I admired and wanted to instill in my own kids.

We drove way up to the top of the mountain in Griffith Park where we found an old campsite. I helped pitch a couple of tents when suddenly I remembered that I had an important appointment that evening. I made the command decision that the boys would stay, and I would pick them up in the morning. And so, just as it was getting dark, I left a crew of three Van Pattens from New York City and several Jacksons from Gary, Indiana, all alone to fend for themselves way up in the mountain lion–coyote-infested hills of Griffith Park. To make it worse, later that night a tremendous thunderstorm hit the region which, as I later learned, had its epicenter pretty much right over *Camp Van-Jackson*!

When I came back the next day, I was lucky they were all alive. Shivering, rain-soaked and scared to death, they vowed never to go camping again. I felt terrible.

After the extraction, the Jackson parents still let their kids play with mine—although I'm sure they would have been a little more reticent had Dick Van Patten proposed any more great ideas about toughening-up the kids.

All of our kids were athletic, and they played a good deal of touch football on the street in the cul-de-sac on Queens Road. One day, Nels recalls, they were in the middle of a game when suddenly Michael came running out of his house, followed by Marlon and Jermaine, with a transistor radio in his hands screaming at all the kids: "We're on the radio! We're on the radio! They're playing our song on the radio!" They all stopped and gathered around the little transistor and then began dancing wildly on the corner of Hollywood Boulevard and Queens Road as everyone listened to the Jackson's first chart record—"I Want You Back."

It was the beginning of one of the most extraordinary success stories in the history of popular music. Within months, the Jacksons released, "ABC" which shot to Number 1 on the charts, and soon our friends and neighbors from Queens Road were off to super-stardom, with Michael and Janet eventually rising into the stratosphere of American music and popular culture.

Later, we saw a cloud descend over Michael's life. In truth, I have no insight or knowledge about it—nor do my children or wife. Then, just when it seemed he was turning a new page with hopeful plans for a massive international tour, the bombshell came—Michael was dead. Like everyone, Pat and I were stunned—and deeply saddened. We have only wonderful memories of a precocious, fun-loving, enormously talented and endearing child who carried his own unique innocence and charm into our home on Queens Road. He came from what to us was a wonderful family, and I have only the fondest memories of our time as neighbors.

Through the years, Nels has remained friendly with Jermaine, and on occasion they still get together and reminisce about the days on Queens Road when our families, each looking for a start—in my case a new start—came together quite fortuitously and got to know each other before the good and bad of celebrity status made those kinds of relationships more difficult to sustain. Looking back, we were blessed to have had the Jackson family as our neighbors and our friends at that precarious moment in our lives. And with millions of others we will miss the enchanting young boy whose enormous charm and talent was so evident to all of us from the very beginning—a talent that despite his often troubled life would shine brighter than we could have ever imagined.

38

THE PHONES ARE RINGING AGAIN

The Los Angeles run of *Next* was a success. Fortunately I received good reviews as Jimmy Coco's replacement and was happy to be back with a significant part in a successful production. Things began to take off when Shirley Booth, whom Joyce had worked with in *Tomorrow the World*, enjoyed the show and recommended it to a talent scout from MGM. MGM was about to produce a television series with Herschel Bernardi, titled *Arnie*.

I auditioned and got a supporting part in the show. At that point we decided to extend our stay in Los Angeles, possibly even making it permanent. I played Arnie's neighbor and best friend and thoroughly enjoyed my work with Herschel. Although canceled after two seasons, it was a great show and brought me some visibility in Hollywood. Soon the phones were ringing for more parts, guest appearances in television series, and even some roles in movies. Over the next six years, between *Arnie* and the beginning of *Eight Is Enough*, I had a tremendous run of good luck. Suddenly the real estate days were gone, and I was back to entertainment full time. As I said, I was happy in New York, but entertainment is what I love, and I could not have been more thrilled at how things were turning out.

The initial breaks were in television. I made an appearance with my old friend Larry Hagman on *I Dream of Jeannie*. I also did guest spots on *That Girl, The Governor and J.J., Making It, Sanford and Son, The Don Rickles Show, The Paul Lynde Show, Hec Ramsey, The Doris Day Show, McMillan and Wife, Cannon, Love American Style, Banacek, Kolchak the Night Stalker, S.W.A.T., Adam 12, The Six Million Dollar Man, The Rookies, Medical Center, Emergency, Barnaby Jones, What's Happening, The Streets of San Francisco, Maude, Ellery Queen, Wonder Woman* and many more.

One of my most enjoyable guest spots was on a show that was just starting to break away from the pack, headed for an eleven-year run that would make it an icon in American television history—*Happy Days*. My first role was in the third season, just around the time the Fonz was coming into his own. Fonzie, played by Henry Winkler, had originally been a minor character in the series, intended as a kind of dumb-guy foil for Ron Howard's character, Richie Cunningham. But as the show progressed, it became clear that Winkler, a Yale Drama School graduate, was accomplishing something really unique, transforming "the Fonz" into a national sensation. I was delighted when I got the call for a guest spot, but even more excited when I read the script and saw that I would be working in a scene directly with Henry.

The episode was called *Fonzie the Salesman*. The premise was that Herb, the owner of the garage where Fonzie worked as a mechanic, decided to sell the garage, and the new owner, Bertly Van Alden, played marvelously by Richard Stahl, was a super-rich eccentric who laid down a bunch of new regulations that Fonzie couldn't accept—including a requirement that Fonz get a haircut. So Fonzie decided to buy his own garage. That's where I came in as Bert Hunsberger, the loan officer at the bank, a Lodge friend of Richie's father, Howard. At Howard's invitation I met the Fonz at the Cunningham home to discuss a possible loan.

The writers got it perfect.

Hunsberger:	*Let's see. What kind of a loan are you applying for?*
The Fonz:	*Money.*
Hunsberger:	*Yes, Well I know that.*
The Fonz:	*Then Why'd ya ask?*
Hunsberger:	*Do you have collateral?*
The Fonz:	*No, man. I ain't been sick a day in my life.*

And so it went on…until Fonzie declared that he'd "had enough of this nerd," and stormed out.

Happy Days, as they announced at the beginning of each show, was filmed before a live audience, and I remember that scene being a big hit. Two years later, they called again, this time for a two-part episode called *The Graduation*, which aired in 1977.

In addition to guest spots, I was landing recurring roles in a variety of series. After *Arnie*, I took a role opposite Don Adams in a show called *The Partners*, where I played Sergeant Higgenbottom. Next, I worked for a few seasons on *The New Dick Van Dyke Show*, an attempt to revive the old show from the 1960s with Mary Tyler Moore. It was also the first time I met the show's creator, Carl Reiner, and we developed a lifelong friendship. Carl, in my opinion, is one of the most intelligent and talented writers in television.

The success I was enjoying in my comeback in the early years of the 1970s also included some interesting opportunities in the movies. A call came for a short role in a big-budget sci-fi thriller with Charlton Heston and Edward G. Robinson titled *Soylent Green*. I had already come to know Charlton from playing tennis with him at Merv Griffin's house. But when I took the part, the one who really interested me was Eddie Robinson. I grew up watching Eddie in all those great gangster films like *Little Caesar* and my favorite, *A Slight Case of Murder*, a comic spoof on his gangster image, which, in my opinion, should have won him the Academy Award in 1938.

I was in awe of Robinson. When I arrived on the set, I was delighted when he motioned for me to come over and talk with him. He was quite deaf at the time, wearing a well-concealed hearing aid, and as I sat with him I had to speak loudly. "I hear you worked with the Lunts," he said. "I started with them too, you know." Actually, I had no idea, but found out that he had worked in five different plays with Alfred and Lynn, including an acclaimed adaptation of Dostoyevsky's *The Brothers Karamazov* in 1927. I told him I wasn't aware of that, and, like so many others, he responded, "Oh yes, they were the very best." I, of course, agreed.

Moments later, we took positions for our scene together. *Soylent Green* was a futuristic story in which the world had been devastated by global warming. Although much of it is a bit dated, *Soylent's* premise is still relevant today. The film takes place in the year 2022. The people are barely surviving, and a police state has been imposed to maintain order. Because of the devastation, food is rationed. But it was not ordinary food. Rather it came in the form of a large pill heralded by the police state as containing all the nutrients necessary for survival. The food was called "soylent green."

Robinson played an aging New York City policeman, Sol Roth, who pestered his young partner, Robert Thorne, played by Charlton Heston, with memories of a world before the global catastrophe. Roth assists Thorne with his investigation of the murder of one of the heads of the company that manufactures "soylent green." He discovers that "soylent green" is actually made from human remains. Upon learning this, Roth loses his desire to continue living and goes to a state-run euthanasia clinic to die. Prior to death, he is allowed twenty minutes to watch beautiful bucolic images of the world as it existed before the warming.

It was my job to lead Roth to the room where he would die. At the time of the filming, I was unaware that Eddie Robinson, who did appear very frail, was actually in the end-stage of terminal cancer. In fact, he would die ten days after shooting stopped. In the movie I was supposed to say, "Come with me, Mr. Roth." And then I would walk him arm-in-arm to the room where he would die. But, I was in such awe of him that I completely messed up the line. Instead, I said: "Come with me, Mr. Robinson." The director, Richard Fleischer, yelled "cut," and we did it again. Later I thought how strange it was that I had made that particular mistake at that moment in time, in effect beckoning Edward G. Robinson to his death, right before he was actually going to die.

That death scene has since become kind of a sci-fi cult classic. Robinson's wife, Jane, who had been coming to the set every day to look after him, declined to come on the day we filmed his death scene. She, of course, knew he was dying and seeing him acting out his own death was more than she could bear. I later learned that Charlton Heston was also aware that Robinson was dying. In that death scene, Heston's character, Detective Robert Thorne, showed up outside the room where Robinson was lying in the bed looking for the last time at a video of the past when the earth was still beautiful. I told Thorne that he couldn't speak with the dying Roth, and we ended up in a fight. Naturally, Thorne won, forcing me to allow him to speak with his partner for the final time through a telephone hookup.

I stood right next to Charlton Heston throughout the scene. In fact, it was just the three of us on camera—Heston, Robinson and myself. As I listened to Heston speaking, I was immediately aware of a deep emotional quality in his acting. I have always thought that Charlton was a wonderful actor, but standing next to him at that moment, watching tears roll down his face, I was, myself, moved by the very real intensity of his performance. Thorne learns that his old, dying friend was right about his memories of a better world in the past. It was easily the best scene in the movie.

But it turned out that Charlton wasn't just performing. As director Richard Fleischer later said of Heston's performance in the scene, "Those were real tears." Fleischer also knew that Robinson was dying.

As I mentioned, Charlton was a regular on the tennis courts. Like me, he had a son who was moving up the junior tennis rankings in California. I remember one day in Arcadia Park, I was watching my son Vincent in a junior tournament, and Charlton's son was also playing. Suddenly, out of the corner of my eye, I spotted Charlton about thirty feet away from the courts, standing behind a tree. I thought that said a lot about the kind of man he was. Charlton was a giant star. He wanted to watch his son, but he didn't want to distract attention from him and the other players by sitting in the stands. So he spent the whole time watching his boy play from behind a tree.

A year later I worked a small part in another of these futuristic films of the early seventies, *Westworld*. Written and directed by Michael Crichton, *Westworld*, which starred Yul Brynner, James Brolin and Richard Benjamin, dealt with a kind of virtual reality vacation resort where guests interacted in fictional worlds based on medieval times and the old Wild West. I played one of the guests in West World. Everything was going fine until the robots started thinking for themselves and began killing the guests.

Today we are more accustomed to the idea of robots taking on human characteristics, a theme used effectively in such hits as the *Matrix*, the *Terminator* and *A.I.* But in 1973, the concept was more striking and *Westworld*, with Brynner as a ruthless robot gunslinger hunting down Richard Benjamin and James Brolin, was an unnerving film.

I played a kind of bumbling guest pretending to be a town sheriff. There was one scene where I was tough-talking to a crowd of townspeople about rounding up a posse. When I finished, I turned to open the door to the Sheriff's Office and deliberately let the door hit me in the head for some comic relief. The director, Michael Crichton, thought my improvisation was over the top and asked me to do it again without the stumbling. I, of course, agreed, and we redid the shot.

Over the many years I've learned to take direction well. I always assume that the director has a better overview of the picture and knows what's best. This time, however, I was surprised when I saw the final version in the theater, and there I was banging my head into the door. Another sign of a good director is that he can go back in the cutting room, look at the daily rushes of film, and change his mind about what to use. I'm sure that's what Michael did.

39

MEL

Mel Brooks is one of my very closest friends. About two years ago, I suffered the first of two strokes. I was in my home in Sherman Oaks when it happened. Suddenly I became dizzy and unstable, and a moment later I had fallen into the sofa. I was alone in the house, and a thousand thoughts raced through my head. I was scared to death. I didn't know what was happening, but I sure knew it wasn't good. I managed to fumble my way to the cell phone on the kitchen table. When I got hold of it, I did what everyone does when they're having a stroke—I called a comedian. In this case, my friend Mel Brooks.

Mel answered. I said, "I've got a problem." He said, "What's the matter?" I told him, "I think I'm having a stroke. My whole arm is tingling, and now it's going to my leg." He practically took my ear off as he screamed at me: "Get to an Emergency Room! Call the Emergency Room!"

People who know this story always ask, "Why on earth would you call Mel Brooks when you're having a stroke?" Looking back it does seem a little ridiculous. I guess I should've called a doctor, the police, a family member. Instead, I called a comic— maybe I was just looking for one last laugh on the way out.

But Mel is a really smart guy. He's especially street smart—and street-smart guys are fast thinkers. If I was in a tough spot, like the time I was robbed at gunpoint, I'd want to be with Mel. He's such a quick thinker he'd somehow get us out of the jam. Another close friend of mine is Carl Reiner, who is also good friends with Mel. As I've mentioned, Carl is extremely intelligent, but in a more cerebral way. If I was on one of those quiz programs, the ones where you're allowed to call up somebody—a "lifeline" —when you don't know the answer, I'd call Carl. But if I have another stroke—and if I decide to call a comic again—it'll be Mel.

I met Mel through Merv Griffin. Pat and I were invited by Farrah Fawcett to play tennis at the home of Merv Griffin's ex-wife, Julann on Sundays. It was quite a crazy crowd: Gene Wilder, Gilda Radner, Mel Brooks, Anne Bancroft, Carl and Estelle Reiner, and me and Pat. People ask how we could have gotten any tennis played with all those nuts around. But the truth is we all enjoyed the tennis, and it was more serious, even competitive, than you might think. I ended up playing at Merv's for about ten years. After that, I had a court built on my own property, and then everyone came to our house to play.

Mel had gotten his big break in the early 1960s when he and Buck Henry created, *Get Smart*, the classic show starring Don Adams and Barbara Feldon. After that, he turned to movies and made some of the biggest comedy films of the 1970s: *Blazing Saddles, Young Frankenstein,* and *The History of the World.* Around the time we first met, Mel told me he was going to create' a TV series again. With the title, *When Things Were Rotten,* it would be a satire on Robin Hood.

So, one day we were playing tennis at Merv's, and, as we changed sides, Mel suddenly said to me, "You know, Dick, I've got a part for you in my new series." I asked, "What part?" He said, "I want you to play Friar Tuck." I thought that was a little strange, so I said, "Mel, Friar Tuck was a fat man, and I'm not fat."

Mel responded emphatically: "Yes, Dick, but you have a fat man's face. You have a round, fat man's face."

I wasn't sure if that was a compliment or not. But he went on: "Don't worry about it, we'll pad you up."

Mel gathered together a talented group, some of whom had worked with him before, including Dick Gautier, who played Robin Hood. And he brought in Marty Feldman, who had played Igor in *Young Frankenstein,* to direct. Marty did a great job bringing out the best from Mel's tremendous scripts. It was a terrific show—at least I thought so. We made thirteen episodes, which aired in the fall of 1976 and received some critical acclaim as well as decent ratings for a first-season show. We all thought it was going to run for years.

Still, it hadn't been the smash hit that Mel envisioned, and ABC's new president, Fred Silverman, decided to pull the plug. Mel was furious. The cancellation was sudden and unexpected, and Mel lashed out at the network: "They're standing in line to see Mel Brooks movies, and I'm giving them free Mel Brooks on television and they cancel it." He was so angry he swore he would never do another television show again—and he never has.

Mel enjoyed a long and very happy marriage to Anne Bancroft. He has never really gotten over her tragic death from cancer in June of 2005. At the funeral services, he was inconsolable. He asked all the mourners to please not come up and tell him how sorry they felt. Somehow he thought those small packaged comments we all make at these awkward moments, when there really are no adequate words, were trivial and, in some cases, even insincere. I don't agree, but everyone grieves in their own way and, we all respected Mel's wishes.

The extent of Mel's mourning was evident one day about a year after Anne's death when we were together at the Santa Anita racetrack. It was getting late in the day, and I made a call to Pat to see if she wanted to go to a restaurant that evening. When I hung up, nothing was said about it, and shortly afterwards I went home.

The next day, I saw Mel again, and he said to me: "You know, Dick, you really hurt my feelings yesterday. That was very inconsiderate." I was stunned. I had absolutely no idea what he was talking about. So I asked what I had done to upset him. "You have a wife to go with to a restaurant," he responded, "and I don't."

It had already been clear just how deeply Anne's death had wounded Mel. I felt terrible that I had inadvertently caused my friend to reflect on his own loneliness. At the same time, it made me realize just how much we all take life's simple things for granted. Mel wasn't sad he couldn't go to the Oscars with Anne or meet the President or work on a Broadway play; he was sad because he couldn't eat dinner with her. I've been more sensitive to those seemingly small things ever since.

40

Memory of a Dark Time

During the comeback years, I had an opportunity to work on a wonderful production that made me think about my childhood. Eleven months after I was born, the United States fell into the greatest depression in its history. It's become more relevant to us today, as we now find ourselves in the midst of another widespread economic crisis. Still, we have not, and hopefully will never, reach the depths of what occurred in this country, and around the world, in the 1930s.

As things unraveled, people across the country, and especially in New York City, were being reduced not just to impoverishment, but despair. At a New Year's Eve party in the late 1930s, I remember someone asking my father how long he thought the crisis would last, and all I recall him responding was, "It can't get much worse."

I've mentioned earlier that to a very large degree I was insulated from the most terrible aspects of the Depression. As a child model, radio and stage actor during the 1930s, I simply never knew poverty in the way so many around me experienced it. I recall taking the E-Train to my modeling jobs in Manhattan pretty much oblivious to the fact that just a hundred yards from the train window there were people who made less money in a month than I was going to make in an hour. Although passing it nearly every day, I never saw the makeshift camps that turned Central Park into a squatters' village—movingly depicted in the recent film, *The Cinderella Man*, which told the story of the great boxing champion James J. Braddock, who, for a time, fell victim himself to financial desperation. As a child, the depth of suffering around me was outside both my reality and my imagination—and perhaps it was better that way.

The first time I really thought deeply about that terrible economic plague was in 1971, when I took a part in a made-for-TV stage production of Arthur Miller's, *A Memory of Two Mondays*. Although not one of his most recognizable works, I remember Miller telling me and some of the other cast members on the set that of all his plays, *Memory* was his personal favorite. No doubt because it's largely autobiographical, telling the story of a young man, Bert, working in a New York City warehouse in 1935, as Miller, himself, had done. The youngster obsessively saves his paltry wages in order to get into college and, hopefully, work his way out from under the despair that was crushing the workers around him.

Kristoffer Tabori gave a wonderful performance as young Bert, and the supporting cast, including Estelle Parsons, Jack Warden, George Grizzard and a young Harvey Keitel, were extraordinary. I played the foreman, a decent but limited man who tries the best he can, or at least the best he knows how, to protect his nearly dysfunctional collection of workers from the anger and financial despair that repeatedly triggers their destructive behavior.

At the opening of the Public Broadcast Television production, Miller spoke briefly about the Great Depression, explaining what he believed that period in our past means to Americans: "I can only think of two times in American history," said Miller, "when we were all in the same boat—the Civil War and the Great Depression." Miller died just a few years ago, but I imagine he would have added the days following the attacks of September 11, 2001, as another of those moments when Americans were once again "all in the same boat."

But my life was an exception to Miller's idea. I certainly lived through the Great Depression, and there was a terrible poverty and despair all around me, but I didn't feel it the same way that most everyone else did—and certainly not the way Miller had. For most Americans, the Depression meant poverty, hunger, and, most of all, a faltering, if not a complete loss of hope. Hope is always our light to find a way out of a dark place. And in the Great Depression hope meant one thing above all—having a job. Miller's play is so powerful because he understood the importance of work; he recognized that unemployment, even the fear of being without work, has the power to reduce all of us to something terrible. A hungry man with a family to support will endure every manner of indignation, or break in the process.

My life was different. It would make a more dramatic story if I felt as though I was riding in that same boat or if this book was a story, like Miller's own life on which the play is based, of a man overcoming terrible adversity and triumphing in the end. That's a story many of my contemporaries can tell, some of whom really suffered impoverished childhoods or were devastated as young adults by the crisis. But it wasn't my story. The truth is that I don't remember those fears in my childhood. They would come later in life for me and under different circumstances, but not growing up in New York City in the 1930s.

In fact, my biggest problem was juggling all the different jobs—running from the modeling agency to the theater, to the radio station, always conscious of hard deadlines. I was paid what was considered an enormous amount of money at the time. I honestly cannot recall a moment when money was not coming in on a regular basis. I'm sure my parents were worried about it, but for me, I never knew anything different. And my father was never out of work, and so I didn't experience that sense of foreboding, that terrible feeling that disaster was just a moment away; that mindset that had poisoned so much of the world that surrounded me.

But it did affect other kids in the shows. The full Depression hit a year after I was born. But it lasted right up until the start of the Second World War, with some of the deepest parts coming in the late 1930s, nearly ten years after it started. Because it lasted so long, Joyce, who was five years younger than me, saw its effects—often with greater clarity than I did. She remembers the kids who were onstage because their jobs were their families' only source of income. Many of these kids never had speaking lines in the plays, and their participation carried little of the glamour associated with being an actor on Broadway. Joyce was shocked when she first went to visit some of the other kids at their homes—many of whom lived in crowded tenements on New York's lower east side.

The production of *Memory of Two Mondays* was a powerful reminder of how fortunate we all are. It also spoke to the fragility of our present circumstances. With the advent of the Second World War, the Great Depression finally lifted. Hopefully, we will find a way out of the present crisis without having to endure a similar catastrophe.

41

BACK TO BROADWAY

With the phones ringing again in Hollywood, an opportunity suddenly arose to return to Broadway. Marlo Thomas, the daughter of one of my all-time favorite comedians, Danny Thomas, had enjoyed great success with her television show, *That Girl*, a situation "dramedy" about a single, aspiring actress in New York City. It was a groundbreaking show, and I was fortunate to have made a couple of guest appearances during its final season. With its focus on the difficulties of being a single woman making her own way in the big city, *That Girl* was unique to television. The show quickly attracted millions of viewers and made Marlo a star.

I had enjoyed working with Marlo. On the set, I mentioned my admiration for her father, something I'm sure she heard often. I also told her that I had seen him perform in Boston many years earlier. In 1974, after *That Girl* had been off the air for a few years, I received a call asking if I'd be interested in a part in a theatrical production that Marlo was bringing to Broadway called *Thieves*. It dealt with a marriage that after twelve years was falling apart. I would play a neurotic neighbor.

It was a difficult decision. I was getting busy in Hollywood, and my family had adapted to the change from New York. Taking the part would mean an extended time away from them. But my agent Mary Ellen White and I both felt that a successful run on Broadway would be good for my career in Hollywood. Many film and television actors take time to work in theater. It increases their visibility and enhances their reputation as an actor. I also thought that working with Marlo would be wonderful.

In the spring of 1974, I returned to my old apartment in the Des Artistes. It felt good to be back in the old neighborhood and working again on Broadway. During one of the rehearsals at the Broadhurst Theater, Marlo's father, Danny Thomas, came backstage. As is well known, throughout his life, Danny had been a tireless advocate for children's charities and particularly for St. Jude's Hospital in Memphis, Tennessee, where children with cancer are treated. Danny spoke to us about the charity and encouraged us to contribute, which most of us did.

Thieves opened in April of 1974. It was an instant hit and ran for seven months. I received wonderful reviews, and some of the critics even remembered me from the old days. "Dick Van Patten was a child star only a few seasons ago," wrote Jack O' Brien of New Jersey's *Star Ledger*. "Where did the years, and his hair, go! His gifted stage skills didn't." Other reviews were terrific, and we used them on a redone résumé that Mary Ellen sent around as 1975 approached.

42

CONNING THE CON MAN

When *Thieves* closed, I headed back to Hollywood. During the early years of my West Coast comeback, two of my sons, Vincent and Nels, were fast developing as standout tennis players. As a result, we all became involved in a number of celebrity tennis tournaments. When we attended an event in Denver, Colorado, in June of 1975, Vincent was seventeen years old and still known mostly as a teenage actor who happened to be a good tennis player.

Bobby Riggs was also there. One day he approached me and said: "I hear your kid is pretty good. I'll betcha ten thousand he can't beat me." I laughed and told him I couldn't afford that kind of bet.

Riggs was, of course, near the height of his notoriety as a tennis con man. But he was much more than that. In his prime during the 1940s, Bobby Riggs was the number one tennis player in the world. I happen to be friendly with the great tennis legend Jack Kramer, and Jack has always touted Riggs's stature, claiming in his book that Bobby is the most underrated tennis player in history. Jack would know since he was the one who eventually took the top position in the world away from Riggs in 1948.

Riggs's second life began when he started a career as a tennis con man. He was really more of a showman, making outrageous comments and challenging everyone to bet on a match, often giving his opponents some crazy advantage like placing a set of chairs on his side of the court, which he would have to run around to hit the ball. His star rose in the spring of 1973, when Margaret Court, very possibly the greatest female player in tennis history, agreed to meet Riggs in an exhibition match. We don't hear much about Margaret these days, but she is still the all-time leader in major tournament singles titles with twenty-four, including a real Grand Slam, which means winning all four majors in the same year. Only Margaret, Steffi Graff and Maureen Connolly have accomplished that feat. And only two men have done it: Don Budge and Rod Laver, who did it twice!

It was a mistake for Margaret to take Riggs's challenge. But at the time it probably didn't seem like much of a big deal. She lost badly on Mother's Day, May 13, 1973. It ended up grabbing more publicity than anyone expected, making the cover of *Sports Illustrated* and *Time*. Instead of being an isolated, modestly-publicized event, it became a prelude to the match everyone now wanted to see, Riggs against Billy Jean King, not because Billy Jean was better than Margaret—in fact Margaret had won the French Open before her match with Riggs and the U.S. Open before Billy Jean's match with Riggs. But Billy was far more outspoken on women's issues than Margaret, who was shy and reserved. Margaret, now long retired, works as a pentecostal minister in Australia.

Riggs versus King was everything the promoters hoped for. On September 20, 1973, Billy Jean King beat Bobby Riggs at the Houston Astrodome in the most watched tennis match in history. Even though Riggs had retired from professional tennis over twenty-five years earlier, the result was still a shock to many. Billy had played smart. Like Margaret, Billy Jean preferred to charge the net. But in the Riggs match she decided to stay in the back court, a brilliant strategy causing the fifty-five year old Bobby to tire out. Although he lost, Riggs quickly became one of the most recognizable people in America, and he parlayed his new fame into even more challenges on and off the tennis courts. The truth is I liked the guy, and we shared a penchant for betting.

So while I didn't take Riggs up on his first offer, after speaking with Vincent, we agreed to a smaller amount. So they played. Vincent won a close match in a tie breaker, and Riggs paid me right after the match—which also means he had ten thousand dollars ready if I had taken the bigger bet!

Riggs wanted a rematch, but it didn't happen until October when Vincent met up with him in another celebrity tennis tournament. And Vincent beat him again—this time, like Billy Jean—he won by using his head. After his match with Billy Jean, Riggs had published a book, *Court Hustler*, teaching the tricks of winning with your mind. Vincent read the book and employed some of Riggs's own tactics against him. When the match ended, Riggs told the press: "The kid reads my book and knows all my tricks." He also paid Vincent a very nice compliment, telling the press: "I've got to stop giving away my trade secrets. No wonder I couldn't beat you. It was like playing against myself when I was in my prime." In his "prime," Riggs was the best tennis player in the world, so that was certainly high praise.

They played a final time at the LA Convention Center. It wasn't advertised, but there were hundreds of people watching. Vincent won again, and Riggs gave me the thousand bucks on the spot. But he was annoyed. Nels and Casey both went to the match, and one thing stood out in their minds. In the early stages, Vincent was handling Riggs fairly easily. And so Riggs, in an attempt to upset Vincent's rhythm, changed from his standard Dunlop Maxply to a huge oversized racket. We had never seen anything like that, and Nels wondered if it was legal. Later, of course, the oversized Prince racquet would be enormously popular, and today most players use a racket bigger than the old wooden ones. But at the time, it looked ridiculous. It was designed to throw Vincent off his game. But it didn't work, and Bobby, as always, paid up when the match was over.

I enjoyed my dealings with Bobby Riggs, and not just because my son got the best of him. The truth is we shared an appetite for putting it on the line. He was a real character. Vincent also stayed friendly with him and years later worked with him in a movie starring Ron Silver titled *When Billy Beat Bobby*. I also respected Riggs. In his youth, he had been a great champion, the best player in the world. But he also showed that a guy could still get out and play and enjoy athletics into his old age. I played tennis nearly every day of life into my late 70s—right up until my first stroke. There was more to Riggs's message than just the overly-publicized battle of the sexes. And in the end, he also became close to Billy Jean. She spoke to him right before he died in 1995, and the last thing she said to him was "I love you." I give her a lot of credit. In the end, Bobby Riggs, despite his sometimes controversial antics, was a class act.

43

FARRAH

Each generation has its feminine icon. There's no way to fully understand the phenomenon, but the world—and particularly the world of men—seem to regularly come together like a wolf pack to elevate some woman to a status above all others. The women they choose are the women who have "it." What exactly "it" is remains a mystery, but of all the women I've seen through the years, Marilyn Monroe had it; so did Jean Harlow, Betty Grable, Sophia Loren, Liz Taylor and Raquel Welch. In the 1970s Farrah had "it."

One thing these women have in common is, of course, beauty—in fact, stunning beauty. But that doesn't tell the half of it. They also have that special something, a charisma that eludes precise definition. And yet despite its elusive character, we all know exactly who they are; we all know because each one of them projects a self-image that somehow manages to ignite the imagination of entire generations.

I first met Farrah Fawcett while my son Vincent was doing a show, *Apples Way*, with my good friend and longtime neighbor, Ronnie Cox. One day this beautiful young woman did a guest appearance on the show.

In the meantime, Farrah and my wife Pat, who was sitting with Vincent on the set, were also becoming very friendly. In time Pat would choreograph some of the dance skits on *Charlie's Angels,* and she and Farrah remained the very best of friends up until Farrah's death.

I remember early on telling Bill Sheppard of Disney that I knew a young actress who might be good to have in one of their movies. They met with Farrah, and I recall his humorous and prescient response when he said to me, "Dick, we're trying to promote a wholesome look over here. This girl's a knockout."

That was, of course, true. In fact, it was around this time that Farrah made that transition into something bigger than life with her historic poster, which within months was the biggest seller in the world, eventually smashing all records for poster sales. It was even shot into outer space as part of a time capsule launched in a NASA space probe in 1977. At around the same time of the poster's release, September of 1976, Farrah debuted on *Charlie's Angels*. And with the new role, the poster and her own marvelous charisma, Farrah transformed into the biggest sex icon of her generation. It was amazing for us to watch this fun-loving, witty young woman, who had none of that self-destructive craving for stardom too common among Hollywood celebrities, transform unexpectedly into this giant iconic figure.

In the meantime, Farrah remained a close friend of our family, especially to Pat. In recent years she had been a model of dignity and courage as she fought her battle with cancer. Pat was by her side throughout much of her struggle, even visiting her in Germany while she received treatment. One of our most treasured possessions is a beautiful picture of Farrah in her famous red bathing suit in which she signed: "For my second family, I love you, Farrah."

I always believed that if anyone could win that fight it would be Farrah. Survival involves the will to live, to persevere against the odds. Farrah had those qualities and more and became a wonderful role model for those afflicted with this terrible disease. Before her death, she made headlines again with her television special, *Farrah's Story*, about her struggle with cancer. Many have expressed different views on whether she should have done it. I don't have an easy answer for that, but I do know that it took guts. And if that show makes it easier for even one person to face this terrible scourge of cancer, then it was certainly worth it. In the end, Pat and I believe that Farrah's courage and dignity throughout her long ordeal will be her greatest legacy.

Upon hearing of her death, Farrah's millions of friends and fans poured out their words celebrating her life and expressing sadness at her leaving. Of them all, Pat and I were especially moved by the beautiful tribute of her former *Charlie's Angels* co-star, Jaclyn Smith, who simply said: "Farrah had courage, she had strength, and she had faith. And now she has peace as she rests with the real angels."

44

GOODBYE

When my mother became seriously ill, also with cancer, she had been living nearby in Los Angeles for the past few years. In the spring of 1976, her cancer had spread, and soon she was in the end-stage and had to be hospitalized.

Hearing the prognosis, my father came to California to see Jo for the last time. When he arrived, Casey took him to see her at the Brotman Memorial Hospital in Culver City. To alleviate the pain, Mom was receiving injections of morphine every three hours and was not always lucid. When Casey and Dad entered her room, she was asleep. Dad knelt down by her bedside and went to kiss her hand. At just that moment her eyes opened, and she saw my father for the first time in many years. "Dick, what are you doing here?" she said. He lied and told her he just happened to be out visiting his family and heard she was not feeling well. Casey listened as they spoke for a few minutes about old times, and I was so happy later when I heard this.

Yet, even at the end, Mom just couldn't leave well enough alone.

"When did you arrive?" she began interrogating Dad.

"Just yesterday."

"How was your flight?"

"Oh, I didn't fly, I took the train."

Mom paused for a moment.

"Why would you take the train, Dick?"

"Well, it's so interesting, you meet people; you get to see the country...."

With that, Mom looked over at Casey with a look of disdain: "I just can't believe it. After all these years, he's still so cheap!"

That was Jo—a straight talker, right to the end.

In truth, Dad really was the kind of man who would enjoy the adventure of a cross-country train ride. But this time, seeing the countryside and meeting an assortment of characters along the way, was, no doubt, a bittersweet experience as he journeyed to see the girl he first loved for the last time.

When Jo died, on May 17, 1976, my father felt there was something that needed saying—some acknowledgment of all she had done for us. He wrote to Joyce and me: "I feel that it is not enough to have lived selflessly all those years, as she did, and then just die and that's the end of it."

But that wasn't "the end of it." Together my parents left an extraordinary legacy. They gave to their children and grandchildren a genuine love of entertainment—a love sparked that magical night in 1928 when Mom and Dad were stagestruck by Edna Ferber's *Showboat*. They went on to create not only young children with stage careers, but an entire family of entertainers. They watched as their grandchildren grew into accomplished actors. Vincent even became a child star. They saw Jimmy and Nels, as well as Joyce's children, Casey and Talia Balsam in numerous shows, plays and films. And my Dad watched his son, Tim Van Patten—my half-brother, although a contemporary of my children—become a teenage star in *The White Shadow* and go on to be recognized as one of the finest directors in television. The legacy my parents left behind was one to be tremendously proud of. Jo didn't just die and, as my father feared, that was "the end of it."

Dad, of course, fully understood Jo's legacy, but he wanted to make sure that we also understood—that Joyce and I fully appreciated the fact that Mom, while flawed like everyone, really had sacrificed so much for us and for all her family. For such a woman, Dad wrote to us, "something more enduring must be stated." To find the right words, he turned again to his trusted muse, ending his letter with Portia's judgment that even a small light of goodness shines bright amidst the troubles and turbulence we make for ourselves. Borrowing from the Bard, he wrote of my mother: "her life will stand out as 'a good deed in a naughty world.'" Dad got it just right.

Since Mom's death, there is one thing that has always bothered me: she never got to see my success in *Eight Is Enough*. She worked her whole life to make that happen. Within a year after her death, I had the lead in one of the most popular television shows of the decade. It would have meant a great deal to her. It might have been a final confirmation that all her sacrifices had been worth it. In fact, my sister Joyce recently commented on what a great shame it was that Jo didn't live just a little longer to watch *Eight Is Enough* take off. Life rarely works out exactly as we plan, but I've never forgotten the role my mother played in preparing me for that success. Nor has a day gone by when I haven't thought of her. She was one of a kind, and saying goodbye to her was the hardest thing I've ever had to do.

45

EIGHT IS ENOUGH

Eight Is Enough was a family show at a time in America when family life had been challenged by a series of social changes, some of which were positive and others less so. When the pilot aired in 1977, Americans were just coming out of the rebellions of the 1960s and early 1970s. The Vietnam War had ended only a few years earlier, and the Watergate scandal had shaken confidence in public officials and institutions. Everyone living through that period knew that many of the values we cherished as Americans had been put to a severe test. As a result, I think there was a genuine desire among many people to restore a semblance of normalcy and stability in American life. That desire was reflected in the kind of television people chose to watch.

The enormous popularity of *Eight Is Enough* was, I suspect, connected to a feeling of comfort people experienced in watching the exploits—often harebrained exploits—of this big, loving and goofy family. The Bradfords were not wrapped up in war, economic crisis or the battle over America's culture that had preoccupied the country for so long. For many people, the Bradfords represented a reaffirmation of the primacy of family life in a world that had long seemed consumed with other things.

But that's not to say the show turned a blind eye to the world. I've always believed the writers of *Eight Is Enough*, particularly the creator and head-writer Bill Blinn, found just the right mix of that idyllic world inside the Bradford household with events outside the home that were not so idyllic. Bill had no desire to create just another family comedy with cardboard characters who lived uncomplicated lives. In an interview, Blinn noted that one appealing aspect of the book, *Eight Is Enough* is that Tom Braden had put up no pretenses: "Braden was flawed," Blinn recalled. "His family was flawed. His kids were flawed. As we all are. And [Braden] acknowledged it." That honesty caused the reader not only to recognize the family as realistic, but also to identify emotionally with the issues they confronted and the often less than perfect way they resolved them.

Being a family television show, *Eight Is Enough* episodes usually had happy endings. Yet in the process we managed to touch on a good number of themes carrying real lessons about the difficulties we all confront in life—especially in the years in which our children are coming of age—and how to better manage them in this rapidly changing world. There were episodes dealing with drug abuse, interracial dating, premarital sex, single parenthood and a great number of related topics that would have been considered off-limits for prime-time television just a few years earlier.

We were not the only show addressing such topics. Nor did we address them as strongly as others. *All in the Family* was a truly groundbreaking show, far more stark in raising such issues as bigotry than *Eight Is Enough*. There were others as well. But we did it in the context of a family that was not dysfunctional. If we dealt with divorce, it may have been a softer version, but it was represented in a world that was not angry or hostile toward marriage.

The most important recurring theme involved the difficulties of coming of age. There comes a time when children realize that life is not always what it seems. We began with eight different children, both boys and girls, so the writers could imagine the problems confronted by children at all different stages of development, and they did this with great success.

* * *

The casting of *Eight Is Enough* had been a difficult process. As Bill Blinn described it, the auditions were about more than just finding talented young actors. Bill recalls kids who were terrific standing alone, but less believable when matched with others. The key was getting the "chemistry" right. And even the final selections for the pilot episode turned out to be less than final. In fact, four of the eight original Bradford kids were replaced by the time the first season aired.

My head was also on the chopping block. It turns out Bill Blinn was opposed to my getting the part. He preferred an unknown actor, someone the public would see as a fresh face. And by this time, with my career now revived, that wasn't me.

Through the years I came to greatly admire Bill's work in writing and overseeing the development of the show. More than anyone, in my view, Bill was responsible for the great success of *Eight Is Enough*. But I'll take the liberty of saying that on this one point, and with the benefit of hindsight, Bill may have gotten it wrong. Fortunately—and without my knowing it—I had friends in high places. Actually there was one friend, and he was in the very highest place—Fred Silverman, the President of ABC.

As I heard the story, after working with another actor for a few days, Fred thought the performances needed to be a little more upbeat and comical. Fred, an old fan of *I Remember Mama*, told the producers: "Dick Van Patten has a funny bone." And that was that. As Bill Blinn commented in very good nature: "Silverman, one, Blinn, zero." It certainly made me happy. In fact, I've never hesitated in saying that I owe everything to Fred Silverman. His decision propelled my career back to a place I hadn't known since *Mama* closed down over twenty years earlier.

Like *I Remember Mama*, *Eight Is Enough* was designed to be a show with two parents sharing the task of raising their children. I had learned from *Mama*, as well as *The Goldbergs*, the importance of the mother's character in the center of family life. Peggy Wood's ability to fill that role had been central to *Mama's* success. It was critical that the producers find someone equally gifted to play Tom Bradford's wife, Joan.

I could not have been more pleased to learn that my friend, Diana Hyland, was in the running. Diana was a marvelous actress whom I had worked with in New York on *Young Doctor Malone*. I was delighted the day she called to say she landed the role. She seemed so happy at the time, and, once my own position was secured, we looked forward to working together for as long as the show lasted—hopefully for years.

Diana had just finished filming a television movie, *The Boy in the Plastic Bubble*. She was the mother of a child whose immune system had been so completely destroyed that he was forced to live in a sterile environment. She played that maternal role so beautifully that I have no doubt the producers of *Eight Is Enough* were hoping Diana would bring those same qualities to our show. Diana won an Emmy for Best Supporting Actress for her performance in *The Boy in the Plastic Bubble*. Sadly she would not live long enough to accept the award.

John Travolta played Diana's son in the film. A talented young actor and dancer from Brooklyn, New York, John had not yet exploded into the American consciousness as the principal image of the new disco dance craze and a cultural icon of the 1970s. Although a good deal younger than Diana, the two fell in love on the set of *The Boy in the Plastic Bubble*. At the time there were some skeptics because of the age difference, but I can say from my own observations that John and Diana were deeply in love.

No one connected to *Eight Is Enough* knew Diana was dying of cancer. On every television series, the actors are required to obtain medical clearance from a studio doctor. Obviously it's important for the producers to know if someone is ill. Continuity of characters in a series is critical, and the studios are investing tremendous sums of money, relying on the ability of the actors to continue playing their parts. It's a mystery to me how the doctors could have missed diagnosing Diana's cancer, which must have already advanced to a critical stage. But somehow they didn't see it, and we were all extremely happy that Diana would be playing Joan Bradford.

As expected, Diana was wonderful in the pilot and the three following episodes. I still remember John Travolta picking her up at the studio. They seemed so genuinely happy together, it would have been hard to imagine that she was carrying a terrible burden. But the truth was that her cancer was rapidly progressing.

In retrospect, Diana's final episode, *Turnabout*, held a really ironic twist. In it David, played by Grant Goodeve, began dating an older woman—David was nineteen and his new girlfriend, Jennifer, thirty. Tom was upset by the age difference and raised the issue to Joan at bedtime. He told her: "I just don't understand how a mature, healthy woman can be attracted to someone David's age." Diana, as Joan, took David's side: "Well, men can appreciate a firm young body, why should women be any different?"

I wonder if Diana was thinking of her own relationship with John Travolta during this discussion. In fact, there is a kind of eerie moment when the possibility is suggested in the show that this is some kind of Freudian fixation and that David is really in love with his mother. What makes it stranger, still, is that Grant Goodeve bore a bit of a resemblance to John, and the scenes between Grant and Diana took on an added component in light of all of this. I never asked him, but it's hard to believe that Bill Blinn in writing the episode wasn't in some way influenced by the real-life relationship between John and Diana—if not consciously, then perhaps at some deeper level. In any event, it was another example of *Eight Is Enough* taking on the somewhat controversial topic of age differences in relationships, while still continuing to present an image of family wholesomeness.

Shortly after we began filming the first season, Diana became too sick to continue. At first she seemed to have some kind of injury, but after just four episodes, she would never come back. Her collapse was rapid. Pat and I visited her as she was dying. I'll never forget ringing the doorbell at her home when John Travolta came to the door. It immediately struck us that he was wearing his famous three-piece, white suit from the movie, *Saturday Night Fever*. Apparently Diana loved to see him in that outfit.

John quickly told us it was almost over. We went into Diana's room and tried to give her some encouragement. But as soon as I saw her, I knew this was the end. I asked if she would like to see a priest. John agreed, and I called Father Bob Curtis. He came to the house and administered the last rites of the Catholic Church.

Soon, Diana was unresponsive. In a few minutes, with me, Pat, John and Diana's mother all in the room, she died. It was a terrible moment. John was devastated.

I helped with a few of the practical arrangements. There was a need to have some legal papers signed by her next of kin. Diana had not yet divorced, so that meant they needed the agreement of her estranged husband to proceed with the funeral arrangements. Pat and I drove to his home, and after some initial reluctance, he signed the document in the presence of his attorney. It was all very bizarre. More important, I had lost a friend and colleague, and it affected me deeply. I also gained a tremendous respect for John who stood by Diana throughout her entire illness, never abandoning her for a moment in her time of need. He showed real character, and I know that he suffered immensely.

After Diana's death, many of us believed the show would be cancelled. Already four episodes into the season, it seemed impossible to simply shove another woman into the role as though nothing had happened. But while Bill Blinn and the producers understood things were looking dismal, they came up with the idea of weaving a new love interest into Tom's life. It was a gamble, but one that paid off in the end. We all felt lucky that the show wasn't pulled right off the air.

In the pilot, the part of my oldest son David had been played by an unknown actor named Mark Hamill. At the time, Mark was filming the lead role in a new science fiction movie by George Lucas, the director of *American Graffiti*. The film was having production difficulties, and they kept putting off its release date. Still, there was a buzz in the air that it was going to be something special. Just two months after the first season of *Eight Is Enough* began airing in March of 1977, *Star Wars* hit the theaters, catapulting Mark from my son David in a pilot television program to one of the most recognizable actors in the world as the swashbuckling Jedi knight, Luke Skywalker.

But before the world came to know Mark as the hero battling Darth Vader and the "dark side," he did his share to help us market *Eight Is Enough*. In fact, the pilot is largely centered on the strained relationship between David and Tom. The pilot was actually the first of many of those "coming of age" storylines on *Eight Is Enough*. It reflected the tensions arising when a young man's need to break from the restraints of home collides with a parent's resistance to his efforts for independence. When this happens, something has to give way. In the pilot, David moved out of the house and rented his own apartment.

The final scene was, in my view, one of the best in the entire series of *Eight Is Enough*. Realizing that he may have been too restrictive, and not wanting to lose the affection of his son, Tom swallows his pride and visits David at his new apartment. Upon entering, things immediately take a turn for the worse as Tom notices a piece of woman's clothing on the floor. It's obvious David has female company. In this scene, Bill Blinn wrote some beautiful dialogue reflecting the bond between a man and his son—a bond stronger than the disagreements they have about how to live their lives.

That central tension between father and son remained with the show until the very end. Much later my old friend David Wayne would help out in a two-part episode of *Eight Is Enough*, where, once again, the age-old conundrum of parent/child discord was front and center. Coincidentally, David, who came in as Matt, Tom Bradford's estranged father, had also played my father in *The American Way* in 1939. Now, forty years later, and with a little more grey, we did it again. I wonder if there have ever been two actors who played father and son with a forty-year gap.

In the show, Tom's father was a dreamer, a man who abandoned his family in search of something more—some elusive dream he would never find. He ends up in Hawaii, where we shot on location. In a beautiful scene reminiscent of that poignant moment with Mark Hamill in the pilot, David and I—father and son—nursing drinks in an empty Hawaiian barroom, found a way to reconcile. David Wayne was a wonderful actor whose career over many years oddly and fortuitously intersected with my own. I was sad to hear of his death in 1993.

The pilot, thus, established the thematic framework for the rest of the series. With my son, David, gone from the home, the rest of the children fought over his room, the first of many domestic squabbles over scarce family possessions. It was an idea that persisted throughout the series. In addition to this innocent bickering, one of the daughters, Susan, played by Susan Richardson, was arrested for marijuana possession.

With the pilot raising issues about both premarital sex and drugs, *Eight Is Enough* was marketed not just as a show representing family values, but as one that would not shy away from difficult topics simply because they were controversial. In *Eight Is Enough* these issues were rarely viewed as black and white. Just as Tom Bradford was conflicted over his son's right to independence, Susan's drug possession was presented as an obstacle to be overcome, rather than a pronouncement of moral outrage against any teenager who experimented with marijuana.

* * *

It's impossible for me to point to any one of the kids in *Eight Is Enough* as better than the others. But it's certainly true that casting Adam Rich as little Nicholas was a stroke of genius, dumb luck—or both. At age eight, Adam was an uncanny natural. He melded childhood innocence with the acting skills of a seasoned adult. His enormously powerful screen presence prompted the phenomenon of "Nicholas-mania" among throngs of women infatuated with his irresistible charm. Years after the show, one of our premier directors, Harry Harris, described an incident during the shooting of an episode in San Diego. Adam needed to use the bathroom, but there was a mass of women between him and the door. When Adam saw them, Harris recalled, he was literally "shaking." Harris had to ask a local policeman to escort Adam to and from the men's room.

Even thirty years later, people still comment on Adam's unique charm. In fact, it's no surprise that in response to President Obama's reference to the show, Michael Malone wrote that the President had "smiled a bit," perhaps "because you can't not smile when a picture of young Adam Rich in a bowl cut comes to mind." He's right. There was a quality Adam brought to the role of Nicholas that was simply unforgettable. He really did leave you smiling. In my nearly eighty years in the entertainment business, I've seen thousands, if not, tens of thousands, of child actors, but I don't think I've ever seen anything more magical than Adam Rich playing Nicholas Bradford. The success of *Eight Is Enough* was the result of a wondrous convergence of so many marvelous performers, writers and producers, but, in my mind, it was Adam more than anyone who kept the viewers coming back for more.

In the second season, I recall being pleased when I received a script for an episode, titled: *Who's on First?* As mentioned, I had been a lifelong fan of Abbott and Costello. Lou and Bud had so many great skits, but one of my favorites, and perhaps their most enduring, was their famous "Who's on First?" It was one of those fast-paced routines in which timing is critical.

The storyline for the episode involved a school variety show in which Tom and Nicholas perform the famous "Who's on First?" routine. I have to admit I was initially a bit apprehensive. Having seen the great Abbott and Costello do it so many times, I just wasn't sure we could pull it off. It requires a good deal of skill, especially Lou's Costello's part, which would be played by Adam. I wasn't at all convinced that any child Adam's age could make it work. But I should have known better. It took just one rehearsal to convince me I should be worrying about me and not Adam.

The writers had changed the premise from a baseball game to a school variety show. So I came out onstage and asked Nicholas about the lineup for the show—one that would feature acts by three different groups calling themselves, "What," Who" and "Yes."

Nicholas:	*There's going to be three groups playing.*
Tom:	*What's the name of the first group?*
Nicholas:	*Who.*
Tom:	*That's what I want to find out?*
Nicholas:	*What's that?*
Tom:	*Who's the group that's going to play—the first group?*
Nicholas:	*Well, if you know, why are you asking me?*
Tom:	*Wait a minute! The second group, do they have a name?*
Nicholas:	*Yes.*
Tom:	*Well what's their name?*
Nicholas:	*Yes.*
Tom:	*Okay, you told me, now who's the second group?*
Nicholas:	*No, Who's the first group.*

And so it went…Adam, with his impeccable timing, had everyone in stitches.

Another very special and memorable episode featuring Adam, as well as Willie Aames as Tommy, was the two-part Christmas show, *Yes, Nicholas, There Is a Santa Claus*. The title came from a Christmas article Tom wrote for his newspaper in which he affirmed that Christmas is not only a time for celebration, but "a time for reassessing the value of our lives." It had been a difficult year for the family since Joan's death, and their Christmas would be the first one without her. Because of that, and because the kids were getting older, many of them wanted to spend Christmas day elsewhere, or were less than enthusiastic about the holiday.

Tommy was particularly disinterested and cynical. Abby, now his stepmother, saw that Tommy's indifference was a front for a far deeper problem—the loss of his mother. She discovers a gift hidden in a silver chalice on a kitchen shelf. She realizes it was left there for Tommy by Joan before she died. Tom explains to Abby that throughout the year Joan was always looking for a special gift for each of the children. When she found one, she would hide it away for the following Christmas.

In one of the most touching moments of the series, Tom, at the end of the show, gives the gift to his son. Tommy realizes it's from his deceased mother. In one of the strongest performances in all of *Eight Is Enough*, Willie Aames managed to touch a special emotional chord that resonated with all of us and is still beautiful to watch today. The gift from his mother is a book of poetry. And it's particularly special to Tommy because his mother knew he had a sensitive side, which at times made him feel less masculine than his older brother and friends. The book contained a message from Joan. She wrote to Tommy: "It is not unmanly to be sensitive. Be happy that you are. It makes you even more of a man...." As I read the message out loud, it was impossible for everyone on the set to keep the tears away.

A large part of what made the scene so very wrenching was the strange coincidence of reality and fiction. The character Joan Bradford had died, just as Diana Hyland, who played her in the show, had died. All of us, except Betty, had been on the show at the time of Diana's death. I know that as the camera panned the room and paused at each of the saddened, tearful faces of all those kids, there was a mix of acting and genuine sadness. I know that's how it was for me.

To complicate matters, the Bradfords were robbed that night by a burglar. The thief was a cynical old man played by the veteran actor and political activist, Will Geer, who died shortly after the show aired. Geer had become famous as Grandpa Zeb in *The Waltons*, and his character, a lonely guy who had come to despise the holiday spirit, added a special poignancy to the Christmas episode. In many ways the show recalled the famous Christmas episode of *I Remember Mama*. And as with the thieves in *Mama*, the Bradfords end up bringing the thief into their home to celebrate the holiday.

* * *

Just as Nicholas won the hearts of millions of viewers, his oldest sibling, David, was also making fans. But now it wasn't Mark Hamill. In fact, as it became more apparent that *Star Wars* was going to be a hit movie, with the likelihood of sequels given Lucas's original conception of a series of trilogies, Mark wanted out of his contract with *Eight Is Enough*. ABC, however, had other ideas. They naturally thought it would be great to have a big movie star in the show, and so they refused to let him go.

But fate intervened. In December of 1976, just as we were about to start shooting the first season, Mark was in a terrible car crash, suffering serious injuries that required reconstructive surgery on his face. I'm sure it was an awful time for Mark, but in time he pulled through and was eventually able to return to those Star Wars sequels. But the accident did end his days as David Bradford. With Mark recovering in the hospital, and the TV schedule pressing, ABC hired a talented young actor named Grant Goodeve to step in as the oldest Bradford child.

Grant was an immediate sensation. Much of his success, I believe, was due to his ability to successfully portray two different aspects of the character. He conveyed the maturity of an older brother, who often took on the role of substitute father, while still struggling with his own transition to adulthood. In an episode titled, *Fast and Loose*, David is stunned when his friend drops dead of a massive heart attack right in the middle of their conversation. For the first time in his life, he is confronted with the harsh reality that life is fragile and death often arbitrary. He asks his father: "What's it all worth, Dad. All the hassles and work you put into making something good out of life if it can all just end like that?" My only response is, "It's worth as much as you can make of it." But that's not nearly enough. David will have to find his own way through this crisis.

Like many young people searching for meaning in their lives, David rebels. At his friend's grave he promises: "I'll live enough for the both of us. From now on it's going to be fast and loose." And so he begins a journey of reckless and self-destructive behavior. He spirals downward until he finds himself on the brink of alienating and even losing his own family. In the end, David finds his way back, recognizing that despite inexplicable and senseless tragedies, people have to move forward, no matter how painful.

David will never be quite the same. But he will learn to cope with the blows life deals us. I think that's a passage we all, sooner or later, have to make. In the wake of tragedy, there's always a temptation to lose faith in the meaning of our lives. Grant's portrayal of a young man at that crossroad was, in my view, an example of *Eight Is Enough* at its best.

On a lighter note, the family itself takes a big step forward toward normalcy when, in the second season, Tom married Abby. One of the biggest television episodes of the 1970s, more than half the television sets in America were tuned to the Bradford nuptials during a two-hour special titled, *Children of the Groom*. The wedding was the happy fruition of Bill Blinn's idea that ultimately saved the show. According to Bill, his sister had told him about a friend who tutored the children of a widower and then ended up marrying the guy. Bill grabbed the idea, and, in a wonderful instance of art imitating life, it worked perfectly.

Still, there were complications—particularly with the younger children. Both Nicholas and Elizabeth view the marriage as putting a further distance between themselves and their real mother. As the whole family enthusiastically prepares for the wedding, Elizabeth bitterly complains: "No one even mentions Mom." Nicholas is just as dejected—still believing his mom will be mad at all the commotion when she finally comes back. In a poignant scene, Elizabeth, played by Connie Newton, explains the truth to her little brother: "Nicholas, Mom isn't coming home." But, Nicholas refuses to believe it: "She's a good mother, and good mothers don't leave their kids for ever and ever."

Connie, Adam and the writers successfully captured not just the sadness of Joan's death, but the guilt we all experience from moving on. After such a tragedy, I think it's always difficult to believe that the acceptance of a new person no longer counts as a betrayal of the one who's gone. Elizabeth had to understand and internalize that idea before she could ever accept Abby. In the end, she does, but only when Abby persuades her she will never try to replace Joan. With that understanding, they begin a new and better relationship as Abby asks Elizabeth to be her Maid of Honor at the wedding.

* * *

Eight Is Enough aired during a time of changing racial attitudes in the United States. By the 1970s, things had certainly progressed from the days on that train in Baltimore when the black cast members of *The Skin of Our Teeth* were moved to the "colored car." The civil rights movement had made great progress, and many of the legal barriers to discrimination had been removed.

But we all know there's a difference between laws and attitudes. Often people enthusiastic about eradicating legal discrimination were less flexible when it came to their own deeply-rooted notions about race. *Eight Is Enough's* attempt to deal with the problem of what some have called "soft racism" came in an episode, *All's Fair in Love and War*, in which Tom believes his daughter Mary is about to embark on a serious, long-term relationship with the African-American son of one of Tom's old war buddies.

The episode has another important thread since the young man, Richard, played by Dorian Harewood, is a captain in the Army, who is in Sacramento to set up an ROTC recruiting office in the local college. When this episode aired in 1978, memories of the Vietnam War were fresh on everyone's mind, and attitudes in society were quite different than what we experience now. In today's America, regardless of one's political views concerning the wars in Iraq and Afghanistan, Americans tend to separate the military from the political. There is rightly a widespread feeling of appreciation for the tremendous sacrifices made by our young men and women in the armed forces.

But in the wake of Vietnam, things were different. The war left deep divisions in American society and culture, including a diminished respect for the military. The armed forces were seen by some—wrongly in my view—as responsible for the disastrous consequences of a war that cost nearly 50,000 American lives and a great many more permanently injured.

Those bitter feelings are powerfully presented in *Eight Is Enough* when Mary reveals that her hostility toward the ROTC has its roots in the loss of a friend in high school—a young man of eighteen, who died in the war before ever having a chance to live his own life. While initially hostile toward Richard and his ROTC recruiting office, Mary nevertheless comes to admire him as a person. In a tender scene, she reveals the tragedy of her high school friend's death, and Richard and Mary embrace. What they don't know is that Tom is watching from the window. And he manages to completely mistake the comforting embrace of friends with a budding romance.

Tom's misperception creates conflicted feelings causing him to question his own integrity. While he admires Richard, Tom finds himself unable to shake the thought that something is somehow wrong. Trying to explain to Abby, he argues that an interracial relationship between Mary and Richard would have "complications." But after fumbling for a moment, he reluctantly gets to the heart of the matter: "Abby," he asks, "am I a bigot?

Abby assures him he's not. And she's right. His preoccupation with the "complications" his daughter would face in an interracial marriage is motivated by genuine concern for her welfare. It is, he reasons, the general attitude of society that creates these "complications." But on this, Tom misses the mark. After all, those attitudes only change when individuals take the first steps. The prejudice on that Baltimore train only stops when someone refuses to move to the "colored car." There is, of course, a risk in being that person, and Tom is not quite willing to have his family assume that danger.

In the end, Tom learns the truth: Mary and Richard are not romantically involved. In fact, Richard is about to become engaged to a girlfriend back in Berkeley. The revelation is a great relief to Tom. He can barely contain his joy as he admires a photo of Richard's girlfriend. But the very fact of his relief is a reminder of the distance still to travel before race is no longer creating divisions among us. Even today, and even with a black President, there's still plenty of room for improvement before we get it right. But I do believe that America, despite its flaws, has brought us closer to realizing that day.

As we have seen, *Eight Is Enough* was willing to address thorny social issues, but only to a point. Had Mary and Richard actually embarked on a serious relationship, or even marriage, that would have set the stage for a far deeper exploration of the landscape of interracial relationships. Still, the episode does reflect Bill Blinn's idea of a family show where the characters, like all people, are flawed. Tom is a good and decent man, but he's far from perfect. Nor was he ever intended to be. Rather his imperfections help all of us better understand ourselves and that, in my view, is what makes his character so compelling.

* * *

Another hot topic of the 1970s was single mothers. In one episode, Tom's third daughter Susan discovers she's pregnant just as she's experiencing serious problems with her marriage. The family crisis brings out the tremendous gulf between father and daughter—a difference very much reflective of attitudes about marriage and fatherhood in the 1970s.

Tom sees the pregnancy as an opportunity; a chance to heal the marriage. With no small degree of naiveté, he tells Susan that the coming child "changes the whole complexion of the separation. Everything is different now," he tells her. But for Susan a bad marriage is worse than a fatherless family. In Bruce Shelly's excellent script, they argue the point:

Susan: *I'm not going to risk the future happiness of my child.*

Tom: *Then how come you're overlooking the fact that children need fathers?*

Susan: *Children need love. And Merle and I didn't have enough of that to keep us together.*

Tom: *A child might give you a new reason to find that love.*

Susan: *No, Dad, a child is the wrong reason.*

But Tom persists: "Susan, you don't understand," he says. "A man feels very differently about a woman who's going to have his child. Merle might change." Unconvinced, Susan fires back: "Babies don't change a bad relationship, they just add more strain."

Tom later looks for support from Abby. His daughter, he argues, has a naïve and unrealistic view of marriage. In playing the role, I was reminded of Richard Castellano's character, Frank, back on Broadway in *Lovers and Other Strangers*—a man utterly mystified by his son's dissatisfaction with a marriage that was no longer considered "fun." For Tom, it all seems ridiculous: "What do they expect? A few minutes of romantic fever earns them happiness forever. Nobody has to change! Everybody gets exactly what they want!" To many in Tom Bradford's generation, that's not only foolish, but a recipe for dissatisfaction. Unrealistic expectations will only continue to erode the importance of the nuclear family and marginalize every child's need for a father.

In the end, Susan and Merle reconcile. With a renewed willingness to compromise, they become hopeful their love will prevail. *Eight Is Enough*, as I've mentioned, was willing to take on the difficult issues, but they usually ended happily. Had the producers opted for something grittier, Susan's marriage might well have fallen apart. But that would have been a mistake. *Eight Is Enough* was not an unvarnished examination of marriage. Its great success, in my view, was an ability to raise these important issues, while still retaining that magic of a wholesome, whacky, loving, and ultimately functional American family.

* * *

At the Bradford house, there were always lessons to be learned. Perhaps the first rule in raising any family is that there are certain principles that override our individual and often selfish wants and desires. We frequently speak of passing along "values" to our children, and it is my belief that these values are the bedrock of our morality.

But what happens when the best principles suddenly collide with each other? That's what takes place in *The Devil and Mr. Bradford*. There, Tom takes Nicholas to see *Snow White and the Seven Dwarfs* at the local theater. But it's not the *Snow White* Tom thinks; not by a long shot. In fact, he quickly finds out that it's the porno version—and he comes tearing out of the theater, furious and holding his hand over young Nicholas's eyes.

At home, Tom mounts the soap box. Enraged about this porno theater in his community, he announces, with great indignation, his intention to write a column denouncing those rascals who've brought smut to his town. But so high on his horse, Tom doesn't see just how far he's going to fall.

Tom's daughter Joanie, played by Laurie Walters—who was actually six months older than Betty Buckley, who played her stepmother—works for a local news station and recounts the incident to her boss, who then insists that she beat her father to the punch. Joanie feels terrible about trying to scoop her dad, and finally she asks him for advice. Being a man of principle, he tells Joanie to go right ahead with the story. His only condition: that she do it right. He doesn't want to see her put out some superficial, poorly researched piece of sensationalism, the kind of stories he sees all too often on her boss's television program.

Following her dad's advice and her boss's prodding, Joanie digs deep. She discovers not only the corporation that owns the porno theater, but all of its stockholders. If these people are bringing smut to town, they should be fully exposed—her dad's principles of journalistic integrity would require nothing less.

So Joanie glances at the list of these filthy shareholders and nearly falls out of her chair when she recognizes one of the names: Tom Bradford. Her righteous father, the one who demanded she dig deep into the story, is part owner of the porn theater.

Once she recovers, Joanie brings it to Tom, who is, of course, mortified. Tom then confirms it as his accountant explains that there had been a corporate merger: the company Tom had stock in purchased a smaller company which owns the theater. Tom, of course, had no idea. But that won't get him off the hook.

Tom properly decides Joanie should run the story regardless of the damage it may do him: "I can lose my reputation," he explains, "but I can't lose my daughter."

But when he arrives at the television station, Tom learns that Joanie has quit her job. In her internal battle between journalistic ethics and family loyalty, the family won; Joanie gave up the job she loved rather than be the instrument of her father's disgrace.

In the end, Joanie's boss backs off provided Tom writes the full, unvarnished story in his column. It is a magnanimous gesture from someone whose journalistic principles Tom never respected. Tom agrees. Both he and Joanie have learned that while principles are great, life has a way of complicating things.

* * *

One small disappointment of *Eight Is Enough* is that I never met Tom Braden, whose real life story of raising eight children, recounted in his book, *Eight Is Enough*, provided the inspiration for the show. Braden actually had a far more exciting life than his television alter ego. Born and raised in Iowa, Braden was an American soldier who worked with the British Army in 1940 during World War II. With a penchant for intelligence work, Braden was later recruited by the Office of Strategic Services, the predecessor of the CIA, and in 1950 he became a CIA operative managing an international division that focused on promoting anti-communist movements in countries across the world. He was a key member of what was called Operation Mockingbird, an initiative that funneled huge sums of money to CIA partners in foreign countries.

Braden later revealed the nature of these operations, as well as the enormous power of the CIA. If the Director wanted to reward some foreign politician or journalist, Braden's team would take a large sum of cash, "hand it to him, and never have to account to anybody." Braden noted that "there was simply no limit to the money it could spend and no limit to the people it could hire and no limit to the activities it could decide were necessary to conduct the war—the secret war."

After leaving the CIA in 1954, Braden opened a newspaper, *The Blade Journal,* in San Francisco. He became a prominent columnist, for the most part promoting moderately conservative views. In 1966 he lost a bid to be California's Lieutenant Governor. Later Braden was one of the original hosts of the political program *Crossfire* with Pat Buchanan. By this time, Braden's politics had moved somewhat to the left, and he and Buchanan had fierce debates that established the show's unique format that lasted for years to come. Still, many were not convinced that this former CIA operative was a genuine representative of the show's liberal point of view. Curiously, it was Timothy Leary, the father-figure of the 1960s psychedelic drug movement, who commented that watching the show was like seeing "the left wing of the CIA debating the right wing of the CIA."

Braden published his memoirs titled *Eight Is Enough* in 1975. Although Braden recounted some of his interesting career exploits, it was primarily a domestic story of the travails of raising eight children. It was that aspect of the book that interested William Blinn, who felt the time was ripe for an old-style family show, but one that addressed some of the dicey issues that had put traditional institutions under attack. Bill convinced the producers at ABC to purchase the rights to Braden's book.

Blinn wanted to remain true to the book, but in the end, I'm not sure that was really possible. He did keep the first names of all the children. But the actual similarities between Tom Bradford and the real-life Tom Braden were limited. The resemblance was pretty much just the fact of raising eight children, as well as being a journalist in Northern California—Braden in San Francisco, Tom Bradford in Sacramento. No doubt, Blinn carefully read the various stories Braden wrote about his family life with an eye toward weaving some of Braden's anecdotes into the television show. But the similarities stopped there as *Eight Is Enough* took on a life of its own. Blinn created an entirely different character in Tom Bradford, with a wholly different family and history. *Eight Is Enough* was originally derived from Braden's book, but Bill Blinn was the show's true creator.

There came a time when Fred Silverman tried to arrange a meeting between me and Tom Braden. I was looking forward to it, but Braden backed out. Regrettably, I believe he wasn't happy with the show. I recall one time hearing that he had said that Dick Van Patten's not an athlete, whereas he was a real athlete. I have no doubt Braden was an excellent sportsman. He was, in fact, a multifaceted man with many talents. Still, at the time I recall taking some umbrage. After all, I'd spent my whole life involved in athletics. I have two sons who were among the world's elite athletes, one of whom, Vincent, played at Wimbledon and the U.S. Open and held his own—occasionally beating many of the greatest tennis players in the world. And Nels has dedicated his whole life to athletics, teaching tennis, winning national racquetball tournaments and promoting fitness for over thirty years.

It's true that some of the touch-football games we played on the show were a bit goofy. And I certainly didn't look like Johnny Unitas out there. But that was never the point. The games on *Eight Is Enough* were designed to incorporate life lessons for the children—as well as the parents.

Tom Braden wrote an exceptional book. In my view he was doubly fortunate that a guy as talented as Bill Blinn took the book and created a tremendously successful television show centered around the family life similar, in some respects, to what Braden enjoyed. Braden's declining to meet me for a quick promotional session was unfortunate, and his comment about my athletics was petty. But that aside, he was an exceptional man, a patriot who provided the original inspiration for a wonderful television show that made a significant impact on many Americans. That became clear with the amazing moment at Denver's Invesco Field when the first African-American presidential candidate accepted the Democratic Party nomination before a record 80,000 people and many, many millions more in America and all over the world. And what was the one cultural reference he used in that remarkable speech? *Eight Is Enough.* In arguably the biggest speech of his career—one that epitomized a massive fervor for change in America—Barack Obama had the whole stadium chanting Tom Braden's words over and over again: "*Eight is enough...Eight is enough....*" That didn't happen because of Braden's book, but because the book spawned a television show that struck a chord with Americans. There was something in those zany—even unathletic—family games, antics and travails, as well as a family's caring, respect and love, that made enough of a contribution that a presidential candidate would make a deliberate reference to it. Braden had been a key part of all that. They were his words. Tom Braden has passed on now, but I sincerely hope his family—especially his children—enjoyed that extraordinary moment as much as I did.

* * *

While *Eight Is Enough* was a show extolling family values, things were happening off camera that were not so wholesome. The 1970s was a period when drug usage exploded. It was particularly damaging in Hollywood, where young people had both the time and money to indulge these dangerous appetites. It was also true that the kind of familial discipline promoted on the show, and critical to the development and shaping of moral character, was simply absent in many cases. While I have always rejected extreme positions against child acting, I also recognize that without proper supervision, young actors, especially stars, can have a difficult time resisting the endless temptations that surround them.

At the time problems of drug abuse began on *Eight Is Enough*, I was unaware, not just of their extent, but that there was any problem at all. I was simply blind or naïve. Later as the truth came to light, I was genuinely astonished. I suppose if I had noticed a rash of lateness, missed cues, forgotten lines or other behavior affecting the quality of the performances, I might have noticed it. But the truth is that, despite the drug problems, the kids seemed to me to be professional both during rehearsals and in the filming of the shows.

Now having said that, I also know that some who were not involved with these problems have said the very opposite— that the drug abuse did affect the performances. On the *E! True Hollywood* documentary, Dianne Kay says: "Drugs will do it. Drugs will change your way of thinking and so it does affect your performance." She is, of course, entirely correct. Later hearing Willie Aames talk about how many of them showed up for work high on cocaine and other drugs, I have no doubt that all of this did affect them professionally. Perhaps because of my age and the fact that I did have a kind of father-figure relationship with many of them, they tended to hide it from me. If I had known, I really don't know that I could have changed things, but I certainly would have tried.

After the show, things came crashing down around some of them. While Willie went on to another successful show, *Charles in Charge* with Scott Baio, his own descent into addiction brought him to the brink. Willie has publicly described his difficult journey back, including his religious conversion. Today, I'm delighted to know that his life is on a far better path.

Susan Richardson also fell on hard times. During the show, Susan became pregnant and gained an enormous amount of weight. She began to think the weight gain put her job in jeopardy and started using drugs to lose it. Her difficulties continued after the regular series ended. In 1989, while filming the second and final reunion episode, Susan, then 37, made a disturbing, even bizarre, allegation about being kidnapped and held hostage by filmmakers in Korea. Susan continued to think they were pursuing her. "They had a lot of insurance policies out on me," she claimed, "and they tried to blow me up in a church." Skepticism about her story was damaging to her acting career. And later she suffered a nervous breakdown. But Susan recovered, and the last I heard from her she was enjoying her life, working as a caretaker at a retirement home in Pennsylvania.

The most tragic case was Lani O'Grady, who played Mary Bradford. She always seemed to me to be a happy and outgoing young woman, who was professional in every way. But later Lani revealed that her problems ran much deeper. She said she had suffered from panic attacks and began taking large quantities of tranquilizers and alcohol to calm her before each show. One thing led to another, and by the time the series ended, she had become a full-blown addict.

After *Eight Is Enough*, her life spiraled downward. Once, my nephew Casey and his wife Pat went to the Brown Bagger Restaurant in Venice Beach, and Lani was there waiting tables. There's certainly nothing wrong with working as a waitress, but it did seem from her appearance that Lani was heading toward rock bottom.

Lani also spoke candidly about her addiction in an interview in 1994. She was hopeful of breaking her habit and had checked into the Cedars Sinai Medical Center for treatment. But, in the end, she lost the battle. Lani was found dead of an overdose in her home on September 25, 2001. It was a terrible shock, and I was deeply saddened when I heard the news.

Perhaps the most publicized post-*Eight Is Enough* problems have come from Adam Rich. All of us who have children experience a little sadness as they grow up. If only they stayed like that forever. In Adam's case, it wasn't just parents watching him grow up, but the whole country. Everyone wanted little Nicholas to stay just like he was, but in a few years, that irresistibly charming little boy was gone. Rarely has anyone in this industry suffered so greatly from that transition.

Following *Eight Is Enough*, Adam fell into that familiar cycle of addiction and self-destructive behavior. In April 1991, Adam, now twenty-two years old, was arrested for breaking into a pharmacy to steal drugs. I remember receiving a call that Adam was in jail, so I went down to the Van Nuys Courthouse and bailed him out. No sooner was he on the streets when he was arrested again for shoplifting. In the end, the judge gave him a break. He wound up with a suspended sentence and a court order to enter a drug treatment program, which he completed. In fact, he even lived in my guesthouse for a while as he was trying to clean himself up and find work. Unfortunately, he's had difficulty getting parts as an actor. No doubt, the ghost of young Nicholas is a tough one to shake.

Not all the post *Eight Is Enough* stories are so stormy. Grant Goodeve made a number of guest appearances on popular shows before he and his wife, Debbie, moved with their three children to Seattle, Washington. Grant really loves the beauty of the great outdoors. From his home, far from Hollywood, he's had success with a number of local television programs, including as host of several popular shows for Home and Gardens television. And like Willie Aames, Grant found great support in his Christian faith. I still see him occasionally. Last year, while in Seattle for an Old Time Radio convention, Grant and I had dinner, and I was delighted to see how happy he is with his life and work. He's every bit as good a person as he is an actor.

Laurie Walters, Dianne Kay and Connie Newton have left Hollywood and settled down with their own families. I truly enjoyed working with all three and am delighted to hear they lead happy and fulfilling lives. All of the young women on *Eight Is Enough* were, in my view, beautiful—but none more so than Dianne Kay. In fact, in one episode she entered a Sacramento beauty contest. I secretly used to hope she would hit it off with one of my own boys. It was easy to see Diane as a mother, especially after her performance in *A Little Triangle*, where she developed a special rapport with little Wendy, the three-year-old daughter of another widower. In the end, she comes to the sad realization that she loves the child more than the father. It's a poignant and beautifully performed scene when Diana as Nancy explains to the little girl that she won't be coming back anymore.

One family member who enjoyed an astonishing post *Eight Is Enough* career is Betty Buckley. One year after the show ended, Betty went back to her roots on Broadway and stunned the world with her now classic rendition of *Memory*, in the smash hit *Cats*. Her success has been so great that she's often referred to as "the voice of Broadway." When I listen to her soaring voice, it reminds me of how many times she begged the producers to let her sing on the show and how many times they said no. Betty sure had the last laugh on that one.

* * *

Eight Is Enough was a marvelous show, and I was proud to be part of it. Despite the problems, there was always a genuine affection existing among all the cast members. Those Bradfords were an important part of my life, and, more important, I believe they also entered the American consciousness in a very personal way. I still have people stop me on the street and ask about the Bradford kids as if we were all still living back in Sacramento. And the women always ask: "How is Nicholas?" Sometimes mothers come up to me and say: "I cut my son's hair just like Nicholas's."

Time has passed quickly. It's nearly thirty years since the last episode of the series. Still, I think people will continue to look back at the show and feel that maybe it represents something we've lost in today's world. Brian Patrick Clark, who played Merle the Pearl on *Eight Is Enough*, described the show as a "relic" of another time. It was a time when life was just as complex as it is today, but somehow the support of that big, loving family made it all seem simpler. As Bill Blinn has noted, having ten people around a dinner table every night is something we not only look back on with nostalgia, but that leaves us yearning for all that was good in the magical world of the Bradfords.

With Mom and Dad at the Broad Channel tennis courts in Queens around 1933. That's me sporting a shock of blond hair and holding my first wooden tennis racquet. (Photo from Dick Van Patten's collection)

Breakfast at home in our Kew Gardens apartment with Mom and Joyce around 1940. (Photo from Dick Van Patten's collection)

A private performance for Mom and Joyce at the Belasco on Broadway in the Edward Chodorov drama, *Decision.* At the time, February, 1944, I was fifteen and Joyce, just nine, was already starring in *Tomorrow the World* three blocks away at the Ethel Barrymore Theater. (Photo from Dick Van Patten's collection)

My first television family, the Hansens, on Steiner Street in San Francisco. The popular show, *I Remember Mama,* ran from 1949 through 1957. (Left to right: Judson Laire, me, Peggy Wood, Robin Morgan and Rosemary Rice) (Photo © CBS/Landov)

No privacy in the Hansen family, as Peggy Wood, Judson Laire, Rosemary Rice and Robin Morgan enjoy themselves at my expense. (Photo © CBS/Landov)

The cast and crew of *I Remember Mama*, breaking for dinner. My good friend, and Academy Award–winning director, Ralph Nelson, who had written *The Wind Is Ninety*, is standing on the right. (Photo © CBS/Landov)

Nels Hansen taking some wise counsel from "Papa" (Judson Laire).
(Photo © CBS/Landov)

Pat knocking them dead in 1953 out on W. 44th Street between The Majestic and Saint James Theaters. With the dancers from Rogers and Hammerstein's *Me and Juliet*, Pat is in the front on the right. Third from the left in the back is a marvelous young dancer with a big future, Shirley MacLaine. (Photo from Dick Van Patten's collection)

The combined New York, London and touring casts of *Mister Roberts* in 1950. I'm in the second row on the far right. Henry Fonda is front and center, Tyrone Power is on the left, John Forsythe is behind Fonda, and Jackie Cooper is in the front row on the right. (Photo from Dick Van Patten's collection)

Christmas at the Bradfords. (Left to right, front: Adam Rich, Dianne Kay, Connie Newton, Willie Aames, Susan Richardson, me, Betty Buckley; Back: Grant Goodeve, Lani O'Grady, Laurie Walters.) (Photo © American Broadcasting Companies, Inc.)

ADAMS, AVIATION, BAYSIDE, BOWNE, BOYS, BRONX SCIENCE, BROOKLYN TECH, BRYANT, BUSHWICK, CANARSIE, CARDINAL HAYES, CARDOZO, CENTRAL COMMERCIAL, CLINTON, COLUMBUS, COMMERCE, EASTERN DISTRICT, ERASMUS HALL, EVANDER CHILDS, FAR ROCKAWAY, FDR, FLUSHING, FOREST HILLS, FT. HAMILTON, FRANCIS LEWIS, GEO. WASHINGTON, GIRLS COMMERCIAL, GREAT NECK, CLEVELAND, HAAREN, HUNTER, JAMAICA, JEFFERSON, JULIA RICHMAN, LAFAYETTE, LANE, LAWRENCE, LINCOLN, L I CITY, MADISON, MALVERNE, MANUAL TRAINING, MIDWOOD, MONROE, MORRIS, MOTHER BUTLER, M&A, NEW UTRECHT, NEWTOWN, PERFORMING ARTS, POWER MEMORIAL, RIVERHEAD, SCARSDALE, SEWARD PARK, SHEEPSHEAD BAY, SOUTH SHORE, STUYVESANT, TAFT, THEO. ROOSEVELT, TILDEN, TOWNSEND HARRIS, VALLEY STREAM, VAN BUREN, WALTON, WASHINGTON IRVING, WINGATE, WOODMERE, YONKERS

NEW YORK ALUMNI
presents

WORLD'S BIGGEST HIGH SCHOOL REUNION
and

"Night of New York Nostalgia"
honoring

DICK AND PAT VAN PATTEN

Special Guests
Fernando Ferrer
Bronx Boro Prez

James Dawson
Headmaster
Professional's Children School

LIMITED SEATING
AVAILABLE
Saturday, September 28

Chairman of the Board
MILTON BERLE

Executive Producers
Lou and Fran Zigman
Co-Chairs
Louis Gossett Jr. and Jon Voight
Produced by
Buddy Arnold and Johnny Francis

HONORARY COMMITTEE
Steve Allen, Patty Andrews, Bea Arthur, Dave Barry, Gene Barry, Daniel Benzali, Mr. Blackwell, Julie Budd, Red Buttons, Sid Caesar, Jack Carter, Dane Clark, Kim Coles, Dom DeLuise, Charles Durning, Herb Edelman, Fyvush Finkel, Roy Firestone, Tony Franciosa, Jackie Gayle, Hank Garrett, Estelle Getty, Elliott Gould, Michael Gregory, Huntz Hall, Varlerie Harper, Herb Jeffries, Lainie Kazan, Marvin Kaplan, Harvey Keitel, Bernie Kopell, Martin Kove, Martin Landau, Ed Lauter, Thelma Lee, Len Lesser, Peter Lupus, Rose Marie, Garry Marshall, Steven Macht, Barbara McNair, Rita Moreno, Jan Murray, Don Newcombe, Tony Orlando, Freddie Roman, John Saxon, Jack Scalia, Neil Sedaka, Sammy Shore, Jimmy Smits, Connie Stevens, Fred Travalena, Brenda Vaccarro, Jerry Vale, Bea Wain, and Jesse White.

Masters of Ceremonies
Johnny Francis, Budd Friedman & Stanley Ralph Ross

in the playground, they sell New York hot dogs, and all new york foods —

House Manager
Arlene Marcus Schachter

Technical Directors
Jon Alexander & Ed Schachter

Saturday, September 28, 1996
(310) 276-2754

Reunion | 4:00 - 7:00 P.M.
Show   7:15 P.M.

Tickets
$40, $50, $100

N.Y.A.A.
8306 Wilshire Blvd. #596
Beverly Hills, CA 90211

Tickets will be sent to ticket holders by September 14

OUR PREVIOUS HONOREES		
PHIL FOSTER	MARTIN LANDAU	RUBY KEELER
MILTON BERLE	STEVE ALLEN	GENE BARRY
SID CAESAR	JAN MURRAY	JOE BOLOGNA
HUNTZ HALL		RENEE TAYLOR

Better late than never! The program cover from the day I received my diploma from New York's Professional Children's School. The event was chaired by alumnus, Milton Berle, and the diploma was presented to me by the head of the school, James Dawson, around sixty-five years after my last class. Pat was also honored, and together with June Taylor, Marilyn Gleason and Dorothy Adams (Don's wife) did a few impromptu dance steps. (Photo from Dick Van Patten's collection)

Pat and I loved to go for a brisk jog on the beach along the beautiful Santa Monica coastline. (Photo © John G. Zimmerman)

The flying Van Pattens sail over the net captured by the great sports photographer, John Zimmerman. (Left to right: Nels, Pat, Dick, Jimmy and Vincent)

(Photo © John G. Zimmerman)

46

Breakfast at Wimbledon

Just as *Eight Is Enough* was getting underway, my son Vincent's tennis game was also launching into a new gear. It was now clear that he wasn't just talented, but had a special gift for the game and was quickly turning into a world-class athlete. Vincent, Jimmy and Nels are all good athletes, but I never expected this. By age seventeen, Vincent was beating everyone in the lower level "satellite" tournaments and was soon highly ranked among Southern California junior players.

The following year he joined his brother, Nels, at Pepperdine University. There, both Nels and Vincent worked with Coach Larry Riggs, son of the great tennis champion, Bobby Riggs. Pepperdine had a terrific program, but in a short time, Vincent's game had rapidly moved beyond the college level, and in 1979, he turned professional.

Suddenly Pat and I found ourselves following all the tennis news. We began taking calls from Vincent from all over the world as he played on the Pro Tour against the top players. It is hard to describe our excitement. So many times I had gone to watch my father play tennis at Hempstead Park in the 1930s and 1940s where I'd developed a real love for the game. I'd also gone with him to see the great legends like Don Budge and Ellsworth Vines at the National Championships just down the road at the stadium in Forest Hills, Queens. Now, my son was on those same courts, competing against the greatest players in the world, and I was ecstatic.

In his first year on the tour, Vincent made it into the main draw at the U.S. Open. I still remember the thrill of heading off to Flushing Meadows to watch him play. It was even more exciting because my Dad was with us. Tennis was one of the great loves of his life, and he was never prouder than when we all took our seats in the player's box on that first day at the U.S. Open.

In the opening round, Vincent was pitted against another newcomer named Ivan Lendl, and we actually thought it was a bit of good luck. After all, this quiet kid from Czechoslovakia was as new to all this as Vincent. Everyone at a major tennis tournament has talent. That's a given. But it's the calm under pressure that comes from experience which is usually the deciding factor. Drawing another novice seemed fortunate.

Boy, were we wrong! We got a little sense of Ivan's personality before the match began when he surprised us by walking over to our player's box. His family was still back behind the Iron Curtain. So here he was facing our extended family, all there to root for his opponent. I'll never forget as Ivan approached us, he reached out and took Pat's hand in his. With that serious look on his face, he literally bowed from the waist and kissed her hand. Then he smiled and said in his then broken English, "Hello, family," and walked off to play the match.

In the 1970s, the youth culture in America had undergone tremendous change. Too often there was a disregard, even disrespect, for elders. Frequently, as I mentioned regarding *Eight Is Enough*, that sentiment was accompanied by a diminution of the importance of family. But young Ivan Lendl's family was living under a dictatorship in Eastern Europe. He was a young man who understood real difficulties in life, and tennis was his way out.

While I instantly gained respect for him from that brief incident at the family box, there was still no way we could have known he was destined for greatness. Still, when he came over to our box and did his bow, he looked like a serious, respectful and self-disciplined young man—one to be reckoned with. Suddenly, we were all a little more concerned than we had been a few minutes earlier.

It was a tight first set. Vincent and Ivan both played well, but Ivan pulled it out at 6-4. After that, the match was a bit of a blur. I guess we all got a glimpse of the greatness that was yet to come from Ivan. The match ended quickly, and we later consoled a disappointed Vincent with assurances that his own prodigious talents would continue to sharpen and that many more chances lay ahead for him here at Flushing Meadow. As for Ivan, notwithstanding his brilliance that day, he was still not quite ready for the very biggest stage, and he lost in the next round to the far more experienced southpaw with a blistering serve named Roscoe Tanner.

By the end of 1979, Vincent had played in his first ATP finals in Montgomery, Alabama, where he beat a series of excellent players. He also had impressive wins against an array of former champions like Stan Smith, Bob Lutz, and Tom Okker. Smith had been number one in the world, and Okker, a veteran from Holland called "The Flying Dutchman," had the honor of being a finalist in the very first U.S. Open, won by the great Arthur Ashe. Vincent's explosive rise in the ranking, from number 450 in the world all the way up to number 42 was one of the most dramatic in tennis history. By the end of 1979, his precipitous, rapid and stunning explosion into the world's top fifty earned Vincent the ATP newcomer's award—similar to Rookie of the Year in other sports. For me, it was the thrill of a lifetime.

It turned out that one of the biggest tennis fans in Hollywood at the time was Johnny Carson. I had become a regular guest on *The Tonight Show*, and with Johnny's encouragement, I could barely contain myself and my enthusiasm for this marvelous new stage of world-class tennis where my son was now performing—an accomplishment that I like to think was the result of the values he learned at home—values impressing the fact that talent will only take you so far. The rest is hard work, discipline, and commitment. Vincent was proving he had it all, and Pat and I were as proud as any parents could ever be.

Over the next few years, Vincent established himself on the professional tennis tour. While he played at tournaments all over the world, there was nothing more exciting than having a child playing on the fabled grass courts of Wimbledon, the same magical turf where great Americans from Bill Tilden to Pete Sampras have made tennis history.

But the biggest thrill occurred across the world in Tokyo, Japan, in October of 1981. As a boy playing with a local team of friends from Bellerose Village, Vincent recalls being excited about a match with a more powerful team from Douglaston, Queens. When the big day came, Vincent and his friends were trounced by the Douglaston kids—and this was only their B team. That day, however, he recalls the club members at Douglaston talking about a young ten-year-old prodigy who was already showing signs of potential greatness. The little kid's name was John McEnroe.

Around thirteen years later, when Vincent arrived in Japan for the ATP's Tokyo Indoor Championships, that kid they whispered about back in Douglaston had risen to the very top of the tennis world. In October of 1981, John McEnroe was not only the number one player in the world but was reaching the peak of his extraordinary career having just won both Wimbledon and the U.S. Open, beating the great Bjorn Borg each time in the finals. And now McEnroe was also arriving in Japan. For Vincent it might have seemed a bit like Douglaston all over again, except this time it was the A team.

It was an incredible week at the Van Patten home. Each night Vincent would call from Tokyo—and each night it got more exciting. In the second round, he barely survived a barn-burner after losing the first set to a great Argentine player, Jose-Luis Clerc, who would rank as high as number 4 in the world, 6-7, 7-5, 7-6. In the quarterfinals, it again seemed like he was headed home after losing the first set 6-0 to the legendary Vitas Gerulitas. But Vincent came roaring back to beat Vitas in the final sets, 6-3,6-3.

Suddenly he was in the semi-finals, and across the net was that prodigy from Queens, now the greatest player in the world. John McEnroe was supremely confident—and arrogant. In fact, this was just after he had made tennis history for not being offered membership in the Wimbledon Tennis Club after winning the title due to his obnoxious behavior. McEnroe not only believed that Vincent didn't belong on the same court with him, but his condescending attitude was on full display. On that day, however, it was the kid from Bellerose who was unbeatable. Vincent took out McEnroe in straight sets, 6-3,7-5, in one of the biggest upsets of the year. And the next day, Vincent kept rolling as he won the tournament, beating Australia's Mark Edmonson in a close three-set finals. When the week ended, Vincent had risen to number 26 in the world. More important, he had proven that he could play with anyone, a world-class athlete who made his parents proud.

But what delighted Pat and I even more than his winning was the fact that he behaved with such class and dignity at a time when too many tennis players felt it was okay to act like jerks, mistreating umpires, linesmen and tournament officials. And still more important for us was the camaraderie that existed between all three of our sons, then and throughout their lives. Just as exciting as Vincent's rise to the heights of the tennis world was the fact that he and Nels could still enjoy playing together. As satisfying as Vincent's accomplishments in singles was the triumph of Nels and Vincent at the ATP Grand Prix doubles championship in Athens, Greece. In fact, they are among the very few brothers ever to have won an ATP Tour tennis tournament. I had gone from watching my father play against his friends at the old courts back in Richmond Hill in the 1930s to seeing one of my children step onto the grass courts of Wimbledon fifty years later. Tennis is a wonderful game, and it has brought much fun and joy to the Van Patten family.

47

AFRICA

When *Eight Is Enough* was at its peak, I found there were now great demands on my time. Running from one celebrity event to another, there was barely time to reflect on all that was happening. I was also aware that people with good fortune have an obligation to give something back, and such an opportunity came along for me in the spring of 1981.

Father Michael Kaiser was a Catholic priest who hosted a television show in which he would frequently feature celebrities to talk about various issues. His association with so many stars led to suggestions that he was too frequently hobnobbing with Hollywood celebrities. Father Kaiser had an office in Malibu Beach and was viewed with mixed feelings by many—some thought he was too attracted to the glitter of celebrity, while others were convinced that he was a deeply spiritual man, dedicated to many praiseworthy charities.

I guess I believed a little of both. Still, I genuinely liked Father Kaiser, and we enjoyed going on his show. One day he told me he was planning a missionary trip to Africa and asked if I would like to join him. He had already signed up LeVar Burton, the star of *Roots*, and Patty Duke, and there were a number of other people committed to going as well. At first, I declined. I don't recall what excuse I made, but it stayed on my mind.

Later that day, I met John Forsythe, a friend since we did *Mister Roberts* together on Broadway back in the early 1950s, after Henry Fonda had left the show. I told John about Father Kaiser's proposal, and John immediately said I'd made a mistake. He thought it would be a wonderful experience for me, as well as it being a very worthy cause. After that, I kept thinking about it, and finally, later in the day, I went back to Father Kaiser and told him I would go. I'll never forget his response: "Dick, after you left I said a prayer that you would change your mind. And here you are."

We all flew into Dijibouti, the capital of Ethiopia. I had never been to Africa or any other place where people lived at a subsistence level. We brought food and other supplies that were desperately needed. I remember that Patty Duke was particularly wonderful with the children, and we all grew very attached to them.

In the short time I spent with these wonderful African children, I was struck by the fact that they seemed to have never been exposed to humor—at least not in the way we're accustomed to. The day we were leaving, on the spur of the moment, I pretended to bump into a tree. Suddenly all the kids went crazy. So I kept doing pratfalls and put on a little show as they just kept laughing and laughing. I had the impression they had never seen any kind of organized show or act that was designed just to make them laugh. It seemed to me that this was something outside their life experience. It may sound insignificant, but in the midst of all their terrible privation, I found myself introducing these kids to comedy.

I've had many different audiences over my lifetime, but I don't ever remember one more appreciative. More important, I never appreciated an audience more than I did those kids. Laughter really is good for the soul. And I hope the children in that village, with all the enormous burdens they carried, felt a little bit better for having laughed at this crazy American who was bumping into trees and tripping over logs.

I won't be so pretentious as to say that the African trip changed my life forever or made me a better person. But I did leave with a fuller understanding of the giant gap between those who have and those who don't. I also see my own life a little differently. Most of us are self-absorbed when we're young. I know I was. And yet, there are those rare and magical people who seem to be born altruists. To care deeply about the plight of others requires that we temper concern about ourselves. In the Catholic Church, the clergy take vows to ensure that state of mind—vows of poverty and even celibacy. These are commitments that help these wonderful people turn their own focus away from themselves and toward others. Other religions, I believe, have some variant on this—moral teachings and ethical principles requiring that people forego their own pleasures for the comfort of others. One of the advantages of growing older is the ability to see oneself more clearly. As I look back, I see that the time spent with those unlucky children was more important than all my appearances on radio, stage and television. That clear introspection leads to regret for not having done more. I'm sure many people feel that way. By the time we emerge from the self-obsession of our youth, we find ourselves on the homestretch—and wondering why we didn't do more.

48

Life after Eight Is Enough

As a result of *Eight Is Enough*, I became a regular on all the talk shows. My favorite was *The Merv Griffin Show*, where I appeared many times. Merv was a good friend, and, as mentioned, we played tennis together for years.

One day Merv was going on vacation and asked if I would be the guest host. At first it sounded great, and I agreed. But as the date approached, for the first time in my entire professional life I began to feel nervous. This was different than what I was used to. I always had a script to lean on. Or, if I was the guest on a show, it was up to Merv or Johnny Carson or whoever to make sure things went smoothly. But now it would be up to me, and I was scared to death that I would run out of conversation.

One way to ease things was to book people who were already friends. So my first guest was Don Adams. Now Don was a great guy, but he could also be a bit ornery at times. I was sitting in the dressing room trying to think about what I would say to him when I came up with an idea. Before the show went on the air, I went into the audience and asked them to play along. I told them when Don Adams comes on I'm going to introduce him—and then dismiss him in ten seconds.

So Don came out. He sat down, and I asked him how he was. He responded that he was fine. And then I immediately said in the most serious voice: "Well thank you very much for coming, Don. It was wonderful having you." Don gave me that ornery look as if I was completely out of my mind and then yelled at me: "That's it?"

The audience loved it, which made me a lot more relaxed. I also remembered some advice that Merv gave me which is important for any interviewer—and is also important in real life— which is to really listen. Rather than thinking about what you're going to say next, listen. There's always a tendency as a host to be so concerned about the next question that you tune out what your guest is saying. In the end, that just makes it worse. I appreciated that advice, and it helped get me through my week as guest host of *The Merv Griffin Show*. But I also acquired a new respect for those people, like Merv and Johnny, who have that rare ability to keep a conversation going and to make it interesting to the viewers. I believe that everybody has something interesting about them and people like Larry King or Oprah have a special gift for bringing it out—and doing it day after day. I enjoyed my week in Merv's chair, but that was enough for me. It's a lot more comfortable being the guest.

* * *

Around the same time, I learned that whatever the occasion, whether as a talk show host, in an African village or anyplace else, an entertainer entertains. That's the job description. And sometimes you've got to be ready at a moment's notice.

My son Jimmy loves to tell a true story about some quick improvisation. Jimmy had a friend who introduced him to a very wealthy individual, recently retired, who had moved from Washington to Beverly Hills. Apparently, the man was very much taken with the idea of "celebrity." He would throw giant parties with hundreds of people at his mansion and invite as many Hollywood stars as he could find.

One day he dropped dead from a heart attack. Jimmy was asked to be a pallbearer at his funeral, which he thought was odd since he didn't know him all that well. But he agreed. Then it got even stranger when one of his friends asked Jimmy if I would come. Now I had never met the man in my life. Still, his family insisted that he was a big fan of mine, and they would really appreciate it if I attended. Jimmy thought it was ridiculous, but he asked me anyway. It happened that I had nothing scheduled that day, and the story intrigued me, so to Jimmy's surprise, I told him I would go.

A few hours later, we arrived for the services, which were held at the cemetery. I sat down next to Jimmy, glanced at the program and nearly had a heart attack, when I saw in big black letters: "Eulogy by Dick Van Patten." I looked at Jimmy and said: "What is this, some kind of practical joke?" He assured me it must be a mistake, and he would talk to them.

So the service started, and I was waiting for someone to announce an error in the program. Instead, the man's friend who was speaking to the crowd was suddenly overcome with emotion and was unable to continue. At this point everyone looked at me. I didn't know what to do, so I just got up, walked to the lectern and delivered a eulogy for a man I never met.

I began by saying what a wonderful guy he was. I then started making things up. I told about our many trips to the racetrack together and our long games of all-night poker. I explained to them about how we had talked so frequently about his interest in sports and the arts and many other aspects of his life that had been so tragically cut short. By the time I was done they were all in tears. Afterwards his mother and father came up to me, and with great appreciation, said: "You told us things about our son, we didn't even know!"

* * *

In May of 1985, I had to say goodbye again, this time to my father. Following World War II, Dad remarried and had several more children: Johnny, Marjorie, Byron and Tim. He remained in New York for most of his life, but then moved to Los Angeles where he spent his final years. We had been close throughout our lives, but in the years prior to his death we became even closer, heading out to the Santa Anita racetrack together nearly every day. It was a wonderful time, and I'm so grateful to have been able to share those years with him.

Just as I wished Mom had lived a year longer to see the success of *Eight Is Enough*, I was sad my father died just six months before I received the great honor of having a star on the Hollywood Walk of Fame. The famous bronze stars, set on the sidewalk of Hollywood Boulevard and Vine Street, are awarded by the Walk of Fame committee each year for those making contributions in the categories of film, television, theater, radio and music. It is a special privilege to be among those luminaries, including so many talented people I've admired throughout my life.

Curiously, my star, placed on Vine Street in November of 1985, has just seen some unexpected traffic. It actually resulted from a mistake. There is a star very close to mine belonging to the Los Angeles talk-show host named Michael Jackson. The shocking death of my young neighbor from Queens Road sent thousands of mourners in search of his star. Many of them went to the wrong one near mine and set up a candlelight vigil. (Michael's actual star is located in front of the famous Grauman's Chinese Theater but on the night of his death it was closed off due to a theater production.) I was glad to hear the talk-show host, Michael Jackson, graciously assuring everyone that he was happy to lend his star for the tribute and that he would gladly give it up if it would only bring Michael back.

On the other side of my star, is the lovely actress, Virginia Cherrill, from the silent picture era—best known as Charlie Chaplain's blind flower girl. In the same section are John Wayne, Eleanor Powell, studio mogul Richard Rowland and country music legend Roy Acuff. I'm delighted to share my small piece of Hollywood immortality with all these great entertainers. And while I wish my Dad could have been with us on that memorable autumn day, I believe he was watching from a far better place and whatever little luster there is to my star on Vine Street, it pales next to Dad's star which I know will shine brightly forever in Heaven.

* * *

In early 1987, I received a call telling me that there was going to be a new award in the name of the great actor Pat O'Brien, and I was to be the first recipient. Pat O' Brien was among my very favorite actors, and growing up I remember enjoying him in such classics as *Angels with Dirty Faces, Crack Up* and *The Personality Kid.* And, of course, in 1940 he uttered those famous words, "Win just one for the Gipper" as the legendary Norte Dame Coach in *Knute Rockne: All American* alongside a young man named Ronald Reagan. I had worked with Pat once on a television drama in the early 1960s, and he made a deep impression on me, not only as an actor, but as a truly decent and honorable man.

The event was held at the Beverly Wilshire on Saint Patrick's Day, March 17, 1987, and was hosted by a Catholic priest, Father Michael Manning. As he presented me with the award, Father Manning said that "humor and dedication to wholesome family values were the hallmark of Pat O'Brien" He then added: "Perhaps, no one in Hollywood exemplifies high Christian principles and love of family as much as Dick Van Patten." That was a beautiful thing for Father Manning to say, however undeserved.

The highlight of the evening was a videotaped message from President Reagan. The President recalled his old friend and noted that Pat "typified...all that is good in movies and television. He was a hard-working actor. He loved to use his talent to bring the Good Lord's truth and laughter to his work." Then President Reagan gave his approval to my winning the award, stating that Dick Van Patten had exhibited "high ideals" that are a "model for us all."

I was deeply moved by those words, and I spoke a few that came from the heart that night. "The only reason I'm taking this," I explained, "is because no one else in the world thought more highly of Pat O'Brien and idolized him more than I did." As an actor, I said, Pat "made it look so easy. He was a fast actor, but he was very real." In that sense, I was referencing the differences between those actors like Gleason and Mickey Rooney and the many radio actors who could achieve a real performance in a heartbeat. That was how I saw Pat O'Brien.

"To the public," I continued, Pat "was the cop on the beat or the priest in the neighborhood parish, or the storefront lawyer or the fast-talking private detective.... He made it look so easy that I wonder if his acting was fully appreciated. He was one of the greatest actors that ever lived.... He had such respect for the writers' words." Finally, I noted the thing that struck me most about Pat: "There was no self-indulgence in his acting," I said.

That lack of pretension was what made him such a special person, and I'm sure that President Reagan recognized that same quality. I told the group that in the end Pat really was a model for all of us, a man devoted far more to his family than to the craft he had mastered. "He didn't care what happened to his career," I said, "as long as everything at home was okay."

I would like to accept full credit for President Reagan's generous comment about my "high ideals." And it is certainly true that for me, my family is the one thing that is most precious in this world. But it's equally clear to anyone reading this book that I've had my share of failings. Still, in the end, we are all more than our failings. No one lives a perfect life, but we are, I hope, judged by our best moments rather than our worst.

The receipt of that award also reminded me again of the enormous power of television. The many years on *Mama* and *Eight Is Enough* set forth an image to the world that no one could live up to. Still, I was always conscious of that image. I understood that the world saw me in a certain light and that there was something good about that; the presence of a Tom Bradford in American living rooms was ultimately a positive thing. I don't take credit for it. Credit belongs mostly to people like the real Tom Braden, who lived it and wrote a book about it; Bill Blinn who worked with the book and through his wonderful imagination transformed it into a television show, and Fred Silverman who had the wisdom to see the attraction of something so wholesome at that time in our society.

At the beginning of this book, I mentioned that there is a great distance between a character and the actor who plays that character. That distinction should never be lost. Nevertheless, the actor does have the opportunity to bring some part of himself to the character; to help shape the character. The character in turn can help shape the actor. I've never fully lived up to the "high ideals" of Tom Bradford, but he's always there for me as a model. Cynics often criticize "ideals" as unrealistic. But we create ideals not to achieve them, but to strive for them. Pat O'Brien understood that; so did President Reagan. The receipt of that award was a wonderful moment in my life.

* * *

At around the same time, I received a call from Mel Brooks, who was doing another film. It was going to be a spoof of the movie *Star Wars*. By this time, George Lucas had put out two sequels, *The Empire Strikes Back* and *Return of the Jedi*, so *Star Wars* lore had already become a familiar part of American culture. In Mel's elaborate comedy, I played King Roland of Druidia whose planet is threatened by the planet Spaceball. In an attempt to steal Druidia's air supply, Spaceball sends Dark Helmet, its evil fleet commander, who takes my daughter, Princess Vespa, hostage. He threatens to give her old nose back if I don't tell him the secret access code for the planet's defensive shield.

In one of those great Mel moments, everyone waits with bated breath as I reluctantly give Dark Helmet and his subordinate, Colonel Sandurz, wonderfully played by Rick Moranis and George Wyner, the top-secret code that protects Druidia from all its enemies:

King Roland:	*One.*
Dark Helmet	*One.*
Colonel Sandurz:	*One.*
King Roland:	*Two.*
Dark Helmet	*Two.*
Colonel Sandurz:	*Two.*
King Roland:	*Three.*
Dark Helmet	*Three.*
Colonel Sandurz:	*Three.*
King Roland:	*Four.*
Dark Helmet	*Four.*
Colonel Sandurz:	*Four.*
King Roland:	*Five.*
Dark Helmet	*Five.*

Dark Helmet pauses. Then looks at me with contempt: "So the combination is...one, two, three, four, five? That's the stupidest combination I've ever heard in my life!"

Some of *Spaceballs*'s critics complained the movie was a few years late. After all, the last of the *Stars Wars* original trilogy had been released in 1983, four years prior to *Spaceballs*. By then, there had already been a number of *Star Wars* spoofs, and, indeed, the box office numbers at the time were not as good as we had hoped. But time has proven friendly to *Spaceballs*, which turned into a kind of cult classic, extremely popular with kids today even though it's been over twenty years since its release. In fact, I sometimes meet young people who know of me primarily—or even solely—as Druidia's King Roland.

* * *

In the years after *Eight Is Enough*, I also became further involved in various tennis events, particularly those associated with Nancy Reagan's campaign against drug abuse. During the Reagan years, Nancy made headlines with her famous, "Just say no," policy. Some people criticized the First Lady for what they perceived as a simplistic message. But I think they were wrong.

While it's certainly true that addiction is a complex phenomenon, and for the hard-core drug abuser, getting clean requires more than just will power, Nancy's message was designed to reach the millions of children who are not junkies but have been tempted to experiment. At that point, the very best advice to those kids is to "Just say no." No matter how slick and enticing the drug purveyors can make their deadly product, kids need to have engrained in them a zero-tolerance attitude—one strongly reflected in those simple words.

In June of 1987, I had the great fortune to actually run a tennis tournament at the Reagan White House under the auspices of the Nancy Reagan Drug Abuse Fund. It was a terrific event, with a great group of celebrities and politicians, including Tom Selleck, Chris Evert, Dorothy Hamill, John Forsythe, George Shultz and many others. As it turned out, I was partnered with Secretary of State James Baker, who was an excellent player. We made it all the way to the finals. But that's when our luck ran out as we lost to actress Catherine Oxenberg—who was married to my friend, Bob Evans, for a full nine days in 1998—and the ringer of the foreign dignitaries, Count Wilhelm Wachtmeister, the Swedish Ambassador to the United States. Later Wachtmeister would become a favorite doubles partner of President George H. W. Bush.

And the worst part of losing was that President Reagan and Nancy were there in the stands watching our demise. Anyway, it was great fun and all for a wonderful cause.

* * *

Life is full of dreams, and mine as a child wasn't of stardom on radio, stage, television or in movies; what I really wanted was to be a jockey. I learned to ride horses at an early age, and one of the greatest thrills of my entire life was the day I bought Penetrator, my first horse, back in 1946. I rode constantly throughout the years and became an excellent horseman. I mentioned earlier how I got in trouble when I did my own horse stunts on *Rawhide*.

I was sixty years old in 1989 when ABC asked me to participate in a show called *War of the Stars*. There had been television programs called *Battle of the Stars* that pitted the cast of *Eight Is Enough* against the cast of other shows. These were fun, but they were just quiz or game formats designed to promote the programs. This was different. ABC had lined up a group of celebrities and great athletes, and they wanted to have some actual competition. Obviously the athletes would win, but we were to go all out—which suited me just fine.

The lineup was impressive. They had Milton Berle, who was a great pool player, matched up against the legendary Willie Mosconi—it was Mosconi who, as technical advisor to the film *The Hustler*, taught Paul Newman how to act like a pool shark. Willie even made the most difficult shots for Paul's great character, Fast Eddie. Jackie Gleason, who played Minnesota Fats, made his own shots. They also had Jack Lemmon set to tee off against Arnold Palmer, Martin Sheen playing basketball against Michael Jordan, and Gabe Kaplan to bowl against the legendary Dick Weber.

Probably because of Vincent's reputation as a world-class tennis player, they decided I should play a match against the great Bjorn Borg. I remember they were really enthusiastic when they suggested the idea; they were also certain I would share their enthusiasm.

But I'd already played tennis with great players—including my own sons and other tour players at a large number of celebrity tournaments. So they were surprised when I said I really wasn't interested. But I proposed an alternative: I'd love to run a race against a great jockey. At first, they balked. But I persisted, and after a while they started warming up to the idea. Soon they suggested getting Willie Shoemaker, the all-time great jockey whose loss at Belmont Park on Gallant Man had sent me into the real estate profession. Despite that debacle, I'd always loved to watch Willie race.

I had developed a friendship with Chris McCarron, however, who was fast becoming one of the great jockeys of his generation. I explained to them that Chris was going to be a Hall of Fame Jockey—which he now is—and that he had just won the Kentucky Derby and the Preakness in 1987. When they gave me the green light, I called Chris, and he immediately agreed. Finally, I would get the chance to be a real jockey. I only wished my grandfather, Jimmy Vincent, was alive to watch.

The race was held at Hollywood Park. Everything was all set, but on the big day, Marge Everett, the owner of the track, came running out, saying we couldn't race. It turned out she was unable to get me insured. The insurance company wouldn't indemnify the track if something happened to me in the starting gate.

Most people think horse racing is dangerous because of the speed and the proximity of the horses to one another. But the most perilous moment is actually just as the horses are coming out of the gate. A few years later there was a tragic accident at the Santa Anita track, the track made famous in the film, *Seabiscuit*, when a jockey, Alvero Pineda, was adjusting his helmet in the stall. His horse reared and threw Pineda upward so he hit his head on the steel top of the starting gate. The blow killed him. Since then the roofs have been changed to rubber. To add to the tragedy, Pineda's brother, Roberto, also died in a race in Pimlico, Maryland.

Someone suggested we could still do it if I started with the gate open. We all agreed. The cameramen set it up so it appeared as if the gate was closed. Everyone was ready. They gave me a faster horse because at 165 pounds, I was much heavier than Chris who weighed just 110 pounds. He was a real thoroughbred racehorse who was competing in major races at the time. In fact, Chris had ridden my horse a number of times, and it turned out to be a good thing for me that he had. As we waited for the start, Chris said to me: "Dick, when he gets under the finish line, he has a tendency to bear out, and if you're not expecting it, he'll throw you. So when you pass the line, take a good hold of him up here, so he doesn't turn out on you," pointing to the place on the reins he wanted me to grab.

That was just what I needed to hear: my horse had a mind of his own! My son Nels was terrified as his sixty-year-old father prepared to take off for the full, five furloughs on a real thoroughbred horse in a race against one of the top jockeys in the world.

The bell sounded, and we were off. I'll never forget those two minutes. My horse ran like the wind. We actually kept even with Chris all the way around the track. When we hit the homestretch, we were neck and neck. For a brief moment I actually thought I might win. But the truly great jockeys, like Chris, know just what to do in a pinch, and Chris pulled it out in a photo finish.

And just as Chris predicted, the moment we crossed the finish line, my horse began bucking violently to the right. Had I been unaware, he would have thrown me. Instead, I pulled up on the reins just as Chris showed me, and the horse immediately straightened out. It's a good thing Chris warned me, or I would have been splattered all over Hollywood Park.

I've always admired jockeys. They really are terrific athletes. Many people think it's all the horse, but that's not true. If they're riding Secretariat or, more recently, Big Brown, or my grandfather's favorite, Man o' War, then, naturally, the horse is the key. But a great jockey will almost always beat a lesser jockey who's on a faster horse.

Several years ago, Tim Conway, who is not only a dear friend but one of the great comic actors, along with Chris McCarron and his wife, Judy, started a charity called the Don MacBeth Fund. It was named after a jockey whom Tim and Chris both admired for the help he had given to other jockeys when they were down on their luck. MacBeth died of cancer in 1987, and the Memorial Fund was immediately begun, helping out injured and disabled jockeys. Unfortunately, accidents happen far too frequently, and often the jockeys don't have the means to support themselves. There's a special place in my heart for the courageous athletes who mount a thousand-pound thoroughbred and put themselves on the line day after day.

* * *

In 1990, I began my final television show, *WIOU*. This was the sixth straight decade that I took a recurring role in a TV series. I don't know if that's a record, but it must be close. In fact, I nearly had it going for seven. My dear friend Joe Urbanczyk, a cameraman on the popular *That '70s Show*, recommended that since it dealt with the 1970s, they might have a spot for me. It turned out they liked the idea and brought me in to play a recurring role as "Murph" a drinking buddy of Red Foreman, played by Kurtwood Smith. Unfortunately, after appearing in just one episode, I had a stroke and that ended that.

WIOU seemed like a hit in the making. A situation dramedy created by Kathryn Pratt and John Eisendrath that took place in a Chicago television newsroom. There was some real authenticity to it as both Pratt and Eisendrath were themselves former news reporters in Chicago.

I played the wacky weatherman, Floyd Graham, who had a penchant for creating new-fangled words by combining two words—like snow and rain as "snain." Floyd's good-natured malapropisms made him enormously popular with the news audience.

But Floyd had another aspect of his character that I discovered when I auditioned: he was going blind. Kathryn told me that he would be a very funny character, but that he was going to have this serious story line as well. At first, I was concerned. It was risky, and I remember asking Kathryn if she really thought the character could continue to be funny after he had gone blind. Later she told *L.A. Times* reporter, Diane Haithman, she had doubts about it herself.

During her career in a newsroom, Kathryn had actually known a pair of newsmen who provided the inspiration for Floyd—one who lost his hearing and another who was replaced because of his age. Watching both these men struggle with those obstacles left an impression on her, and she very much wanted to convey that struggle to the audience.

When the script for the episode where Floyd goes blind was completed, they decided to try it out on a test audience—but not any old audience, one that Haithman rightly described as "a usually ignored demographic group: people with disabilities." In January of 1991, we did a special performance at the TODD/AO Studios for an audience of people who were blind, deaf and even in wheelchairs. It was an interesting night. One thing we all learned was the importance of being open about disabilities. I'd been using expressions like "sight-impaired" and "hearing-impaired," which, I found out, didn't go over well with the crowd. One of the audience members told Haithman: "I think there's not a single one of us in this room who hasn't denied their disabilities," but, he continued, that's not something that should be encouraged. One person said flatly: "I'm blind. I'm not sight-impaired."

Throughout the duration of the show, I met quite a number of blind people, and it reinforced for me just how fortunate I'd been in my life. Many of them thought I was doing something wonderful by helping bring disabled people out of the shadows. But it was Kathryn who deserved credit for whatever contribution the character of Floyd Graham made toward greater acceptance of disabilities in the workplace. More important, it's one thing to play a blind person in a television show, it's quite another to be faced with the terrible obstacles that confront people with disabilities all day, every day. During my time on *WIOU* I learned a lot about the courage of so many people who face and overcome their disabilities.

WIOU received terrific reviews. The *New York Post* praised the casting of John Shea and Helen Shaver in the leads. They even found some nice words for the aging weatherman: "[B]y casting Dick Van Patten [as Floyd Graham] WIOU has filled that role with perfect, almost perverse, precision."

But nothing in life is certain. There have been shows I never thought would last, and they went for years and others, like *WIOU*, that were well-received by the critics, enjoyed good ratings and seemed to have the kind of story lines and writing that can turn a show into a hit, and yet they get cancelled. *WIOU* lasted for two seasons, and suddenly we were all shocked to find out it was all over. It's too bad. It was a great show and should have lasted for years.

* * *

Meanwhile my life path once again led me back to my friends in the animal kingdom. In 1989, I had lunch during a guest appearance on the *John Davidson Show* with the band's drummer, Joey Herrick, an animal lover deeply involved with rescuing abused and neglected dogs and cats. Joey piqued my interest with an idea for developing a healthier pet food, and so we soon started up our own company, Natural Balance. For the past twenty years, I've been traveling across the country hawking healthier meals to a curious clientele of cats and dogs, as well as lions, tigers, cheetahs, polar bears and even snakes.

Working with Natural Balance has made it possible for me to become more involved with the wonderful people who raise and train seeing-eye dogs. Natural Balance lends support for many groups like Guide Dogs of the Desert and Guide Dogs of America, all wonderful organizations, that provide well-trained dogs for the blind free of cost. These groups, made up of many hundreds of hard-working volunteers, really do make a difference in people's lives, and I'm so proud and grateful to be a part of it.

* * *

Recalling the abrupt cancellation of WIOU, I just commented that nothing in life is certain. But perhaps, that's not entirely true. There is one thing we can all count on—sooner or later that reliable old pump inside our chest, faithfully working its magic every moment of our lives, will one day grow a little weary. When that happens, the blood stops flowing, and suddenly life is never the same again. That happened to me in January of 2006, when I suffered the first of two strokes.

I won't deny that it's been a struggle. I've had to hang up my beloved tennis racket, and pizza with all the toppings is pretty much a thing of the past. It's true we don't realize just how much the small pleasures mean until they're gone.

A second stroke followed in July of 2007. Afterwards, the doctors worried that medication alone was insufficient—the valve had to come out. And, of course, that meant a new one had to go in. Those who face this surgery will appreciate my skepticism when Dr. Greg Kay, my dear friend, who after retiring from medicine joined us at Natural Balance, explained that they were going to replace my old valve with a new one—and it would come from a pig!

My family insisted, and in September of 2008, I had the surgery. Dr. Alfredo Trento, the brilliant Director of Cardiothoracic Surgery at Cedars Sinai Hospital, saved my life. While my health's not perfect, I'm immensely grateful for the miracles performed by so many dedicated people—nurses, doctors and volunteers—for me and millions like me. Getting through this ordeal has meant leaning heavily for support on those I love, having confidence in my doctors and faith that God has a plan. In the end, they all came through!

49

EIGHTY IS NOT ENOUGH

Each person writes his own life-script. No one formula fits all. If we look for a single path, a perfect model on how to respond to the joys and adversities that confront us, we'll always be disappointed. In the end, we all have to find our own way; the way that works best for us. I've never dwelled on the paths not taken. It's a waste of time and energy. It's today and tomorrow, not yesterday, that matters most.

Life, of course, is complicated. But I think that's a blessing. It reflects the fact that we are all so very different. It's true in acting, just as in life. My friend Ralph Nelson, whom I worked with in *The Wind Is Ninety* and *I Remember Mama*, once told me a great story that's right on point. After directing the film *Requiem for a Heavyweight*, Ralph said to me: "Dickie, it's the funniest thing. I was doing a scene with Jackie Gleason, Anthony Quinn and Mickey Rooney. Now before the scene, Anthony Quinn said to me, 'I have to get in the mood before I do this.' So he went off by himself to take some time alone and think about the character and the scene. And while Quinn was getting in the mood, Gleason was practicing his golf swing, and Mickey was on the phone with his bookie. Then as soon as Quinn said, 'All right, I'm ready,' we started shooting. And the amazing thing is that all three were terrific."

What worked for Gleason or Rooney didn't work for Quinn—and vice versa. No one was right or wrong. It simply reflected different approaches to acting, which in the end produced good performances all around.

After eighty years, I've come to believe that life is similar. I've been caught up—perhaps too much—in the debates about child acting. My sister Joyce and I have very different attitudes about growing up as actors. It would be foolish to believe there are no problems with such a childhood. Clearly, behind the scenes of *Eight Is Enough* there were terrible difficulties, some tragic, that almost certainly were, to some degree, rooted in the pressures arising from those children being thrust into celebrity status.

On the other hand, I recently saw an interview with Danny Bonaduce from *The Partridge Family* talking about his own struggle with drug addiction. He was asked whether his being a child actor was at the heart of his problem. Danny responded passionately: "That's a lot of baloney. I was in a rehab with ninety other people, and none of *them* were child actors."

Danny's response reflects the fact that people in all walks of life are confronted with the same difficulties. The question is not how those difficulties arise, but how we respond to them when they come. More important, in my view, than whether we were child actors, is whether we have the right people around for that moral support and guidance, so indispensable for the shaping and developing of good character. That's why having a sound family structure—one we can lean on when the challenges of life come knocking—is so essential. If that family structure is absent, we're going to have problems whether we're onstage or not.

This family framework of moral guidance was at the heart of both *I Remember Mama* and *Eight Is Enough*. For precisely that reason, each show struck a chord with millions of Americans. In the case of *Eight Is Enough*, I believe this came at an opportune moment when traditional institutions had been under attack, and Americans were hungry for a restoration of a healthy family life. Of course, we can never fully live up to the ideals of these fictional characters, but the very fact that we are imperfect is all the more reason to have something better than ourselves standing as a model. The ideal of Tom Bradford was clearly more than I could match, but he's most certainly an ideal to which I can aspire.

While I've lived the first eighty years with a great appreciation of life, still there are times when I'm saddened by the terrible losses that are inevitable when you hang around so long. It troubles me greatly to look through the old playbills from my childhood on Broadway and realize that pretty much all the people in all those great productions are gone—all the marvelous directors, Max Reinhardt, Joshua Logan, Elia Kazan, Guthrie McClintock, and George S. Kaufman, as well as the great actors, Alfred Lunt, Lynn Fontanne, Fredric March, Henry Fonda, Tallulah Bankhead, Melvyn Douglas, Ethel Barrymore and so many more. They were adults then, but they were as much a part of my childhood as the kids around the neighborhood, and when I reminisce about the past, those are the people I think about, next only to my own family.

But I certainly don't dwell on it all. It's not in my nature to be morose. While many are gone, there are so many more to meet. I'm a natural optimist. I still look forward to another day's work on a set; watching a great horse turn it on down the homestretch; seeing a new magician dazzle us at the Magic Castle; hearing about the exploits of my children and grandchildren; and, above all, a quiet dinner with my wife, Pat. I've spoken a great deal about my Mom, partly because I loved her so and partly because she was so instrumental in my success. But my life's happiness, I owe entirely to Pat Poole Van Patten, who has been there by my side every day for fifty-five years.

Eighty is **not** enough! Not by a long shot. Life is so rich and interesting, and I'll need another eighty before I'm ready to call it quits. But, of course, if I got my wish, I'd want even more. That's why in the end, we have to learn to be satisfied with what we've had. In my case, that's been a truly wonderful life, a loving family and the great fortune of entertaining millions of people. As I close, I'm reminded again of my parents at the Ziegfeld in 1928, stagestruck by the marvelous and groundbreaking story, song and dance of Edna Ferber's *Showboat*. I was just on the way in that night, but now I'm a little like that timeless Mississippi—an old comic who just keeps rollin' along. And with a little luck, I might even be around to take a few more bows. I hope so!

EPILOGUE:
A SPECIAL TRIBUTE TO DICK VAN PATTEN

Throughout my life, I've marveled at the outpouring of love and affection from millions of people for my remarkable uncle, Dick Van Patten. What those people don't know, however, is that Dick's warm, caring and joyful public persona also reflects the private man. In fact, the real Dick Van Patten is even better!

I have strong personal reasons for saying so: Dick and his wife, Pat, took me in when I was just two and half years old. At the time, Pat was pregnant with their first child, Nels. Today, as a parent with two children of my own, I marvel at what a loving and unselfish act that was. Soon two more boys were born, Jimmy and Vincent, and I was able to grow up with them as four brothers in one close family—and I owe all that to Dick and Pat.

Privately, Dick is every bit as modest as he is in public. In the past few years, however, he began opening up to me a little more about his astonishing history in the entertainment world. Then in August of 2005 he was interviewed at the Screen Actors Guild. Not a single person present that night will ever forget it. Dick mesmerized the audience with story after story, often poignant, and just as often hilarious, tracing his amazing life-journey and spicing it with incredible "insider" tales of the many legends he had worked with for more than three-quarters of a century in American entertainment.

At the close of the SAG interview, a thoroughly enchanted moderator, Ilyanne Kichaven, queried Dick, "Why don't you write a book about all this?" In his typically modest way, Dick shrugged it off.

But, I didn't. In fact, I became totally committed to the idea that a book must be written about this remarkable life. I pressed Dick, and finally he agreed. After speaking with our good friend, Joe Urbanczyk, we enlisted a mutual friend, Robert Baer, who made that happen. In time, a dream became a reality.

I am so proud to have played a part in this project. But I am even prouder of the special bond I've come to share with my uncle. He's been my Best Man, a grandfather to my children and, simply put, he is the best friend I have in all the world. And I know his children, Nels, Jimmy and Vincent, who are all so proud of him, would join me in saying that there is no one more deserving of having their story told than this great man who has been a father to all of us. My own contribution in kick-starting and assisting with this project is my most precious and heartfelt gift to Dick. But Dick's life has been a gift to us all—and his remarkable book is his own loving gift to so many millions more who for nearly eighty years have been entertained by this supremely talented and beloved man.

God bless you, Dick.

Casey King

ACKNOWLEDGMENTS

My nephew, Casey King, first raised the idea of a memoir several years ago. For his confidence in the possibilities of this book, and his commitment and hard work throughout this long process, as well as for being a nephew, who is far more like a son, I am deeply appreciative.

Along the way, we received help from many people. Most important, were my own family. I want to thank my wife Pat, my sister Joyce, my three sons, Nels, Jimmy and Vincent, as well as my daughter-in-law, Nancy Valen, who all spent hours recounting their memories and jogging mine.

I also owe a very special thanks to Rosemary Rice, my dear friend from *Mama*, who was a tremendous help as we put together the section on my very first television family.

Additionally, I want to express my gratitude to Joe Urbanczyk, a great friend to our entire family, who introduced me to my co-author, Robert Baer, some fifteen years ago, and has helped out in countless ways throughout the course of this project.

I also wish to give very special thanks to Fred Silverman, Mel Brooks, Carl Reiner, Cloris Leachman, Wayne Carson, Joe Bologna, Renee Taylor, Mary Ellen White, Jeff Ballard, and Bill Sheppard, who helped out along the way at critical moments in my career. Without the support of these friends, and many others, I would not be writing these memoirs.

On a sad note, our publisher and my long-time friend, Michael Viner, a great innovator in his field, passed away just before we were going to print. Michael, the President of Phoenix Books and Audio, was the very first to read our manuscript, and we will forever treasure his enthusiasm for the book.

We have also been tremendously fortunate to work with Phoenix's talented editor, Dan Smetanka. Dan's commitment, hard work, enthusiasm and skillful editing have certainly made this a better book.

I am also grateful to the entire hard-working Phoenix staff, especially Darby Connor, who has relentlessly hunted down every error in the draft, and Stephan Matson, an outstanding director in the recording booth.

I also deeply appreciate the support of Dwight Opperman and Julie Chrystyn, who have been so gracious in their reception of our book.

Finally, I want to thank my co-author, Robert Baer. He is a truly exceptionally writer who was able to crystallize my thoughts and feelings with wonderful insight and eloquence. Most important, Robert and I became great friends along the way, and I will be forever grateful.

INDEX